How to Make Opportunity Equal

For Mary

How to Make Opportunity Equal

Race and Contributive Justice

Paul Gomberg

Blackwell
Publishing

BLACKWELL PUBLISHING
350 Main Street, Malden, MA 02148-5020, USA
9600 Garsington Road, Oxford OX4 2DQ, UK
550 Swanston Street, Carlton, Victoria 3053, Australia

First published 2007 by Blackwell Publishing Ltd.

1   2007

Library of Congress Cataloging-in-Publication Data

Gomberg, Paul.
   How to make opportunity equal : race and contributive justice / Paul Gomberg.
      p. cm.
   Includes bibliographical references and index.
   ISBN 978-1-4051-6081-0 (hardback : alk. paper) – ISBN 978-1-4051-6082-7
(pbk. : alk. paper)   1. Social justice.   2. Justice (Philosophy).   3. Social ethics.
4. Political science–Philosophy.   5. Race discrimination.   I. Title.

   HM671.G64 2007
   172′.2–dc22

                                                                            2006034412

A catalogue record for this title is available from the British Library.

Set in 10.5/13 pt Galliard
by Graphicraft Limited, Hong Kong
Printed and bound in Singapore
by COS Printers Pte Ltd

The publisher's policy is to use permanent paper from mills that operate
a sustainable forestry policy, and which has been manufactured from
pulp processed using acid-free and elementary chlorine-free practices.
Furthermore, the publisher ensures that the text paper and cover board
used have met acceptable environmental accreditation standards.

For further information on
Blackwell Publishing, visit our website:
www.blackwellpublishing.com

Contents

Preface

You have opened the cover and are looking at the preface. Is this book meant for you? I believe so. If you are a professor or advanced student of philosophy, it addresses you by offering a new way of understanding justice and racism. If you are a beginning student, it addresses problems you may have thought about – that some folks seem to have a better chance to succeed than others – explores the reasons why, and proposes a solution. If you are a student or general reader untrained in philosophy, it is meant for you too. I have tried to write so that anyone can read and understand the argument.

At times the argument may be difficult. After all, it is a philosophy book. But I have included stories and examples to illustrate what I am saying. You may decide to read just the parts that interest you. That's fine with me. The argument is politically and socially radical: I believe that problems of racism and unequal opportunity cannot be solved in capitalist society. The central practical proposal is simple: we need to share labor, including the boring work most of us like to avoid, if everyone is to have an opportunity to develop all of their abilities. The central philosophical innovation is also simple: philosophers have thought that justice is about what people get; I think it is about what people are able to do, particularly how they are able to develop their abilities, give those back to society, and be respected for their contributions.

Some chapters are harder than others. I believe that chapters 4, 11, 12, and 13 are harder because they discuss details of other philosophers' ideas. Sometimes what I write may not make sense to you. If it does not, there could be at least three reasons. First, it could be that I wrote something that makes no sense. If I had thought about it better or longer or more clearly, I would not have written it. Second, it may make sense, but I may not have explained it as fully or clearly as I should. Third, it may just be a complex idea or argument. In any case, if something does not make sense to you, mark it and move on. There should be much else in the book that you will find useful. You can come back to it later, if you wish, to decide whether it does in fact make sense and whether I was right.

I have tried to make this book as good as I could. But some things I wrote are wrong or confused. If I knew which these were, I would not have written them, but I am quite sure that in a year or two I will wish I had written some of the book differently. I offer the ideas in the book for you to explore with me: help me to figure out where I am right and where I am wrong. Then, on the next try, we will do better. You may contact me at <gombergopp@earthlink.net>.

Because the book is meant for teachers and students of philosophy and because many others may wish to investigate these questions further, it includes a "scholarly apparatus," which I will explain, in case you are unfamiliar with the one I use. I use the name of an author and the date of publication – for example, Rawls 1999 – as an abbreviation for a book or article. At the end there is a list of references. There, all the authors I cite are listed alphabetically with the date of their work and a full citation. (References that can be accessed electronically on the World Wide Web are marked with an asterisk (*).) If I am quoting or referring to a particular passage, I will follow the citation with the page number – for example, Rawls 1999: 464. If it is obvious what book or article I am referring to, I will just give the page number in parentheses. If you are not interested in these citations, just ignore them. You can use them later if you wish.

I hope you enjoy the book, find it useful, and can help to solve the problems of racism and unequal opportunity.

Chapter 1

Who Toils? Race, Equal Opportunity, and the Division of Labor

A radical proposal

The book you are reading is an essay in utopian political and social philosophy. Equal opportunity is usually understood as equality of *competitive* opportunity to attain limited positions of advantage such as those of doctor, journalist, professor, or software engineer. Ideally, no one should have unfair advantages in the competition. Although the ideal is popular, people disagree about what constitutes an unfair advantage or disadvantage.

Usually the demand for equal opportunity opposes advantage and disadvantage associated with race and gender. We think it wrong that men should get the best jobs because they are males and that the best educational opportunities are in overwhelmingly white schools, while many black students in segregated schools are "tracked" for unemployment or low-wage jobs. (Here, the "we" is intended to represent agreement between my reader and myself, not unanimously held belief.) Gender discrimination and forms of residential and school segregation that create unequal life chances violate our ideal of equal opportunity.

Yet equal opportunity can be a conservative ideal: the more talented should prosper; incomes and wealth can be unequal. Equal opportunity is "American" egalitarianism, in contrast to "European" or socialist egalitarianism that would create equal conditions for all; this alternative is sometimes called "equality of welfare" as opposed to the individualist ideal of equal opportunity that makes each responsible for her own life.

I will argue, to the contrary, that the ideal of equal opportunity can be quite radical if equal opportunity is not competitive. Competitive equal opportunity is impossible. Non-competitive opportunity must be for goods available in unlimited supply. I propose equal opportunity to attain a constellation of goods: to develop complex abilities, to contribute those developed abilities to society, and to be esteemed for those social contributions. This constellation can be of unlimited supply only if we share both routine and complex labor. Necessary tasks of cleaning public spaces, of producing food, clothing, shelter, and durable goods such as appliances and trains, and of providing services such as health care require contributions of routine labor. This routine labor should be shared by all capable of it. When routine labor is shared, no one's working life need be consumed by routine labor. All have opportunity to develop complex abilities and contribute these to society provided that this labor too is shared.

Some history

The phrases "equal opportunity" and "equality of opportunity" are relatively new. The first listings of their use in the *Oxford English Dictionary* are from the late nineteenth century in an economics journal, then from the early twentieth century in discussing the demand of Fabian socialists for equality of opportunity for women. Searching the University of Illinois catalog, I found two books from the 1930s and early 1940s with the phrases "equalizing educational opportunity" and "equalization of educational opportunity" in their titles, addressing anti-black discrimination in the American South (Aly 1934; Ray 1941). After World War II, 24 states passed fair employment laws prohibiting racial discrimination in employment (Chen 2001); at the federal level the Equal Employment Opportunity Commission was established by the Civil Rights Act of 1964. Historically, the demand for equal opportunity opposed discrimination that narrowed opportunities for women, immigrants, and racial or religious minorities. The demand was specific, usually directed against discrimination in employment or against the effects of racially segregated or gender stereotyped education.

There was a nineteenth-century notion of America as the "land of opportunity," expressed in Tocqueville's *Democracy in America*: a country of free-wheeling economic competition where fortunes are made and lost, aristocratic privilege is absent, and poor men can move to the frontier to build a new life (Blum 1988). This older conception represented, among other things, the opportunity of white males to "make their fortune" by exploiting African-descended slave labor on new plantations in Alabama and Mississippi – land obtained by the removal of native peoples (Oakes 1983; Takaki 1979). In the words of the historian Alexander Saxton:

> By the time of Jefferson and Jackson the nation had already assumed the form of a racially exclusive democracy – democratic in the sense that it sought to provide equal opportunities for the pursuit of happiness by its white citizens through the enslavement of African Americans, extermination of Indians, and territorial expansion at the expense of Indians and Mexicans. (1990: 10)

In the 1820s and 1830s many white males gained voting rights; at the same time, many black men in the North lost voting rights. Anti-black pogroms occurred in northern cities and towns; segregation in public places increased (Takaki 1979). This "opportunity" is not equal opportunity as we now conceive it.

Already at the end of the eighteenth century something like our contemporary ideal of equal opportunity was emerging. Immanuel Kant opposed aristocratic privilege and favored a civil service where positions were based on individual merit (Kant 1798: 328–9). These ideals were popularized in the French Revolution and Napoleonic period under the slogan "careers open to talents." This slogan rejected aristocratic privilege but countenanced other advantages and disadvantages, particularly associated with gender, that we would now reject.

Why our conception of equal opportunity changes

The meaning of the phrase "equal opportunity" changes. Two hundred years ago, egalitarians demanded an end to aristocratic privilege. From the mid-nineteenth century, educated women demanded gender equality. Other struggles opposed slavery and racism: in the nineteenth century, after the American Civil War, there was a demand for "40 acres and a mule;" later, anti-racists fought to end segregation in schools and public places and racial job exclusions (skilled construction trades were often dominated by a particular national group, making it difficult for others to enter; black workers were excluded from all these trades). Now immigrants without residency documents demand health care and education. People with disabilities demand equal access to public buildings and transportation. Gay people demand the right to marry.

The content of "equal opportunity" changes for two reasons: power and logic. At different periods, different "outsiders" assert power, making demands related to demeaned status – commoners in eighteenth-century France, women, people of African descent, undocumented immigrants, people with disabilities, gays and lesbians. Yet the legal issues raised by the disenfranchisement of women are different from those raised by segregated (de jure or de facto) schools, by denial of health care services to immigrants without residency papers, or by lack of access to buildings or buses for people in wheelchairs. Still, these issues have been raised under the phrase "equal opportunity."

The content of "equal opportunity" also changes because of logic. Once one form of unequal treatment is recognized as unfair, it can be difficult, particularly in the face of protests by people who are left out, to explain why poor white men should have the right to vote but not women; why mastery of the relevant skills admits men to journeyman status in a trade but not women; why neighborhood of residence makes one child eligible for a school but not another child with a different racial identity. When the audience is not inclusive and no one questions exclusion, marginalization, or segregation grounded in gender or racial identity, the practices may not seem illogical. But once challenged by people struggling to leave the social margins, these practices can seem illogical.

Power and logic are connected, and power is more important. To change the composition of the audience for a discussion, an "outside" group must assert its power. Because the audience becomes more inclusive, justifications are needed that would be unnecessary when the audience was narrower. For example, if women are not considered equal persons, no justification will seem necessary for limiting the apprenticeships to males. The issue of women in the trades will be *invisible*. If "she is a woman" is *not* a valid reason to exclude an applicant for an apprenticeship, this is likely because women have insisted on their inclusion in the audience: an assertion of power. Inclusion in the audience gives women the same rights as others. Because women have those rights, it is "illogical" to give as a reason for exclusion, "She is a woman."

In the United States today equal opportunity is thought incompatible with explicit racial exclusion: one cannot (plausibly) claim to be an equal opportunity employer and then say, "We don't hire black folks." Yet once we understand how black people are deprived of opportunity, it is difficult to limit our objections to *explicit* racial exclusion. For example, racial identifications are prominent in housing choices: most white people are reluctant to live in neighborhoods with many black residents (most black people prefer neighborhoods about 50 percent black). This reluctance causes white people to move out when a "tipping" percentage of black people is reached. For example, 10 percent of white families may move out as soon as a single black family moves in. If these families are replaced by black families, another group of white families that would tolerate a single black family but not a neighborhood that is 10 percent black would move out. If they are replaced by black families, this may "tip" another group of white families. The process might continue until the neighborhood becomes nearly all black.[1] Because people act according to this perception of race, segregation often occurs also in schools, churches, and voluntary associations. But much educational and employment opportunity depends on the characteristics of the schools we go to and the friendships we form in neighborhoods, churches, and elsewhere. Racial segregation of neighborhoods and the consequences of segregation for other opportunities put many black people at a disadvantage (Wilson 1987; Massey and Denton 1993; Cashin 2004).

Considerations such as these can make us feel confused: *how* do we combat unequal racial opportunity? Must we break up ghetto neighborhoods and demand complete residential integration? If so, how is this to be achieved? Alternatively, should we bus children to integrate schools? Many integrated schools are internally segregated through honors programs, advanced placement classes, and other forms of "tracking." Should elite colleges and universities give preferences to disadvantaged minorities? Should employers give similar preferences? Many argue that intervention must begin earlier, but, despairing of integration's promise, call for better urban black schools. Once we understand

---

[1] For the theory, see Schelling 1971 and 1972. For applications, see the writings of Farley and his co-authors 1978, 1993, and 2002, and National Research Council 1989. Not all neighborhoods change quickly from white to black, and this too needs explaining. See Easterly 2005 for an argument that challenges the Schelling model.

the complexities of racial disadvantage, we feel that opposing explicit racial barriers is not enough. We need other policies. But it is hard to know what these other policies should be.

"Logic" can push us further. Once we understand how racial marginalization works through residential segregation, we realize that parallel processes deprive disadvantaged white people in similar ways: young people growing up in "welfare towns" in Appalachia or suburban trailer parks often have inferior educational and employment opportunities, just as black people do. They can be socially branded and slurred. Young people may see few models of economic success and be confined to schools where demoralization prevails or, in economically mixed schools, be treated as inferior. What should the phrase "equal opportunity" imply?

Moreover, when we review the many social practices and institutions that have created disadvantages, the thought occurs: wouldn't it be better to have *equal* opportunity whereby success and failure are not at all affected by disadvantaged social circumstances? This has come to be called the "level playing field" conception of equal opportunity; it acknowledges limited opportunity – some positions are more desirable than others – but seeks to eliminate the social disadvantages that make it unlikely that some will realize those opportunities. The "level playing field" conception gives a radical content to the ideal of distributing limited opportunities in a fair way.

We see, then, that, for reasons of power and of logic, it is hard to fix on a single, simple meaning of "equal opportunity." This situation makes it possible to reinterpret equal opportunity in new ways. This book will *oppose* the "level playing field" conception of equal opportunity. It proposes a more radical view: a non-competitive conception of equal opportunity.

Racism and the costs of unequal opportunity

In the United States in 1999, life expectancy for black women was 5.2 years less than that for white women, for black men 6.8 years less than for white. At the time of writing, 1 in 20 black men is in prison, and 1 in 3 aged 20–29 is in jail or prison or on probation or parole; black men are incarcerated in state prisons at a rate 9.6 times the rate for white men. Black people report poorer health but fewer visits to doctors. The unemployment rate for black people is double that for white people; the poverty rate is two and a half times greater. While income inequalities between black and white families narrowed slightly in the 1990s, the racial gap in control of disposable wealth is huge; so is the advantage that wealth brings.[2]

---

[2] Most of this information is in the *Statistical Abstract of the United States*, which is now on the web at <www.census.gov/compendia/statab/>. I will sometimes use data from the *Statistical Abstract* without citing it. Discussion of wealth differences are in Oliver and Shapiro 1995; Conley 1999; and Shapiro 2004. The information about incarceration is from a Human Rights Watch report at <www.hrw.org/reports/2000/usa/Rcedrg00-01.htm>.

These racial differences in how well people fare are largely the result of the ghettoization of black residents in the major cities of the United States; no other national, racial, or ethnic group in the United States experiences a degree of residential segregation like that experienced by black people (Massey and Denton 1993).

In the United States, and elsewhere, social inequality is organized through categories of race or allied categories. Poor health services, widespread incarceration, unemployment, and low wages – all affecting black people disproportionately – constitute racist harms; these inequalities affect longevity and quality of life. Related inequalities affect *Gastarbeiter* (workers without citizenship rights) in Germany, North Africans in France, Asians in Russia, Koreans in Japan, and minority workers from the Commonwealth in Britain.[3]

The words "racism" and "racist" are used with many different meanings. The idea of race is central, but "race" is not a biological concept; it is a socially defined concept that cues into a person's appearance and ancestry (Taylor 2004). In the United States someone is said to be black if she displays enough of the stereotypically "black" features of skin color, hair color and texture, shape of lips and nose, and if at a family reunion many of her kin would also display some of those same characteristics. Racial identification works through physical appearance, unlike, for example, the distinction between Serb and Croat or Muslim and Christian.

As I will use the word, what is racist in the central sense is a *society*. A society is racist when a person's racial identification affects her likelihood of having a good life. Thus a society is racist if some members suffer lower life expectancy, more disease and injury, greater poverty, and higher unemployment *as a consequence of* a racial identification. There is much more to racism than this. Racial identification is associated with stereotypes of racial difference; so in the United States today, many more white people than black people believe that the higher rate of black poverty comes from lack of motivation or willpower (Sigelman and Welch 1991: 53, 91).[4] And stereotyping may be part of the causal nexus I am calling "racism." But no particular story of prejudice, discrimination, or stereotyping is part of the *definition* of "racism" as I use the term.

When I use the word "racism," I will, with rare exceptions, be referring to anti-black racism in the United States. This usage is a distortion, but one that

---

[3]   The classic discussion of immigrant workers in Europe – in Castles and Kosak 1973 – is helpful to comparisons with racism in the United States but is now outdated. A study focused as much on movement of capital as on movement of labor is Sassen 1988. The development of the European Union and the collapse of the old Soviet bloc have led to more migration. More recent literature includes Calavita 2005; Geddes 2003; Kopina 2005; Lahav 2004; and Lucassen 2005. For the British case, see Solomos 2003.

[4]   In one survey, 70 percent of black people but only 40 percent of white thought that disproportionate black poverty was due mainly to discrimination, while 60 percent of whites but only 34 percent of blacks thought it was due to a lack of motivation or willpower on the part of black people. Compare to Kinder and Sanders 1996: 107, which surveys only white opinion. See also Kluegel and Smith 1986.

I can justify. From the beginnings of their exploration, Europeans noticed that the peoples they encountered differed from them in appearance. Many of the first conceptualizations of these differences were biblical. The "racial" view of difference does not emerge until the late seventeenth century, and it becomes prominent in European thought by the late eighteenth century (Smedley 1993). Ronald Takaki's *Iron Cages* gives a greater sense of the varieties of racism in the United States in the nineteenth century, including the stereotypes of native peoples and Chinese. I focus on the case of anti-black racism in the United States for two related reasons. First, it was in the United States that racism was first woven so thoroughly into social structure. Jefferson's *Notes on the State of Virginia* (1781) is remarkable because an important founder of the new republic interprets social structure through categories of race. That inter-pretation is popularized and consolidated in the nineteenth century (Takaki 1979). Second, in the United States anti-black racism has always been central because the economy depends upon black labor. Black people are stigmatized and segregated far beyond any other group.

A large part of the story of racial inequality is inequality of opportunity to attain more advantaged social positions. Black students attend schools that are becoming increasingly segregated (Orfield 2001); black children are less likely to graduate from high school; black high school graduates are less likely to attend college, and those who attend are less likely to graduate.

The writings of Jonathan Kozol (1967, 1991, 2005) have documented the conditions in particular schools. I too have relevant personal experiences. I teach at a low-status, urban, public university with a student population that consists overwhelmingly of disadvantaged black students from public high schools (the six-year graduation rate for incoming freshmen is less than 20 percent). In an introductory class in philosophy of science, I ask students to measure photographic images of the sun taken throughout the year (evidence that the sun and earth are further apart during northern hemispheric summer, con-trary to a common belief) and report their measurements in millimeters. Several years ago one student expressed puzzlement how to do this: she did not know how to measure with a ruler. Outside the classroom, I asked whether she had taken geometry in high school. She said she had. I asked what she had learned. She said that they spent the entire year with a substitute teacher who never taught geometry. She went to a black public high school in Chicago within three miles of my campus. Whenever I tell this story to my classes, some stu-dents report similar experiences with unqualified teachers. More general stud-ies show that low-income students, and black students in particular, are more likely to be taught by teachers who lack proper credentials in the subject (Haycock 2000: 5).[5]

---

[5] Specifically, high poverty (more than 75 percent) schools were compared with low poverty (less than 10 percent) schools, and high minority (more than 90 percent) schools with low minority (less than 10 percent) schools; in schools that were either low poverty or low minority, 13 percent of classes were taught by teachers without certification in the subject; in schools that were either high minority or high poverty, 27 percent of classes were taught by teachers lacking certification in the subject.

Students are subject to frequent suspensions, particularly since the implementation of a "zero-tolerance" policy. One student told me how this worked in the case of her 7-year-old son, then completing second grade. He had just been suspended from school for the third time. The first time occurred when he was in kindergarten: he had put cheese on his French fries in the cafeteria line when he did not have a quarter to pay for it; he was suspended for "theft." In first grade he was suspended for talking during a fire drill. In second grade he was suspended for running in the hallway. Another student told of her brother being suspended for fighting and being told that he would not be allowed to re-enroll unless he was on Ritalin therapy. Ritalin is prescribed for students diagnosed as hyperactive, but my students report that children in Chicago public schools are not given recess.[6] Zero-tolerance policies greatly increase the number of suspensions and expulsions; in the first six years of zero tolerance in Chicago public schools, annual expulsions increased from 14 to 737 (Civil Rights Project 2000: 3). In a survey of 12 cities throughout the United States, in every city (except one that had no black enrollment) the percentage of black students suspended or expelled exceeded the percentage of black students in the schools, in one case by more than 300 percent. The overwhelming majority of such suspensions and expulsions are for "attitude" and minor behavior issues, not for violence, weapons, or drugs (Gordon and others n.d.).

A math teacher at a different high school within three miles of my campus reports that, in an effort to raise test scores, the schools have adopted a "triage" method: she was told to concentrate her efforts on the students who are performing best; the ones who are behind in mathematics were to be written off.

These anecdotes reinforce Kozol's writing, which is also specific and anecdotal. The overall effect of overcrowded classes, demoralized, unqualified, or absent teachers, punitive disciplinary policies, efforts to raise test scores by pushing students out of school, and cultural alternatives that diminish the importance of education is that 43 percent of black girls and 61 percent of black boys do not graduate from Chicago public high schools in four years (Allensworth 2005). Those who do are often unprepared for college work and under-equipped with job skills.

In pointing out that black children have inferior educational opportunity, I do not mean that unqualified teachers and inferior segregated black education are the *major* causes of lower performance by poor minority students. There is evidence that better qualified teachers have a positive impact on student performance, particularly for low-income and minority students (*Chicago Tribune*, June 9, 2006 based on Presley and others 2006). But there is also evidence that lower performance by disadvantaged children has multiple causes not easily remedied (Rothstein 2004), and this shows, I believe, the need for more radical

---

[6] According to a 1999 article in *The Chicago Reporter*, 80 percent of Chicago public grade schools do not offer recess, especially those with large minority populations. See <www.chicagoreporter.com/1999/06-99/0699healthextra.htm>.

change. Still, the lack of certified teachers is evidence that there is insufficient effort to educate poor and minority children.

I mentioned earlier, parenthetically, that the six-year graduation rate for incoming freshmen students at my university is less than 20 percent. The most important reason, according to surveys of student dropouts, was financial. They had to earn more money, or could not afford the (relatively low) tuition, or both. Also it has seemed to me that my students are often the most "together" members of families with problems related to poverty. So when there is a difficulty that others more affluent might solve by paying for professional help (child care or counseling), family members turn to our students as reliable and sensible people. This creates an additional difficulty in completing college.

In addition to completing fewer years of schooling, at every level of educational attainment black people earn lower incomes than white (Carnoy 1994: 123). This difference combines with the difference in educational accomplishments to create inequality in access to income and wealth. Lower incomes and greater poverty, organized through and exacerbated by ghettoization, lead to shorter and worse lives.

One reader of this book responded to these points by saying that the issue is class, not race. And Dalton Conley, after showing that when family wealth (not income, but assets) is taken into account, black students did as well as white in school, wrote:

> This situation only emphasizes the importance of carefully separating out the effects of class from those of race . . . differences in average levels of educational attainment between blacks and whites are not about race *per se*. They are about socio-economic status. Blacks are not disadvantaged in the educational system; rather, they are disadvantaged in the resources they bring to the system. Race matters, but only indirectly – through the realm of class inequality. (Conley 1999: 80)

This language generates confusion. Analysis of variance defines static categories such as "class" and "race" separately and then looks at what effects correlate with each category. But race arose historically and is constantly recreated in decisions such as where to live. Race is a class phenomenon, but a special one. Race *is* class made visible and vicious. Race identifies demeaned class status with a human *body* that has a certain appearance.[7] Inequality within the working class is organized through race; perception of the racialized body divides the working class. One cannot understand class in the United States (or, increasingly, anywhere else) without seeing how it is constructed through racial categories. For example, disproportionate black poverty is not just another class phenomenon. Legislation before and after World War II exempted jobs held primarily by black workers from labor protection; it created educational opportunities and housing equity for working-class white people, while black people were largely excluded. They were excluded *because they were black* (Katznelson

---

[7] See the discussion in chapter 11 below on English efforts to create a visible mark of class status.

2005). Racial inequality is *re*created daily through decisions that maintain segregated black neighborhoods and schools (Fields 1990; Cashin 2004; compare
my view to that of Reed 2002a and 2002b).

This response may be unfair to Conley. His point is that, once we have
accounted for how race organizes inequality within the working class, race has
no *additional* effect on *educational* attainment. Therefore, it seems, race itself is
not causing differences in school performance beyond the effects of poverty,
which is itself affected by racial identification. However, this conclusion does
not follow. The correct conclusion is that similarly poor white children do as
badly. *If* (as I suspect) anti-black racism does affect school performance, then
what explains why similarly poor white children do as badly? The answer –
again a suspicion – is that something else, *something like racism* is isolating
and *stigmatizing* similarly poor white children, who may be identified by the
way they talk, the way they dress, where they live, or through a quasi racial
category. In St Louis, when I lived there, some called poor white people of
rural origin "hoosiers;" it was as derogatory a term as "nigger" and worked
in a similar way. With black children, it is the racial identification of *the body
itself* that does at least some of this work (although language style and other
behaviors have an effect too).

The harms of racial inequality and unequal opportunity add urgency to the
question of how to make opportunity equal. This book is not concerned just
with abstract social philosophy; it is also an effort to end the harms of racism.

The social context of political philosophy

In the Introduction to his 1993 book *Political Liberalism*, John Rawls explained
the historical background of liberal political philosophy. As Rawls saw it, the
central problem of a modern democratic society was to find a basis for social
cooperation between citizens with different religious faiths, moral beliefs
and values, and philosophies. These beliefs and values are often incompatible;
they cannot all be true or correct. Yet they are reasonable in the sense that
reasonable people embrace them.

Given these profound differences in our "conceptions of the good," how
was it possible to find common norms to govern our shared life as citizens?
Rawls emphasized that his own philosophy of justice as fairness – equal liberty and opportunity and orientation toward improving life for the least advantaged – was a political conception on which citizens with different conceptions
of the good could agree. We all can endorse justice as fairness as consistent
with our more comprehensive philosophies and faiths. For example, while a
traditional Lutheran might believe that the Catholic Church leads people away
from God, she will honor her Catholic neighbor as a fellow citizen with the
same liberty of worship that she enjoys. She believes her neighbor wrong about
the most important things, but, as a liberal citizen, she endorses religious liberty. She believes that her faith is compatible with this tolerance.

For Rawls, the task of finding a common ground for social cooperation was set for us by our history. The religions emerging from the Reformation of the sixteenth and seventeenth centuries each claimed exclusively to have religious truth and the path to salvation. These competing claims led to devastating religious wars. This devastation gave rise to modern notions of freedom of conscience and worship. Liberalism in general and Rawls's liberalism in particular try to articulate the common ground, the conception of fair terms of social cooperation in a liberal democratic society. That conception allows modern people to live together as citizens, while disagreeing about what many regard as life's most important matters.

I tell this story about Rawls's thought for two reasons. First, I share with Rawls the belief that political philosophy needs a social context, an understanding of the key events that set our problems. Second, however, I disagree about the obstacles to social unity. For Rawls, it was religious and philosophical division. I will argue that the racial organization of labor in the history of what became the United States is the key to understanding the main division that impedes social unity.

That does not mean that I believe the main division is racial. Rather, the racial division of labor highlights the injustice of a more general social division. The main division is in how the labor necessary to sustain human society is organized. We divide labor in two ways. First, we separate tasks of organization from those of execution. This separation leads to a command relationship between those who control the labor process and those who labor. An example will illustrate this separation. When a worker starts a new job, the specific responsibilities of the position are explained. Any necessary training is supplied. Then the worker is expected to carry out the assigned responsibility: to stock shelves in a store, to install fenders on an automobile, or to enter data into a computer. The owners or their agents set the various labor tasks and give instructions to workers. This division between the organization of labor tasks and the execution of tasks is the division of society into a class society of laborers and those for whom they labor.

Second, among those who labor, the work is divided into closely supervised labor requiring easily mastered skills and more complex tasks carried out under less supervision. While there are at least two continua – between routine and complex and between close and loose supervision – examples at the extremes help to illustrate these divisions. Data entry involves the mastery of a ten-digit keypad and the entry of numbers into fields in a computer screen. It is not difficult to learn. Once learned, the labor is routine, tedious, and usually closely supervised. In contrast, college teachers may train for many years to master their discipline. They are typically required to produce and distribute a syllabus to students, adhere to the syllabus, and assign grades at the end of the term. The organization of the curriculum, the conduct of lectures and discussions, the specific assignments created, the evaluation of those assignments – in short, all of the day-to-day work – are the prerogative of the instructor, subject to general review. Both the data-entry clerk and the college teacher are employees carrying out assigned tasks according to rules established by those who organize labor. But their labor is at opposite extremes on the continua of routine versus complex and close versus loose supervision.

Before turning to a story that illustrates my own view of the social context of political philosophy, I will quarrel with Rawls's interpretation of the origins of liberalism. He interprets "wars of religion" as battles over religious philosophies, but this is one-sided. Whether we consider the Hussites and Taborites of early fifteenth-century Bohemia, the peasant revolt a century later associated with Thomas Münzer, or the seventeenth-century English Civil War, these conflicts occurred in societies which were not secularized as modern societies are. Hence, to speak of a religious *as opposed to* a social movement does not make sense.

When Taborites objected to the "heresy" of Church luxury alongside poverty and want, when Münzer championed social leveling and the "inner light" against religious and civil authorities of Mühlhausen in 1525, when English Nonconformists protested against the Stuart failure to protect commerce and against the Church that preached that disobedience to the crown was a sin, these were not, as Rawls would have it, simply divisions over "religious, philosophical, or moral doctrines."[8] Contests between haves and have-nots and contests among competing elites are understood and articulated in religious language. How could it be otherwise in those societies? To mobilize public opinion, it is necessary to use the vocabulary of the culture, and this was a religious vocabulary. More important, the churches were centers of what we would now call social or political power. The religious language does not show that the conflicts were over the "highest things."

The context of political philosophy, as I conceive it, is set by the history of the Virginia colony at Jamestown, founded in 1607. The early years of the colony were very difficult. To get a measure of the problem, consider this: between 1619 and 1622, 3,570 people migrated from England to the colony, which already had a population of 700; yet in 1622 Virginia's population was only 1,240 (Morgan 1975: 101). The vast majority who migrated did not survive, partly because they had been inadequately provisioned, but also because in most years the colonists either did not raise enough food to feed themselves or did not distribute the food raised to people who needed it. In January and February 1625, the colony lists 1,210 residents despite continued arrival of new people. Between 1625 and 1640, immigrants to Virginia averaged at least 1,000 per year. Yet the population only increased from 1,300 to 8,100 (Morgan 1975: 159). Life expectancy was very short.

At the same time, after roughly 1620, the colony was continually demanding immigrants. Virginia had discovered the production of tobacco. The crucial ingredient in creating tobacco wealth was labor. Land was plentiful after the native peoples had been driven from eastern Virginia, making available

---

[8] On the Taborites, see Macek 1958. On Münzer, see Engels 1850. On the contests of the English Civil War, see Hill 1940, 1961, and 1972.

several million acres of rich tidewater land. The more bondservants a planter had, the greater the profits from growing tobacco. Indeed, the wealthiest Virginians controlled the most servants – and the government.

The story of the economy of seventeenth-century Virginia is largely the story of the creation of tobacco wealth from English bond labor (and to a lesser extent tenants and African slaves or bondsmen – their status was often somewhat indefinite). Moreover, servants were beaten, raped, gambled as stakes at cards, and killed by their masters; servants had little defense against these abuses. Most of us are familiar with the story of the exploitation and abuse of African or African-descended labor. Yet Africans and their descendants were a minor part of the economy of Virginia until after 1676.

By the 1660s mortality had declined. Slaves for life, although more expensive at the outset than indentured servants and an unwise investment when life expectancy was short, came to be seen as a better bargain. Bondservants were commonly living beyond their years of indenture (despite frequent "punishments" to lengthen the term) and by custom were receiving freedom dues; for males, this included a gun. The rich tidewater lands were now entirely owned by one Englishman or another, and freedmen often had to work as tenants or seek their fortunes to the west, where they were vulnerable to attack from native peoples. Frustrated by their lack of opportunity, freedmen, bondservants, and slaves, English and Negro, united to demand military action to enable westward expansion (essentially an anti-native demand). Bacon's Rebellion in 1676 led to the burning of Jamestown.

Three factors led Virginia's rulers to turn toward African slave labor to grow tobacco, particularly after 1676: given greater life expectancy, slaves were economically advantageous; armed poor Englishmen (also a consequence of greater life expectancy and thus commonly outliving their period of indenture) were dangerous; most important, the dispossessed had united, overlooking differences of status between slaves, bondsmen, and freedmen. English (white) had therefore to be elevated far enough above African to divide the laborers (Allen 1997). In the nineteenth century, as a result of the invention of the cotton gin in 1793, the most profitable plantation crop became cotton, and the exploitation of black slave labor was further intensified (Takaki 1979). Even after the end of chattel slavery, black sharecroppers continued to sustain production of cotton and other crops. Their conditions were different from slavery primarily in that sharecroppers commonly fled debt bondage in the middle of the night, but usually to conditions similar to the ones from which they fled (Jones 1992). In the last third of the nineteenth century black workers were used to break strikes by white workers in industries such as coal-mining, iron, and meatpacking (Gutman 1977; Barrett 1987; Takaki 1979). Henry Grady, editor of the *Atlanta Constitution* in the 1880s, argued that the southern system of labor, where black and white workers came together in the workplace but were socially segregated off the job, led to harmony between labor and capital, preventing the rancor between management and workers so prevalent in the North. In 1886, shortly after the Haymarket Riot, a speech by Grady in New

York was applauded by Andrew Carnegie and other northern businessmen who increasingly imported black labor from the South (Takaki 1979: 204–5).

This trend accelerated in the twentieth century. Black workers were generally in the most dangerous and lowest paid jobs. Since the end of World War II, black workers have suffered double the unemployment rate of white workers. Today, black workers are essential to many industries: driving trucks, buses, and trains; encoding checks for banks; cooking and serving in the fast food industry; sorting and loading parcels; working in hospitals caring for patients, cleaning, and preparing food; and pressing clothes. Wherever essential routine labor is to be done, black workers toil.

I recount this brief history of the role of black labor in the United States because the experience of racism highlights something more general: the labor done by black workers had to be done. Where it was not done by black workers, it was done by others, often immigrants but also, in coal-mining and southern plantation labor, descendants of indentured servants, who were despised nearly as much. On the Pacific Coast and in the west generally, Chinese labor was common. In many northern industries in the Midwest in the 1920s and 1930s, the labor was predominately native-born white; many were failed farmers or their descendants. Workers had no right to organize, and labored long hours, often in dangerous conditions, without earning enough to support their families.

Why is necessary labor often accompanied by intense exploitation and social degradation? These occur because labor is divided in the two ways I stated: the planters did not themselves tend tobacco plants or chop cotton; industrialists did not themselves work assembly lines. But they did give instructions to those who did: they determined at least the general organization of labor, and often its pace. They determined how much of the production is returned to the laborer (thus becoming quite wealthy). This is the division between the labor of production and the ownership and control of production. In the United States this division took a capitalist form, but the general division between organization and command functions on the one hand and execution of labor tasks on the other is universal in class societies, as I will argue later, in chapter 9.

As societies become more complex, and particularly when they become urban, that division of labor is accompanied by another: a division within the laboring classes, between those who do more complex, highly skilled labor, often without close supervision, and those who do the routine, more easily mastered, less skilled labor. Both divisions of labor are tied to race in the history of the United States. Specifically, the capitalist class has included very few black people. And, within the working class (including professional workers), there have been very few black people among the most highly trained and educated workers laboring without close supervision and doing the most intellectually challenging and complex tasks.

This racist organization of labor has been maintained through inequality of opportunity. When need arose for more skilled labor, few black people have been recruited for these tasks.

Anti-racism is now usually understood in the following way: while the general divisions of labor I have described are maintained, it is necessary to insure that disadvantaged minorities are proportionately represented among the owning class and among the more highly skilled workers. Thus affirmative action is understood as a means of creating equality of opportunity between historically disadvantaged groups and those who are not disadvantaged. But if it is wrong that black people are stuck doing mindless labor, why is it better if someone else is doing that work?

Rawls contrasted classical Greek societies, where there was a shared civic religion and shared ceremonies but little emphasis on specific doctrine, with Christian Europe after the Reformation, where competing claims to truth and salvation caused religious wars. As Rawls understood it, the latter historical experience set the problems for modern liberalism. I emphasize a much more general and universal contrast: between societies that do not divide labor (in the ways indicated) and those that do. That is, class societies, grounded in exploitation and command, create a division of labor which the experience of colonial Virginia, and then the United States, captures in one historically specific form. These divisions of labor set the central problems for social and political philosophy: Who toils for whom? Who decides how labor is organized and who works? Who does the more complex and engaging labor? Can those who execute labor plans also make them? Can routine and complex labor be shared?

Contributive justice

David Schmidtz has raised the following problem for Rawls's political philosophy: how can one develop principles of justice governing distribution of the benefits of social cooperation which are independent of the contributions people make to the social product? He suggests that our separateness as persons implies that "justice [is] mainly about what people do, about respecting what they contribute."[9] The social philosophy of Robert Nozick emphasizes respect for the ways people contribute to the good of others (Nozick 1974). But consider the facts about anti-black racism and its effect on equality of opportunity: can there be a just connection between distribution and contribution if we do not have a fair opportunity to contribute?

We may agree with Schmidtz that there should be a connection between contribution and reward – in some way this must be right – but any society which connected reward and contribution but did not give all a fair opportunity to contribute would not be just. We need a theory of contributive justice specifying both opportunities and duties to contribute to a larger social group. This book sketches that theory.

[9]   This quote appears on p. 11 of the typescript of "History and Pattern" (presented at the conference "Natural Rights Liberalism from Locke to Nozick: Essays in Honor of Robert Nozick" sponsored by the Social Philosophy and Policy Center at Bowling Green State University, September 18–20, 2003) but is not in the published version (Schmidtz 2005). I use this quote with the author's permission.

Consider this objection to emphasis on contributive justice: the most stark of the harms of racism – lower life expectancy, poorer health, and lesser access to health care – are harms of a highly unequal *distribution* of wealth. We need to distinguish, the objection continues, between "spheres of justice" (the phrase is from Michael Walzer 1983). The sphere of providing for health, housing, nutrition, and other basic material welfare is not to be confused with the sphere of labor contribution. Each sphere of justice has its own norms. To cite the racist deprivation of material well-being, particularly the differences between black and white life expectancy, and then to propose a solution that involves justice in contribution of labor is to confuse separate spheres of justice.

I disagree with this objection for two reasons. First, as things now stand, in societies dominated by production of commodities for exchange, the spheres cannot be kept separate. While one can distinguish different spheres of human activity governed by different norms – many believe that we should receive health care according to our needs, while designer clothes should go to those who can pay – those demeaned as contributors to the social good will suffer distributional harms. In market societies and money economies, labor that is demeaned will be paid poorly. Essential goods will be more readily available to those who have money. Granted, some societies have loosened this connection, providing all citizens with a minimum of health care, housing, and nutrition. But when this is not associated with elevating all as contributors to society, these reforms tend to be unstable. First in Britain in the 1970s, then in the United States in the 1980s, the "social contracts" that had provided basic needs as a right of citizenship were curtailed or dismantled (admittedly these basic rights were understood differently in the United States). Now these same guaranteed benefits are under assault in France and Germany where, I estimate, they will be greatly curtailed.

Second, a society that made the *appropriate* connection between contribution and reward would not be market-based. David Schmidtz is right: what we contribute to society and what we receive from it will be linked. In the pages that follow I will quarrel with linking contribution and individual *material* rewards, a link that Schmidtz assumes. It is unnecessary and harmful to use the means of life to reward or punish people for contribution or failure to contribute; in chapter 13, I argue that this use of the means of life is incompatible with contributive justice. In market economies the link between contribution of labor and provision of essential needs is hard to sever because money is a universal sign of esteem. I will argue in chapters 5, 9, and 13 that we can respect people's contributions by awarding social esteem, a good that need not be of limited supply. I will show in chapter 6 that there is a natural connection between contribution and other important social goods. A theory of contributive justice makes that natural connection normative.

Contributive justice requires equal opportunity to contribute. It is fair to link other social goods to contribution only if one has a fair opportunity to contribute. Currently, labor is divided in the two ways I described: between control of labor tasks and their execution and between routine, closely supervised labor and more complex labor carried out more autonomously. It is possible to create equal opportunity in a society that breaks down these divisions of labor, creating for all the opportunity to participate in the planning of production and to master complex skills and knowledge. Equal opportunity requires that the most important social goods be of unlimited supply; this is possible if the most important goods are opportunities to contribute and to earn esteem for contributions. Equal opportunity requires a sensible basis for the esteem we may earn from others; this basis is contribution to the good of the social group, including contribution of complex labor. It requires a society where routine and complex labor are shared. To imagine a society of equal opportunity is to imagine something very different from a society dominated by markets, where relationships are mediated by money and commodities. But such a society could be a fully modern one with a complex division of labor in the theoretical and practical sciences.

Race and opportunity

I will suppose that you, the reader, oppose racism; that is, I will suppose that you think it wrong that people should be disadvantaged on account of an ascribed racial identity. "Disadvantage" can be understood in at least two ways: it can mean that people have lesser opportunity; alternatively, it can mean that people have worse lives, fewer material advantages. We believe it wrong that people should experience either sort of disadvantage on account of being thought to be of a particular race.

How are we to understand a society without racism? I will argue in the next two chapters that societies that divide labor and limit opportunities must harbor unequal opportunity. Thus, someone will be disadvantaged in opportunity, and someone will be doing the less desirable routine labor. We believe it wrong that black people, on account of their racial identity, should have lesser opportunity and worse jobs. However, racism just highlights a more general problem. It is wrong that *anyone* should have lesser opportunity and worse jobs. The solution to this dilemma is to share labor. Sharing labor – and only sharing labor – can create equal and unlimited opportunity.

Chapter 2

Against Leveling the Playing Field

Competitive opportunity

Equal opportunity is usually understood as equality of competitive opportunity: there are limited positions of advantage; each should have an opportunity to attain those positions without being disadvantaged by anything irrelevant to one's suitability for the position. This understanding assumes that some social outcomes are generally preferable to others, that it is better to be rich than poor, better to teach than to sweep up classrooms, better to be an electrical engineer than to install electrical cable, better to manage a company than to work on an assembly line. Of course, these judgments are not unanimous, but in the dominant culture there is agreement about which outcomes are better. This agreement attaches (again, in the dominant culture) more prestige to some social positions than to others. In addition, some positions are rewarded with higher incomes and the things that money can buy. As it is usually understood, equal opportunity concerns opportunity to attain a better rather than a worse outcome. The harms of racism cited in chapter 1 are partly the effect of those differences in outcomes. So some outcomes are not only thought to be worse in the dominant culture, but are – we can all agree – in some ways genuinely worse.

Opportunity is competitive because the most desired positions are fewer in number than the people who aspire to them. Since the positions are not determined rigidly by heredity, ethnicity, or caste, there is a competition to determine which aspirants obtain them. The ideal of equal opportunity, in this context, is that each person enters the competition with an equal opportunity to succeed and that no one's aspirations are shaped such that they do not aspire to the more desirable positions. Success in the competition should depend upon merit. It should depend upon personal qualities of those who aspire to positions of advantage, qualities relevant to their carrying out the responsibilities of those positions. It should not depend upon race, ethnicity, religion, gender, family income or background, or any other irrelevant characteristic by which people have historically been stigmatized or otherwise put at a disadvantage.

In the United States philosophers who are regarded as "left," or egalitarian, have put forward a "level playing field" conception of competitive equal opportunity. This conception is defended in John Roemer's *Equality of Opportunity* (1998). Roemer is concerned with opportunity to attain positions of educational and monetary advantage; he tries to devise a policy whereby success in attaining those positions will depend entirely on a person's autonomous choices, not on circumstances into which one is born and over which one has no control. In this chapter I will argue against the level playing field conception. Generally, I argue that the philosophical distinction between autonomously chosen acts and circumstances beyond one's control does not make sense in the political context where Roemer uses it. Specifically against Roemer, I argue that no way of leveling the playing field makes sense. The problems of competitive opportunity cannot be addressed by leveling the playing field.

Roemer on equal opportunity

Roemer's approach to equal opportunity is influenced by Ronald Dworkin, who in 1981 published a widely discussed essay on equality.[1] The governing idea derived from Dworkin is to distinguish between those elements of a person's situation for which she can rightly be held accountable – for Roemer these are autonomously chosen acts – and those elements which constitute arbitrary advantages and disadvantages between individuals – Roemer calls these "circumstances." The governing idea in its most general form – to distinguish those things for which one can, and cannot, rightly be held accountable – is common not only to Roemer and Dworkin, but also to G. A. Cohen (1989) and Richard Arneson (1989).[2] Roemer's "level playing field" conception of equality of opportunity requires that government policy allocate (especially educational) resources to young people in different "circumstances" to insure that all have the same opportunity. Then their achievements will depend on the degree of autonomously chosen effort they make. They can rightly be held accountable for this degree of effort.

Roemer proposes to divide children into a finite number of "types" based on different elements of their "circumstances." One type might consist of "black children, living in the inner city, in single-parent homes with many siblings, whose parent did not graduate from high school," while another might be "upper-middle-class suburban children living in two-parent homes, with two or fewer siblings, and whose parents both graduated from college" (Roemer 1998: 13). Roemer holds that it is unreasonable to expect a child of the first type to make the same *level* of effort (measured, say, in number of hours spent studying) in school as a child of the second type, because:

---

[1] Reprinted as chapters 1 and 2 of Dworkin 2000.
[2] But see Arneson 1999 for qualifications.

> Children form views about the desirability of exerting effort in school by
> observing what others are doing and by making inferences about the value of
> education from observing adults who have and have not achieved education, at
> various levels, and how their lives have consequently gone. These "views" include
> their beliefs and their preferences: preferences themselves may be influenced by
> beliefs, as in the sour-grapes phenomenon [where we cease to desire something
> if we believe it is unattainable]. Influenced by these beliefs and preferences a child
> decides what is a reasonable level of effort to exert. (pp. 13–14)

Roemer proposes (roughly) that educational resources be distributed so that
individuals of different types (for example, the black disadvantaged child and
the white advantaged child) who make the same *degree* of effort (relative to
others of the same type) are rewarded equally with the same educational outcome and expectation of income. The two children of different types would
receive the same rewards even though the level of effort (hours spent studying)
will be less for the typical child of the first type than for the typical child of the
second type. This proposal is based on the sociological premise that the same
level of effort (hours spent studying) represents a much greater effort, relative
to one's peers, for a child of the first type than for a child of the second. In sum,
the child of the first type is unfairly disadvantaged by circumstances; a "level
playing field" policy requires compensation for this disadvantage so that outcomes for equal degrees of effort (relative to others of the same type) are equal.

This much of Roemer's proposal makes sense to me: some people are so
unfairly disadvantaged by family and neighborhood circumstances that they
do not have equal competitive opportunity. This is captured by the contrast
of the two "types" that Roemer draws. At minimum, any society with equal
competitive opportunity would have somehow to undo the unfairness created
by family and neighborhood circumstances.

The fallacy of moralizing politics

Roemer's approach to equal opportunity extends a *moral* belief about what
makes someone deserving to a *political* context. Specifically, Roemer believes
that our degree of effort is an autonomously chosen act for which we can be held
responsible and rewarded (or deprived of rewards) accordingly. This approach
to equal opportunity derives from the moral belief that we can be justly praised
and blamed, rewarded and punished only for acts for which we are rightly
held accountable, that is, for our autonomously chosen acts, not for circumstances over which we have had no control. We may call this the belief that
there is a morally significant difference between the effects of chance and those
of choice; it is commonly held (at least by Dworkin, Roemer, Cohen, and
Arneson) to be central to questions of justice.

We can see the moral belief at work in everyday contexts where we praise
people for their accomplishments or blame them for their failures. Think of an
overly critical parent finding fault with everything his children do, undermining

their self-confidence. Our first reaction might be to criticize any parent who would act that way. After all, the duties of being a parent are nurturing duties, preparing children for adulthood. Constant criticism, undermining self-confidence, makes it hard for children to function as competent adults. So our first moral reaction is to blame the parent, to hold him accountable for his failure to nurture his children, to find fault in his moral character and in the choice he makes to raise his children in this way. Treating him as autonomous, we might confront and criticize him and condemn his behavior to others.

Suppose, however, we find that *his* father raised him in the same way. He grew up learning that a "loving" father is very critical of his children. This is his interpretation of paternal duty, to prepare his children for the harsh world with criticism and exacting standards of behavior that they would meet as adults. As a child growing up, this is how he had learned to understand what it means to be a father. Moreover, knowing him better, we find that he suffers from feelings of being unworthy, feelings that are a continuing effect of criticism he received as a child; he believes his father was an ideal parent, a belief that is a source of both his behavior toward his children and his pain. Knowing his *circumstances*, we are now more likely to think of him as a victim (albeit a victim who is victimizing others) than as morally blameworthy for not being a good father. Rather than holding him accountable and criticizing him, we might urge him to re-examine how he was brought up – the history of abuse which victimized him – perhaps by examining his childhood jointly with a counselor.

So everyday moral life and thought implies this contrast between our *autonomously chosen* behavior and our *circumstances* that make us think and act in certain ways, the distinction between the effects of choice and of chance. In everyday moral thought, we are to be held accountable for our freely chosen behavior but not for the circumstances that have shaped our character in ways for which we should not be held accountable.

Dworkin and those influenced by him transfer this distinction between autonomous choice and circumstance, which makes perfectly good sense in many moral contexts, to a political context. They make the distinction central to their theories of justice. In their view, a just society would minimize the rewards and penalties of chance but allow us to suffer (at least some of) the consequences of our own choices.

For Roemer, equal opportunity is central to justice. So in developing an approach to equal opportunity, Roemer distinguishes between circumstances for which we should not be held accountable but which nevertheless shape the ways we think and act and autonomously chosen behavior for which we are rightly praised and blamed.

We are familiar enough with this transferring of moral ideas into social contexts (I will call this "moralizing" politics) from many examples in everyday life. For example, many blame the unemployed for their plight with language like this: "If you are unemployed, you have no one to blame but yourself. If you try hard enough, you can find a job." This is a familiar sort of example of moralizing politics, of applying the moral category of blame in a social context.

Of course, as any economist will tell us, we need to distinguish between individual and collective rationality. That is, it may be rational for an individual to reason about her unemployment as above and redouble efforts to search for work. Yet this way of thinking hardly makes sense as a *general* response addressed to the unemployed *as a group*; if all the unemployed redouble their effort to find work, it would not have the effect that they all would get jobs. So moralizing politics often makes no sense when moral ways of thinking are applied to a *group* that experiences similar problems.

Roemer would also criticize this particular instance of moralizing politics (blaming the unemployed). In fact, one point of the "level playing field" conception of justice is that one cannot reasonably expect that children who grow up in disadvantaged circumstances will have the same approach to education or have the same motivational resources generally as children who grow up in more advantaged circumstances. Advantaged children are surrounded by many examples of the rewards received by those who put out superior effort. In contrast, children who grow up in more disadvantaged circumstances see many older adults in their neighborhoods who work hard. But their efforts are "rewarded" by jobs with very low wages and with the social contempt that the larger society has for low-wage workers. So Roemer would agree that to blame the unemployed for their plight is to blame them inappropriately for things which are the result of their social circumstances, not their autonomous choices.

Still, if my interpretation of Roemer is right, he is committed to bringing about social organization and policies where it *would* be appropriate to transfer the moral distinction between autonomously chosen acts (for which we can rightly be held accountable) and circumstances (which determine aspects of one's motivation and resources for which we cannot justly be held accountable) into the social realm. That is, he wants to create a society where those who end up with better educations and better jobs are truly deserving of those outcomes. In Roemer's society of equal opportunity, those better jobs are rewards for autonomously chosen behavior. By the same token, in this ideal society those who end up on the bottom of the social heap can rightly be held accountable for their plight; their situation too is the result of *their* choices.

Without going too far afield from issues of equal opportunity, I will argue that we should be skeptical of this distinction between autonomously chosen behavior, for which we can rightly be held accountable, and behavior that is the result of circumstances by which we are unjustly handicapped or advantaged, *when that distinction is applied to the distribution of social positions of advantage.*

To explain why this is so, it is necessary to take a short detour into issues of freedom and determinism. Since the rise of modern science in the seventeenth century, it has been a puzzle how one can rightly hold people responsible for their conduct. This puzzle grows not so much from determinism (all human behavior is determined by antecedent causes, particularly heredity and environment) as from the very nature of explanations of behavior: either behavior can be explained as the result of antecedent events and states, or that behavior cannot be completely explained in that way. That is, every event is either explained by antecedent causal conditions or it is, to an extent, just something that happened without there being any causal explanation of why it happened. If we understand our behavior as being explainable as the effect of causes and these causes as themselves explainable as the effects of further causes and so forth, we eventually get to causes of behavior that are outside the agent's control. But it seems wrong to hold the agent responsible for something outside his control. And if, at any point in this search for explanations, we come upon something that does not have an explanation, that simply happened without being caused, neither can the agent be responsible for that something.

So there is a puzzle arising from the nature of causal explanation and the possibility of random events that have no (complete) causal explanation. Looked at abstractly, apart from practical justifications, it is hard to find a reason to hold people accountable for the things they do. Nevertheless, we hold people responsible.

Many philosophers, going back at least to David Hume in the eighteenth century, have thought that this moral practice makes sense for the following reason: by holding people accountable for their conduct, we hope to modify their conduct and that of others in the future.[3] And, in the light of this way of thinking, the distinction between "autonomously chosen" behavior on the one hand and "circumstances" on the other can be a way of marking behavior that we estimate can be corrected by moral assessment (praise and blame or reward and punishment) and behavior where such assessment would have no positive effect on the behavior of either the person praised or anyone else. When behavior is judged to be "determined by circumstances," we are estimating that moral criticism would be fruitless or counterproductive. When we view behavior as "autonomously chosen," we believe that the agent can respond to criticism or other sanction by correcting his behavior. This seems to be a natural understanding of how we decide to make moral criticism part of the moral training of children. We can naturally extend it to criticisms of adult conduct as well.

The key point is this: moral criticism is about guiding and correcting the conduct of an individual. Moral criticism is directed toward the individual and, when negative, toward behavior that is regarded as individually aberrant. If this is an accurate analysis of why phrases such as "autonomously chosen conduct" make sense in their ordinary use, then such concepts may not make sense when used to decide whether people get the social rewards they deserve. What is the point of saying, in a society with a perfectly level playing field, that people's social positions, their educational and job attainments, are the result of their "autonomous choices"? The statement does not seem to be intended constructively, as it is in ordinary moral praise and blame. It seems to work ideologically, as a moral sanctification of a social order. For this reason, I believe that the move by Dworkin and those who follow him in "moralizing politics" represents a profound error.

---

[3]   This account of the problem of responsibility and this solution is also in Gomberg 1978.

It is the same error of moralizing politics as in the case of someone who is unemployed. Suppose I have a friend who is unemployed. I might advise him to be the first in line every morning at the Job Service. I might feel he is insufficiently committed to getting a job or overly demoralized if he refuses to do so; I might criticize him in this way, either to his face or to others. The criticism has a point. The point is to encourage behavior that will benefit my friend who is unemployed or perhaps, if made to someone else, to encourage that person to continue to try to find work.

As we saw, parallel judgments generally about what the unemployed should do do not make sense in the same way; if all unemployed people showed up at the Job Service a half hour before it opens, the bureaucracy for handling unemployment would break down. In order for that bureaucracy to work as intended, it is necessary that a large percentage of the unemployed should become discouraged. What is meant when people say that the unemployed have only themselves to blame? The statement serves to justify the economic system that harbors unemployment. It does not address what causes the un-employment rate to be higher or lower, thus hiding social forces, institutions, or policies that cause a certain percentage to be unemployed. By hiding the causal role of these institutions and policies and focusing only on the people who are unemployed as causing their own unemployment, the statement that the unemployed have only themselves to blame tends to make the current state of things look as if it is justified.

Consider the parallel with egalitarianisms that propose creating a social order where all inequality is the result of the choices agents make, not the situations "chance" has thrust upon them. In this egalitarian society, our philosophers would judge that those who are in disadvantaged positions are there as a result of their own autonomous choices. We are supposing that these judgments are made within a society which must distribute limited social positions of advantage. The judgments would not be intended to help an individual make better choices; they are not directed to individuals but are assessments of the causes of social inequality. That is why I say the function of such judgments would have to be "ideological." They would, like parallel judgments about the unemployed in our society, be meant to sanctify the social order by assuring us that there was nothing wrong with the society and that anyone in a worse-off position was there as a result of his own choices and hence had only himself to blame.

If some would be better-off and some would be worse-off, if some would live well and others poorly, if some would be janitors and others mathematicians, the judgment that this is the result of people's "autonomous choices" looks at only one factor in determining who is a janitor and who a mathematician. In Roemer's society of equal opportunity, the distribution of positions of janitor and mathematician is a function of two things: (1) the particular "autonomous choices" that explain why one individual ends up in one position and another in the other; (2) the organization of social institutions that create positions such as janitor and mathematician. By saying that the outcome is the result of people's "autonomous choices," we focus on the role of the first of these in explaining the social outcomes and hide the role of the second.

As in the case where the individualist explains unemployment as due to the choices of the unemployed, we hide the causal role of social institutions where *someone* has to sweep up after others. That is why I say that the role of Roemer's use of "autonomous choices" is ideological. By hiding the role of social institutions in creating positions such as "janitor," it tends to justify the social order that would result if society had a level playing field.

The key issue, as I argue throughout this book, is how much opportunity there is for challenging, complex labor. If our social organization creates a few social positions of advantage and many much less desirable social positions and then has a level playing field of competition for those few desirable positions, it is not a simple and transparent fact that people's situations are due to their "autonomous choices." That seems true enough if we take for granted the social organization of positions and roles. But if we imagine how society might be organized differently, if we imagine a society where there are no "janitors" but the labor of cleaning up is woven into other activities that are more challenging and complex, then we see that "autonomous choice" alone does not explain why someone is a janitor.

In Roemer's ideal society, how well people do is the result of their "autonomous choices." But these are the "autonomous choices" of *children*!

Why are we different from one another?

Roemer relies on a distinction between choice and chance to craft an approach to equal opportunity. All are to have equal opportunity, unaffected by circumstances; therefore, those who get the better positions do so because they made better choices and those who get worse positions made worse choices. As a result, those who are in such positions will deserve them. In the last section I criticized this approach.

It will strengthen these criticisms to look at the details of Roemer's approach. His types of circumstance are intended to eliminate the unfairness of the current structure of opportunity. Yet because he accepts limited and hence competitive opportunity, his proposals will not eliminate unfairness. What, for Roemer, constitutes an unfair disadvantage? Consider his first type: black children from inner-city single-parent families. Among individuals who are identical *in those respects* there will be differences relevant to success in *competitive* opportunity; for example, individuals of Roemer's first type will have varying degrees of confidence about their ability to master school subjects, a sense of security in their environment, tolerance of failure, and enthusiasm for competition. All these variations will probably be relevant to competitive success. For some, we may be able to specify characteristics of the environment that we can assume explain these variations. But it is likely that any such explanations are highly specific. Put another way, relevant correlations of school success or effort with factors such as the ones Roemer specifies are always limited (though important). Much of what is relevant is very specific to the life of an individual.

The same rationale that says a single-parent family constitutes an unfair environmental disadvantage will apply with equal force to other factors relevant to competitive success. These factors often cannot be understood apart from a particular narrative account of how one individual became confident while another became doubtful of her abilities. These factors may not lend themselves to generalization, though they make sense within the context of a narrative of a person's life. More specifically, the interactions between two siblings and how they are viewed by the adults around them may have profound effects on the confidence of the two, as one develops a general sense of her own competence while the other may always find her efforts wanting. Once we understand how someone came to lack confidence in her own abilities and hence came to withhold effort in school, we view her lack of confidence as just as much an unfair disadvantage (relative to her sibling) as we do the disadvantage they may share of being from a single-parent family. The rationale for Roemer's specification of types – that young people raised in these circumstances are at a disadvantage (or advantage) when compared with others – only begins to capture the elements that are relevant to how hard students will try in school.

Roemer asks us to accept that two children alike in "circumstances" – growing up in a single-parent home in an inner-city black neighborhood – will be different only in autonomously chosen acts, specifically how much effort they choose to exert to advance in school. But are children who grow up in the environment he describes alike in the way their values are formed? There can be many relevant differences: their parents can have different values (one family an ethic of ambition, another a fatalistic ethic), different skills in conveying their values, different amounts of time to devote to their children, or differences in their networks of support for parenting. The families may be differently affected by drug use or histories of child abuse.

Children have different experiences and learn different things from similar experiences. An example of the first would be that in school one child might form a close friendship with a conventionally ambitious classmate (perhaps partly because the teacher arranged the classroom seating alphabetically, and the two children were seated next to one another), while another may become best friends with a troubled child whose mother is an addict. An example of learning different things from similar experiences is that one child who befriends a troubled classmate might respond by deciding to become a social worker while another child with a similar friendship might be drawn into the troubled world of the classmate. A little imagination should persuade you that any number of factors might be relevant in particular cases. Our development represents a particular lived experience; the narrative of that experience may make sense in retrospect, but it is impossible to anticipate how a child will develop in her circumstances. Most important, it is not the case that the differences between children who develop different orientations toward studying are due to "autonomous choice" of how much effort to make.

Children develop different orientations toward success because of competitive opportunity itself, a sort of opportunity that must produce "failures" as well as "successes." Someone will have to sweep up after others. Who should it be? Once we understand how an individual came to be a "failure," once we grasp the narrative by which someone came to lack enough of the qualities to succeed competitively, we often lose the sense that the competition is fair.

To summarize: Roemer's "level playing field" conception of equal competitive opportunity attempts to equalize opportunity (as measured by the educational and income outcomes achieved) between *groups* (types) differently affected by various advantages and disadvantages. The rationale for the proposal is that some (identifiable) groups are unfairly disadvantaged by circumstances. I have argued in reply that parallel to the considerations that make us feel that group disadvantage constitutes an unfair inequality of opportunity are considerations that affect the relative success of individuals within any such group: once we understand how an individual came to be more or less ambitious, confident, secure, robust, and eager to learn, we cease to think it is fair that one will be relatively better-off and more successful than the other. The problem is competitive opportunity. Competitive opportunity *requires* that some fail, that some be unemployed, underemployed, or in menial, mind-numbing jobs.

Note an implication of "leveling the playing field." The playing field metaphor is derived from competitive games with winners and losers. Level playing field conceptions do not propose to address the number of losers or the severity of their losses but to address who is a winner and who is a loser. If there are still the same number of losers and their losses are similar to those of our current losers, one may wonder how much better than the status quo such equal opportunity would be. The governing idea of the level playing field is that opportunity is a scarce good. The level playing field would distribute that scarce good differently (and presumably more "fairly").

The level playing field conception accepts the assumption made explicit at the beginning of this chapter, that equal opportunity concerns how limited desirable social outcomes are distributed among us. That is, it takes for granted the limitations on desirable social positions and the consequent limitations on opportunity. But how can such limitations be justified?

Chapter 3

Against Limiting Opportunity

Quantity of opportunity

It is important how much opportunity we have to contribute complex abilities. I give three reasons for this conclusion: one abstract, the second practical, the third theoretical. The abstract argument is that even if opportunity were equal, it still would be important how much opportunity there was. Societies should, as far as possible, make it possible for us to exercise characteristically *human* abilities: the abilities to master social and other complexity and to make and execute plans are characteristic strengths of our species; so we should be able to practice those abilities in our work. The practical argument is that limited opportunity will, under any likely circumstances, be highly unequal. Again, if people are to have good lives, quantity of opportunity is important. The theoretical argument is that children are socialized for available opportunities; as a result, if opportunities to contribute complex abilities are limited, children will be socialized not to want to develop those abilities.

The idea of quantity of opportunity is straightforward. The central opportunities are opportunities to attain social positions. Social positions are statuses within a social group defined by rights and obligations or responsibilities (Davis 1948). Usually we think of positions as jobs: architect, professor, auto worker, bus driver, corporate executive, dental technician, administrative assistant, maid, and so forth. Positions of employment come with rights and obligations: an employee has a right to an overtime bonus after working a set number of hours; an employee must carry out the assignments of the job description. But a wife, parent or offspring, PTO member, licensed driver, citizen, and public aid recipient also occupy positions. While we think of the rights and obligations of a licensed driver or public aid recipient as defined by law, we think of the rights and responsibilities of a mother as primarily defined by the ethic of a social group.

For some positions there is unlimited opportunity in the sense that *social structure sets no limits* (except, perhaps, ones related to age or sex) to the number who can attain the position, for example, parent or licensed driver. For others the opportunities are more limited: there is only one position of President of the United States. Most employment positions are intermediate, but there is greater quantity of opportunity to be an auto worker than to be an architect; that is, society employs more auto workers than architects.

The quantity of opportunity for positions is affected by history. In the United States there are fewer opportunities to work in the automobile and steel industries than there were a generation ago. The quantity of opportunity to be a physician in the United States was limited by laws at the end of the nineteenth and beginning of the twentieth centuries; in Cuba, the quantity of opportunity to be a physician was expanded as a result of government policy after the 1959 revolution. To some extent, at least, the quantity of opportunities for particular positions in a society may be due to conscious choices of social policy.

The Meritonia argument

I will argue shortly that where opportunity is limited it will not be equal. So to separate the issues raised by the quantity of opportunity and its equality, we must do an imaginative experiment; specifically, we must imagine a world where opportunity is equal but very limited. Suppose that children are separated from parents and similarly educated; their occupations as adults are determined by tests they take at age 18. Call this world Meritonia. In Meritonia the vast majority of occupations involve mindless, repetitive labor under close supervision; only a few require the exercise of complex abilities, intellectual, literary, artistic, or organizational.

Surely Meritonia is a worse society than it would be if more occupations involved intellectually challenging and self-directed labor. Then more people's work would require them to exercise complex abilities. Other things being equal, more would take pride in what they did, and their work would inspire the admiration of others. It makes a difference how much opportunity there is to exercise complex abilities, and more opportunity of this sort is better than less.

Meritonia is bad because, with so little opportunity to use complex abilities, many who had abilities would be unable to exercise them. The positions in Meritonia constrict too severely the opportunity to exercise our abilities in our working lives. Someone who aspires to be an architect, to design buildings for human needs, may not be able to do so – not because opportunity is unequal but because it is too limited.

When people's working lives are occupied with simple, routine tasks, their lives are, to that extent, degraded. Adam Smith saw this problem, and his description of it is striking:

> In the progress of the division of labour, the employment of the far greater part of those who live by labour . . . comes to be confined to a few very simple operations. . . . But the understandings of the greater part of men are necessarily formed

by their ordinary employments. The man whose whole life is spent in performing a few simple operations . . . has no occasion to exert his understanding. . . .
He naturally loses, therefore, the habit of such exertion, and generally becomes
as stupid and ignorant as it is possible for a human creature to become. (Smith
1776, vol. 2, book V, ch. 1, art. 2, 302–3)

While Smith exaggerates, there is also truth. (We will consider his remedy soon.)
Executing the same routine task *tends* to dull the mind. Nevertheless, workers
may find stimulation elsewhere, and some are active intellectuals. But simple
labor has a negative effect on intellectual development – there is evidence for
this (Kohn and Schooler 1983).[1] Intellectually active workers may incline toward
rebellion, not conformity with norms of labor contribution which degrade them.
When a system of organizing labor confines people to routine, easily mastered
tasks, it harms them.

   Assume that we can affect the distribution of positions that require complex
abilities. What distribution would enable all who have potential to develop
complex abilities to develop and exercise their talents? I believe that we don't
know much about any natural limitations of potential and that, given our ignorance, the distribution of positions that makes most sense creates unlimited
opportunity to develop and exercise these more complex abilities. There is no
reason to think that the potential to develop these abilities is limited to a few.
The point of the Meritonia argument is that the goal of equal opportunity is
best pursued in the context of expanded – if possible, unlimited – opportunity to develop and contribute complex knowledge and talents.

The practical argument

Equal competitive opportunity is practically impossible. When opportunity is
limited and competitive, some positions are more desirable and advantaged,
both intrinsically and extrinsically. That is, some labor is intrinsically more interesting and enjoyable, to almost everyone. (If you doubt this, consider: almost
everyone prefers self-directed to closely supervised labor.) Some labor is carried out in safer and less noxious physical environments. Extrinsically, some
labor is rewarded with greater prestige and income. The opportunity to attain
the more desirable positions will not be equal. Parents will try to convey to
their children cultural and educational advantages that will make the better
positions available to them. More advantaged parents will be able to do this
more effectively. So opportunity to attain these more desirable positions will
not be equal.

   This argument can be made not only abstractly, as above, but also empiric-
ally. Social scientists have argued that hierarchical, including capitalist, societies

---

[1] What Kohn and Schooler show, through a 10-year longitudinal analysis, is that there is a modest
but real tendency for substantive complexity of work to enhance ideational flexibility. See especially
chapter 5.

"reproduce social inequality," through the family, schools, and, more informally, subcultures shared in a neighborhood or community. The "left" has argued that schools are designed to train many for obedience and routine labor (Bowles and Gintis 1976). Others have argued that neighborhoods of disadvantaged people (particularly those identified with a demeaned "race") develop a culture, perhaps psychologically comforting in people's circumstances, that limits aspirations, discourages ambition or deflects it to low-status work, and may disable effective job performance (Massey and Denton 1993). These institutions and informal cultures make it impossible for each child to have the same opportunity to achieve more desirable positions in the hierarchy.

Many, but not all, respond to these arguments with a sense that social structures that organize opportunities in these ways are wasteful, harmful, and unfair. If potential to acquire and contribute complex abilities exists among both rich and poor, much human potential is wasted by such social organization. Moreover, many of the most disadvantaged children are unable to acquire and contribute many characteristically human complex abilities. Potential is wasted, and many people's lives are worse.

And the skewing of opportunity is unfair. Consider: A child from the top 10 percent in family wealth is 16 times more likely to graduate from college than a child from the bottom 10 percent (Haveman and Wilson 2005: 24). If we look at the *prestige* of the colleges from which people graduate, the inequality of opportunity is yet more extreme. (Prestige of the school is surely relevant to one's prospects. Many graduates from the college where I teach are in low-wage social service jobs; recently, I ran into a former student who was working as a security guard a year after graduation.) A survey of 146 elite colleges found that only 3 percent of students are from families in the bottom 25 percent in income, and only 10 percent are from families in the bottom 50 percent in income (Century Foundation 2004). If graduates from these colleges are disproportionately represented in the more challenging, higher-paying jobs, then opportunity is unfairly unequal.

Illustrating the practical argument

Sheryll Cashin's *The Failures of Integration* explains how court decisions, government policies, housing choices, voter preferences, parental concerns, and the culture of anti-black racism have combined in American history to create unequal opportunity, particularly as it disadvantages many black children. In telling this story, I emphasize that there is both necessity and contingency. The particularities of unequal opportunity in the United States arose in the country's history. This is the contingency. At the same time, parents with the means to do so are trying to provide their children with a "leg up" in the competition for limited positions of advantage; some outcomes for their children will leave them with fewer options and probably poorer health and shorter lives. Parents seek as best they can to avoid these outcomes for their own children. This is the necessity. In saying it is a "necessity," I do not mean to imply that the extreme competitiveness of many advantaged parents is necessary; what is necessary is that parents with greater power and wealth give advantages to their children when the worst outcomes are very bad.

Cashin is a law professor at Georgetown University; one of her striking observations is the role of the 1926 Supreme Court decision validating a zoning ordinance in Euclid, Ohio, a small suburb of Cleveland. The Court wrote that excluding other buildings from neighborhoods of single-family homes would "increase the safety and security of home life; . . . decrease noise and other conditions which produce or intensify nervous disorders; [and] preserve a more favorable environment in which to raise children." An apartment house would be "a mere parasite," interfering "with the free exercise of the air and monopoliz[ing] the rays of the sun." Cashin explains the Court's reasoning:

> [T]he increased traffic that would accompany apartment houses would render these neighborhoods less safe, depriving children "in more favored localities" of "the privilege of quiet and open spaces for play." . . . [T]he Court might as well have said that the *people* that would accompany apartment buildings or duplexes would be nuisance-like invaders on the quiet seclusion of favored families. . . . In short, zoning is a means of social control. It plays a critical gatekeeping function. (2004: 106)

Euclid established the right of suburbs to keep out poor people.

Government programs have contributed to racial and economic segregation. While public housing projects have increased the concentration of poverty in ghetto neighborhoods, major highways have built walls of segregation and made it possible for the more affluent to escape the cities while maintaining access to employment and centers of culture. Cashin writes: "Since 1956 the federal government has rained down more than a half trillion dollars on states to subsidize the cost of roads leading out of cities to an ever expanding suburban frontier. . . . [M]assive federal outlays have significantly reduced the real costs of outer suburban development for new suburbanites" (pp. 114–15). Taxpayers, including urban workers, paid for these highways and for sewers and utilities (p. 162). The less advantaged, particularly black people, were excluded from communities made possible by these taxes. Cashin writes: "Monumental highway subsidies, government-backed low-cost mortgages made available on a discriminatory basis, and mostly unbridled exclusionary zoning by new suburban communities all worked in combination to fuel rapid suburbanization by the white middle class and to erect barriers to entry by others" (p. 115).

School districts tend to be segregated by the race and income of the students' families and are unequally funded. In New Jersey the state Supreme Court ruled in 1990 that the legislature was obligated to "assure that poorer urban districts' education funding is substantially equal to that of property-rich districts." The order was never implemented. When legislators passed tax increases to pay for equalization, protest led to a lowering of the increase. Legislators who had voted for the tax increase and the governor who proposed it were defeated in elections. Another governor who advocated shifting state monies from affluent to poor districts to comply with the order, backed off when her supporters rebelled. As of 2002 the reforms mandated by the 1990 order had still not been implemented. There is logic to the process Cashin describes: if affluent parents (and voters) pay large sums to live in homogeneous, affluent neighborhoods with superior schools in order to advantage their children in the competition for limited positions of advantage, why should they then agree to pay more taxes that would undo that advantage?

Cashin depicts parental attitudes. A suburban Utah couple were "focused like a laser beam on doing the best job [they] could for [their] child." The father "didn't want his kid going to school with lower-income children who might lower the standards of education." Cashin writes:

> He had worked hard for his money and had made good choices for himself and his family. "Why should I be penalized for that?" he argued. The father objected to a school busing plan that would bus the children of poor Spanish-speaking students concentrated in one neighborhood: ". . . it doesn't seem fair that people who make good choices to have fewer kids, to work hard and raise them well, get less attention than those people who make bad choices. If a bunch of Spanish-speaking kids are bused into a school, they are . . . going to bring the standard down for everyone else. That is not fair." (pp. 176–7)

The story of increasing school segregation, documented by Orfield (2001), would not be complete without a review of Supreme Court decisions that made resegregation possible. In 1974, in *Milliken v. Bradley*, the Court decided that suburban school districts near Detroit could not be included in desegregation suits unless it had been shown that they had engaged in discriminatory practices. In Cashin's words: "The decision essentially insulated predominately white suburban school districts from the constitutional imperatives of *Brown*, gave suburban citizens more incentive to create their own separate school districts, and offered white parents in urban districts fearful of school desegregation havens of predominately white schools to which they could flee" (2004: 212).[2] In 2000, Detroit schools were 91 percent black, surrounded by 116 suburban school districts. In 1991, in *Board of Education of Oklahoma City v. Dowell*, the Court ended court intervention in a city where the segregation of schools mirrored residential segregation. In 1995's *Missouri v. Jenkins* the Court declined to require the state of Missouri to pay for a magnet school program that might help to integrate Kansas City schools. The de facto segregation that had replaced de jure segregation was not to be remedied. Understanding the Court's position, "school districts across the nation were

---

[2] The 1954 *Brown v. Board of Education* Supreme Court decision declared that separate schools for black children were inherently unequal. The decision was a legal landmark in ending the "Jim Crow" segregation that had been sanctioned in the 1896 *Plessy v. Ferguson* decision.

scrambling to get the benefit of the case's relaxed standard" (p. 216). Between 1991 and 1994, "the nation's schools were resegregating at the fastest rate since 1954" (p. 217). This trend continues.

Black poor people in central cities are residentially "hypersegregated" (in the word used by Douglas Massey and Nancy Denton in *American Apartheid*). Large numbers of black people, particularly the poor, live in huge overwhelmingly black neighborhoods with the very poorest schools. Fully one half or more of black men in Baltimore and Washington, DC are under the criminal justice system (Cashin 2004: 373, n. 19). This is unequal opportunity at its most extreme.

What role does anti-black racism play in this unequal opportunity? In her Introduction, Cashin writes:

> Choosing a neighborhood that separates oneself and one's family from "worse" elements farther down the economic scale has become the critical gateway to upward mobility. . . . Of all of our tacit understandings about separation, the supreme, cardinal principle seems to be that poor black people are to be avoided and that society is better-off shunting them into their own neighborhoods, far away in particular from sizeable white populations. (pp. xvi–xvii)

Racism and the perception of race and poverty in combination are central to housing and school segregation.

Limited opportunity is rationed through segregation. Cashin points out that in the United States children are more segregated than adults and schools are more segregated than children (p. 92). (To understand why this would be so, consider: white people without children might be more ready to live around significant numbers of black people than are white people with children; and white people with children might be readier to live in a significantly black neighborhood if they send their children to parochial or private schools.) To explain these phenomena, including those cases where school integration is stable, I suggest two hypotheses about opportunity and race: (1) racial segregation in housing and schools is driven in part by the desire of white parents to create better opportunity for their children and by negative stereotypes of black children, particularly poor black children; (2) advantaged white parents seeking to secure opportunities for their children will tolerate integrated schools that either are for "gifted" students only or are internally segregated into "gifted" and other tracks.

As I said, there is both contingency and necessity in these phenomena. The rationing of limited opportunity does not require the sixfold increase in incarceration in the United States over the past 30 years. Still, each society with limited opportunity sorts children into winners and losers; the winners tend to be children of more advantaged parents. Cashin's book illustrates the argument that competitive equal opportunity is practically impossible; it shows how differences of wealth and power help the children of advantaged parents in the competitive struggle for limited opportunity.

The socialization principle

The structure of positions limits opportunities. We are trained so that our aspirations and talents, by and large, fit the available positions. If many positions involve demeaned, onerous, and undesirable labor, then many youth are socialized for that labor. Socialization shapes people's aspirations and either develops or blunts talent. Let us call this the socialization principle: human societies socialize youth for their adult positions. Like the superposition principle in geology (younger layers of rock rest on top of older layers), it is generally true but has exceptions. As we will see, the exceptions "prove" the rule in an instructive way.

Suppose – a simplified example – that there will be need for 100 dentists and 300 dental assistants in the next generation. If we train 400 dentists, opportunity is more equal than if we train only 100. Why? As soon as someone is disqualified from further training, that person's opportunity to become a dentist is greatly diminished. So to increase equal opportunity, we encourage each individual to aspire to be a dentist and to train herself accordingly. This is not absolutely irrational. Learning proceeds unevenly; some learn faster at one stage and then later are matched or surpassed by people who had been slower. So increasing equal opportunity, we encourage those who fall behind in early training because they may catch up later. At the end of training we give theoretical and practical tests, selecting the top 100 to be dentists. Then we tell the other 300 that they will be dental assistants.

This is clearly an unlikely approach for any society to take. But why? For at least two reasons: it contributes to discontent, and it wastes resources.

If you want trouble, here is a recipe: train people for positions, particularly advantaged positions, that will be unavailable to them. Would training 400 people for 100 positions as dentists enhance social stability? Not likely. Social scientists have noted that training people for positions they will not fulfill tends to destabilize society (Lipset and Bendix 1959: 262). Educated people whose ambitions have been frustrated have contributed to social unrest; several of those who crashed airliners into the World Trade Center were educated Saudis unemployed in their professions. Thus the socialization principle – that societies train youth for what is available – is confirmed by the exception; where the principle is violated, trouble follows.

Social stability depends on shaping people's aspirations so that, as much as possible, their aspirations approximate what they do. This is more easily done when people are young. So children's aspirations are shaped so that expectations correspond to what is likely to be available.

Jay MacLeod's *Ain't No Makin' It* (1995) shows this process at work. MacLeod observed two groups of youth in a housing project. One group, the Hallway Hangers, many of whose older brothers were in jail or prison, were the "rejects" in school. They responded to demeaned status as students in ways that protected their dignity: they developed a culture and norms which disparaged conventional success and elevated the toughness and loyalty of these petty criminals. Counter-cultures rejecting dominant ideals of success are universal in demeaned groups. They are a consequence of limitations on opportunity. Developing counter-values is psychologically adaptive: if only a few will attain a particular outcome, it is frustrating (for most) to continue to aspire to that outcome. When MacLeod returned to the same project eight years later, the Hallway Hangers tended to blame themselves (and affirmative action – they were white) for their problems. They did not fault the society.

Even more telling, MacLeod relates the outcomes of a second group, the Brothers, mostly black youth who at the time of the original study were aspiring to success through school achievement. After they graduated from high school and entered the job market, aspirations were adjusted downward. The Brother who most blamed the "economic system" for his difficulties was James. Unlike the others, he had specialized training – as a computer programmer; he had been employed as a computer operator and then laid off. James was, in MacLeod's words, "the only Brother to criticize the economic system explicitly and consistently." He had specific abilities for which he was unable to win social rewards, apparently deepening discontent.

Societies such as ours limit opportunities to contribute complex abilities through a lifetime of labor. They train the young so that aspirations correspond to what will exist. Just as some are trained for the professions, so others are trained for trades, unskilled labor, or unemployment. Where many do unskilled labor or are unemployed, this is inevitable. The alternative would be the social unrest arising from the frustration of not being able to do what one has spent years training to do.

For those disadvantaged youth who retain relatively high aspirations into early adulthood there are junior colleges and low-prestige universities; one of the processes that occurs at these institutions is that most students are socialized – at a more advanced age – to diminished aspirations (Bowles and Gintis 1976). As I mentioned in chapter 1, at the predominately African-American urban university where I teach philosophy, fewer than 20 percent of students have graduated seven years after entering the university as freshmen.

Moreover, it wastes resources to provide equal opportunity when opportunity is limited. It wastes social resources to train 400 people for 100 positions as dentists. What applies here applies at all educational levels. Resources are used most efficiently when schooling trains students for the activities of their working lives. The very policies that adapt students' expectations to their prospects are also a more efficient use of educational resources.

No society's politically dominant class will, for long, encourage institutions that waste resources and simultaneously foster unrest. Yet competitive equal opportunity – schools that train large numbers for relatively few positions of advantage – would do both these things. A rationally organized society shapes expectations when children are young and trains children in a relatively efficient way. Hence equal competitive opportunity is impossible.

Much limitation on opportunity is organized through categories of race, at least in the United States. The most disadvantaged tend to be marginalized in neighborhoods where the most visible businesses on commercial streets are churches, currency exchanges, liquor stores, beauty salons, and fast food restaurants. Of the few jobs that are available locally, almost all are at low wages. Unemployment is high. Surrounded by others similarly disadvantaged, not many have contacts with employed folks, contacts that help someone get a job, or a better job (Wilson 1987). Schools are often made up of children from similarly disadvantaged families. Looking at siblings and other young adults, children find it difficult to sustain the optimism required to motivate sustained academic effort, especially when they encounter difficulties – as all do eventually.

The harms of racism underscore the harms of limited opportunity. Earlier, I argued that limited opportunity would never be equal because the better-off would advantage their children. But there is a deeper point. Equal competitive opportunity would be destabilizing and wasteful. So institutions adapt to limited opportunity by making it unequal. In the United States, racial isolation in ghettos and segregated schools organize limited and hence unequal opportunity. The harms of racism display the harms of limiting opportunity.

The strong socialization principle

So far, the socialization principle has been explained in terms of aspirations and expectations. People are socialized to prefer the work that will be available, making it seem chosen. When limited to socialization of expectations and aspirations we may call this "the weak socialization principle." But the principle can be expressed in a stronger form: societies that create a division between routine and complex labor must socialize children to be stupid. The development of talents should correspond to the opportunity to exercise those talents in adult life. Since, as Adam Smith pointed out, much labor tends to blunt thinking, schools prepare children for that labor by killing rather than encouraging curiosity. Since workers spend their adult lives obeying instructions, schools strive to make children submissive to authority. This socialization works not only through the schools but also through other associations in neighborhood, family, and elsewhere. The strong socialization principle is that socialization for routine labor strives to make many children uncurious and obedient.

There is a forceful reply to the strong socialization principle: the "complexity of roles" reply. The complexity of roles reply points out that in modern societies we occupy simultaneously many different social roles. While someone may be a factory worker using only easily trained routine skills, she may be at the same time a mother, soldier, Republican Party activist, church choir member, and student of Japanese cuisine. While one's job may require only rudimentary skills and obedience, the other roles require a more fully developed intellect and personality: the ability to organize meetings, take initiative, assemble and organize information, understand foods and their combinations, and master rhythm and harmony. So, the reply goes, the schools do not prepare us only for the role of worker. They develop in young people a range of skills and abilities that prepare them for other more complex roles. So socialization does not require that children be trained to be uncurious and obedient. The socialization principle, at least in its strong form, is not true. Moreover, complexity of roles explains why many who work monotonous jobs are not at all stupid.

I grant that there is truth to the complexity of roles objection. The problem, however, is this: do these roles sit easily with one another? If there tends to be a conflict of roles, if the qualities needed to be a good worker tend to be *incompatible* with those needed of a spouse or soldier, then either socialization tends to adapt us to our working lives, with the result that many will be poor soldiers or spouses and seek mindless rather than challenging use of leisure time, or socialization will develop more complex abilities, with the consequence that we will be discontented workers. I believe these roles tend to be in conflict. In the sections that follow I argue that the qualities needed for routine labor do not sit easily with the qualities needed for complex roles.

Reply to the strong socialization principle I: Adam Smith

The strong socialization principle asserts that any society that divides labor so that many spend their lives in routine tasks must socialize many children to be stupid. If this principle is true, it represents a strong condemnation of that division of labor. Adam Smith recognized the problem and thought he had a solution to it.

Smith recognized that the "benumbing" of workers' minds was produced by the division of labor he had praised in the capitalism of his time, not by "barbarous societies" where "the varied occupations of every man oblige every man to exert his capacity, and to invent expedients for removing difficulties." In these societies, "Invention is kept alive, and the mind is not suffered to fall into that drowsy stupidity, which, in a civilized society, seems to benumb the understanding of almost all the inferior ranks of people" (1776: vol. 2, book V, ch. 1, art. 2, 303). For the common workmen:

> As soon as they are able to work, they must apply to some trade by which they can earn their subsistence. That trade too is generally so simple and uniform as to give little exercise to the understanding; while, at the same time, their labour is both so constant and so severe, that it leaves them little leisure and less inclination to apply to, or even to think of anything else. (p. 305)

What sort of education should such workers receive? Smith acknowledges that "the common people cannot, in any civilized society, be so well instructed as people of some rank and fortune." Still, they can learn "to read, write, and account" before they are employed in routine labor. He advocated a system of parish schools; if children "were instructed in the elementary parts of geometry and mechanics, the literary education of this rank of people would perhaps be as complete as it can be" (p. 306). Smith seems to intend this education to remedy the tendency of labor to make the worker stupid. Roles such as soldiering require initiative, and society needs soldiers; so education must prepare young people (or perhaps at least males) for these more demanding roles. Smith's proposal relies on the sociology of complex roles.

Apparently Smith wants to mitigate the degradation of the worker by supplying him with tools that would render him less stupid through his entire life. It is hard to be sure. On the one hand, he contrasts the simple education of the common workman with the varied intellectual tasks of some of the elite and their children's access to education through family wealth. On the other, his proposals for educating youth who become workmen seem to mitigate the effect of labor to make a worker "as stupid and ignorant as it is possible for a human creature to become." A worker who understands geometry and mechanics and who can read, write, and do arithmetic calculations is not stupid.

A balanced assessment of Smith would be this: he clearly is not advocating equal access to advantage; he is advocating that the children of common workmen be trained for positions similar to their parents'. But he is denying that "the job of schools is to make children stupid." Thus the worker can be smarter and less degraded than his job might tend to make him. Is Smith right?

To a degree, clearly he is. There are many smart workers doing dull, routine jobs. But the issue is not whether workers are smart, but whether the schools try to make them *less* smart. Are many children trained for stupidity? I believe so. If Smith's proposals for the education of the children of workmen were implemented, the workers' lives would be thereby enriched. But many working-class children are not educated as he proposed. Why not? Because to train them in these ways would tend to develop qualities that ill suit them for the simplest labor.

In her book *The Dignity of Working Men*, Michèle Lamont asked French workers to explain the morality that informs their lives: they valued workers "who are able to sustain efforts even in difficult circumstances. This quality is given value by individuals who describe their work as dirty and physically demanding or as requiring particular will power and perseverance (often because it is boring and repetitive)." One worker tells her that "it is especially important for people who are not highly educated to be hardworking: hard work allows you to demonstrate your worth 'even if you are not very intelligent. . . . It's not because you don't have a *bac* [academic-track high school degree] that you have to stay with your arms crossed, waiting for something'" (2000: 162).

Why the phrase "you are not very intelligent" and the remark about not having a *bac*? The French educational system puts children on different tracks, some being trained for "head" labor, others to work with their hands. While the worker Lamont interviewed is thoughtful and aware, he has been degraded by his labor and his education. He thinks he (or his fellow workers? it is not clear) is "not very intelligent." Many students, particularly the most marginalized African-American children in the United States, are receiving just the education fitted to train them for routine labor. If they stay in school, they become obedient, mechanical, uncurious, and unreflective. Dropping out may be rebelling against an education experienced as demeaning, but it restricts opportunity further. Smith's reply is not adequate. The qualities needed for routine labor may make for poor soldiers, but soldiers with courage and initiative may make discontented workers. If we have to choose between making good soldiers and training contented workers, the conflict of roles might explain why so many schools do so much to blunt initiative, creativity, and curiosity, making many young people hate school.

Reply to the strong socialization principle II: Michael Walzer

Michael Walzer's *Spheres of Justice* defends pluralist egalitarianism. He divides justice into "spheres" – justice in basic welfare, the market economy, bureaucracy, education, the family, religious life, and politics. Each sphere has its purposes and norms. He defends "complex equality": inequality is allowed – is unavoidable – within spheres. *In*egalitarianism – what Walzer opposes – is the tyranny of one sphere over others.

The oppressiveness of "hard work," particularly dangerous, grueling, or dirty work, bothers him, and he considers its being shared. But he is concerned more with soldiering, coal-mining, and garbage-collecting – work that is exceptionally dangerous, grueling, or dirty – than with the routine labor that is everywhere. He rejects as coercive sharing hard labor (1983: 183).

Walzer would regard the argument presented here as tyranny of simple equality: where one sphere is dominant and intrudes inappropriately on other spheres. Other spheres have their own standards of just and unjust conduct and policy. Specifically, for Walzer, equality of opportunity is a principle of justice in the sphere of the distribution of offices, positions sanctioned by institutions such as churches and especially government and that involve public trust. Walzer contrasts offices with positions created by markets, which have their own distinct principles of justice.

Walzer's discussion of education amplifies and defends a thesis that parallels Smith's. Walzer distinguishes two functions of education: as selection procedure for positions of advantage, particularly offices, and as a grounding in knowledge and skills required of a democratic citizen. He does not defend a strong equality of opportunity for positions of advantage; he ignores most inequality of opportunity arising from circumstances of family, neighborhood, social networks, and schools. He stresses equality in preparing children for democratic citizenship. This task, he believes, requires schools to teach all children to read and to master other relevant knowledge. So Walzer's argument, if successful, does not rebut my argument that equality of educational opportunity is impossible. It is consistent with the weak socialization principle that societies prepare children for different roles as adults. In this regard he is like Smith. What he rebuts is the strong socialization principle that where many adult positions require closely supervised routine labor, schools prepare children for these positions by striving to make them uncurious and obedient.

Here it would be helpful to quote a bit of Walzer's description of democratic education for equal citizenship:

> [T]he democratic state . . . insists on *inclusive* schools [because] if there is a body of knowledge that citizens must grasp, or think they must grasp, so as to play their parts, then . . . all of them have to go to school. . . . [A]ll children, conceived as future citizens, have the same need to know, and . . . the ideal of membership is best served if they are all taught the same things. Their education cannot be allowed to hang on the social standing or the economic capacity of their parents. . . . If the teachers are committed to the basic disciplines necessary for democratic politics, they will try to establish a shared knowledge among their students and to raise them to something like the same level. The aim is not to repress differences but to postpone them, so that children learn to be citizens first – workers, managers, merchants, and professionals only afterward. Everyone studies the subjects that citizens need to know. (pp. 202–3)

In line with this, Walzer says that the goal of teaching reading is "not to provide equal chances but to achieve equal results." That is, each student must be taught to read.

Beyond the teaching of reading, Walzer does not tell us much about the curriculum of a democratic education. Still, the argument is clear enough, and it fleshes out the parallel claim in Smith: to participate as a democratic citizen in self-government, citizens need common knowledge and basic skills. This argument, if sustained, defeats the strong socialization thesis that education makes many children stupid in order to prepare them for routine labor. His argument, like Smith's, is based on role complexity: we inhabit not only the role of worker doing routine labor but also that of citizen needing critical faculties for democratic participation. Schools must prepare us accordingly.

Does Walzer successfully rebut the stronger socialization principle, showing that democracies can educate children to be critical, intelligent citizens? Democratic participation now consists in periodic polls. *This* sort of citizenship does not require that citizens be able to read effectively or think critically about policies and alternatives. But our experience of citizenship is not relevant to Walzer's argument; for him, democratic participation is more demanding. Imagine that the situation was as Walzer would have it: positions were distributed as now but children were raised to be active citizens. Critical, informed debate and discussion are encouraged among all, not just a few elites. Imagine someone whose work consists of routine tasks under close supervision with little opportunity to use her own judgment but who is involved in political controversy and engages important questions about government, schools, and foreign policy. Is she likely to be *content* with passivity on her job while being active as a citizen? Hardly; the leisure activities of workers who do very simple, routine work tend to be *less* intellectual (Kohn and Schooler 1983: ch. 9). Routine labor corrodes one's intellect, and this corrosion pervades one's life. Active citizenship is not easily combined with routine labor.

Close supervision works best when workers do not challenge their supervisors. Training children in obedience helps to create workers adapted to this adult life. That is why so many schools, particularly schools of the children of the working class, and most especially schools of black and Latino children, emphasize discipline, following instructions, and not being too curious or questioning. In Chicago, military academies are touted as the best opportunity for disadvantaged black youth.[3] The racism of education is one of the great harms that comes from the division between routine and complex labor.

Walzer's view of education for democratic citizenship does not refute the strong socialization principle. His democratic citizenship would foster qualities that would make workers discontented and rebellious against close supervision and routine labor.

The strong socialization principle asserts that to prepare the young for jobs consisting of routine labor, the schools seek to make children uncurious and obedient. The principle is important because, if true, the division between routine and complex labor does great harm to the young. The complexity of roles reply is that this principle overstates the importance of routine labor to socialization; socialization for other roles requires education that nurtures a variety of abilities. In replying to Smith and Walzer, I have stressed that there is a conflict between the qualities required for routine labor – relatively mindless obedience, mechanical thought, passivity – and those required to be an effective soldier or vigorous democratic citizen. While the situation is complicated, there is some truth to the strong socialization principle: in preparing many children for adult jobs the schools do not encourage curiosity and questioning, and this training harms many throughout their lives. The complexity of roles objection points out limits to the strong form of the principle: many adults in routine jobs display wisdom, creativity, and complex intelligence.

We should not limit opportunity

I have given three arguments against limiting opportunity. The Meritonia argument emphasizes that limited opportunity makes it impossible for many to *contribute* architectural or other ability. The practical argument points out that the opportunity to *develop* abilities is skewed toward the advantaged. Finally, where much labor is routine, many children are socialized for that labor; to the extent that the strong socialization principle is true, socialization for routine labor harms children by blunting curiosity and undermining intellectual confidence. In any event, it is unfair to deprive so many of the opportunity to contribute complex abilities.

---

[3] For example, the letter by Chicago Mayor Richard M. Daley to *Education Next* touting the two Chicago public high school military academies as "provid[ing] students with the order and discipline that is too often lacking at home." Both are in overwhelmingly black neighborhoods. See *Education Next* 1 (3): 4.

Opportunity to develop and contribute complex abilities in music, visual art, landscape design, mathematics, engineering, or any other area should not be limited. While the Meritonia argument stresses the harm of not being able to contribute developed abilities, the other arguments point out that, at an earlier stage of development, potential is squashed as young people are tracked and socialized for routine labor. This skewing of opportunity wastes the talents of the less advantaged. All this is unfair and racist.

Equal opportunity is a virtue where the quantity of opportunity corresponds to human potential. There is no reason to think the potential to develop complex abilities is confined to a few people (a point explained more fully in chapter 10). When we limit opportunity to develop and contribute complex abilities, this harms people and is wrong.

Racial (and similar) categories organize limited opportunity. The least opportunity is in poverty-ridden racially identified neighborhoods. The racial concentration of unequal opportunity divides black people from non-black. Issues of justice are obscured because many non-blacks say that black people create their own problems. Black folks may direct their resentment of racism indiscriminately at anyone who is not racially demeaned. Both those who are racially demeaned and those who are not but who accept demeaning stereotypes direct resentment or contempt at others identified through racial categories. They fail to see how limitation of opportunity creates a world where we compete for positions of advantage. Because racism divides oppressed people and obscures issues of fundamental justice, it contributes to social control.

Racism is a glaring manifestation of a deeper phenomenon: the competitive nature of opportunity causes advantaged folks to see themselves as having an interest (at least through the welfare of their children) in diminishing the disadvantaged. The more advantaged construct a way of thinking that "makes sense" of why advantages accrue to them. People rationalize advantages they perceive to be in their interest. So the same racist contempt for black people will be expressed for "trailer trash," or whatever local term may be used for similarly disadvantaged white people. These points about the social psychology of racism and allied phenomena are developed more fully in chapter 8.

The arguments against limited opportunity raise a central issue of social philosophy: how can social organization reconcile our interests? As long as our interests are competing, inequalities of power will lead to unfairness. People will not risk their children's interests (risk their spending their lives in stultifying labor or unemployment) if they have the resources to try to secure them a better future. Considerations of equal opportunity are set against people's love for their children, a conflict that equal opportunity is unlikely to win. Is there a way around this problem? Could society be organized so that the accomplishments of others, their development of their potential, does not threaten me or my children's prospects but instead enhances it? I will argue that this profound issue of how to reconcile our interests has a solution: creating unlimited opportunities by sharing labor.

Chapter 4

Egalitarianism of Opportunity and Other Egalitarianisms

Two egalitarian traditions

Egalitarianism is the philosophy that people's social conditions should be equal. In some way all political philosophies endorse equality (Sen 1992). Conservative philosophers may advocate only equality of legal rights and freedoms. Egalitarians believe there should be a strong material equality – equality in how people actually live. There are at least two egalitarian traditions.

Neoclassical egalitarianism has dominated recent English-language political philosophy. The tradition derives from classical economics, particularly Adam Smith's thought. For Smith, activity, especially labor, is a bad thing. To labor is to sacrifice one's "ease," "liberty," and "happiness" (Smith 1776: 37). John Rawls suggests a similar idea in explaining the difference principle:[1] the exercise of unusual talents is a burden that may require extra compensation as an incentive. Ronald Dworkin (2000: ch. 2) seems neutral about labor but does not think it is an essential good. I will call this tradition the "neoclassical tradition" because of its roots in classical economics, particularly the assumption that the good is *what* is produced, not production itself.

Because labor – contribution to society – is a burden, what is good are the things we *receive* from society, not what we give to it. Justice is *distributive*: the issue is, who gets what? The egalitarian ideal is that each receives the same benefits from society, or, if less or more than others, deviations derive from special needs or special contributions or should improve the situation of the least advantaged. The conception of the good is *moneyist*: income and wealth are centrally important goods. Neoclassicists embrace – or do not reject – market societies and money as an all-purpose means. Money gives greater effective

---

[1]   In Rawls's philosophy this is the principle that inequalities are just only if they benefit those who are in the worst-off position. The assumption is that by allowing the "more talented" to earn more, they will exercise their talents in a way that benefits everyone else, including those who are in the worst-off position. See Rawls 1999: 67–69.

freedom to those with more of it; they can order their lives and promote other goods as they wish. Each citizen has liberty to pursue her own idea of the good life, using available money or resources. Citizens embrace different values; the state is to be neutral between these differences. John Rawls, Ronald Dworkin, G. A. Cohen, and Richard Arneson, among recent liberal egalitarians, are primarily in this tradition.[2]

The neoclassical tradition typically assumes a *metric* of equality, a measure of whether benefits are equal. For some the metric is money. Utilitarianism proposes happiness, pleasure, or preference satisfaction as a metric. Rawls writes of primary goods as if their quantity could be measured. When the things that make life good have a common measure, they are *commensurable*. Whether the measure is money or something else, egalitarianism derived from the neoclassical tradition assumes that people should be equal or that deviations from equality must be justified.

Dworkin and his followers stress the distinction between brute and option luck. Justice requires different policies toward inequalities arising from brute luck – fortunes or misfortunes not of our doing – from policies toward inequalities resulting from our choices. Some inequalities arising from our choices must be accepted if we are to respect people's autonomy; those arising from brute luck should be mitigated.

Neoclassical egalitarianism is characterized by a constellation of related features: (1) a negative (at best neutral) view of activity, particularly labor; (2) social benefits are what we receive; (3) justice is distributive; (4) governments should be neutral between different ideas of what makes life good; (5) money (or "resources") is a central good and is used to realize one's own good; (6) measuring distributive justice requires a measure of socially provided benefits that is neutral between different conceptions of the good; (7) egalitarianism requires equality by that measure or, if departures from equality are justified, a special justification of inequality.

Egalitarianism of opportunity comes from the tradition of Aristotle, Hegel, and Marx; Amartya Sen and Martha Nussbaum embrace elements of it. This tradition emphasizes *activity* as the greatest good. In strict Aristotelian versions, this is a life of contemplation supplemented by friendship and ethical virtues (Aristotle himself was an elitist; nevertheless, egalitarians have been influenced by his conception of the good life). In one Marxist version, the greatest good is a life of social labor where laborers organized as a rational, self-conscious collective control the labor process. Let us call this the Aristotelian tradition, after its founder.

For the Aristotelian, our good derives from our nature. Good things are distinct from one another and correspond to elements of our humanity. The good of adequate nutrition derives from our biological nature as metabolizing organisms; of our nutritional needs, some are in common with other primates, some with other humans, and some are shared with only a few others.

---

[2] Cohen is skeptical of the justice of markets. See, for example, Cohen 2004.

The good of friendship derives from our social nature; we are the most social of primates. Even our sexuality is as much social as it is reproductive; sexuality can be part of bonds of intimate friendship, often in socially sanctioned arrangements such as marriage or something similar. We need some security, periods where we are not fearful of what may happen to us, and predictability.

The good of contributing complex abilities derives from our nature as social beings who naturally enjoy complexity; our strength as a species is development of social cooperation and complex culture, including moral and technological culture. This culture is learned, applied creatively in new situations, and developed further.

We are self-conscious beings in the sense that, through language, we develop a conception of self as mother, wife, or carpenter, or, more generally, *mensch* or good person. We identify with these self-conceptions; they express who we believe ourselves to be. We need labor with which we identify as self-expression, and we need rest from intense activity. Labor is social labor. Contribution to a social group with which we identify is part of our good. The central problems of justice are duties and opportunities of *contribution*.

Human goods are incommensurable: there is no common measure to compare need for unalienated labor with need for rest. Each need is distinct. Individuals may make trade-offs – choosing to work a hated but high-paying job in order to have more security. The Aristotelian does not interpret this choice as meaning that there is a common measure – pleasure, happiness, preference satisfaction – according to which the trade-off is rational if it leads to a net gain of good by that measure. Rather, one essential need – for security – is met, while another – the need for self-realization through one's daily activities – is frustrated. With a need frustrated, a person's life is less good than it should be.

This tradition judges societies on whether they enable members to achieve human good. In its egalitarian version it strives to make the good life available to everyone. Sen and Nussbaum give the view a liberal twist: the *capability* to engage in good human activities should be provided to all; the individual is free to decide which activities to pursue. Still, this version is Aristotelian because we evaluate *societies* based on the activities of their members.

The Aristotelian tradition, as I develop it, is characterized by these ideas: (1) activity is essential to the good life, particularly labor with which we identify as self-expression; (2) the main good of our social life is contribution to a group; (3) the central conception of justice is contributive: duties and opportunities to contribute; (4) social life depends on shared norms of what is owed to others; (5) everyone should have contributive duties and opportunities; (6) the various things that make life good correspond to our nature and cannot be measured against one another.

The distinction between two traditions in egalitarian thought is rough but useful, and not all writers fall neatly into either tradition.[3]

---

[3] Walzer (1983) defends a pluralist egalitarianism, implying incommensurability between different "spheres" of justice. While Rawls may be the paradigmatic neoclassicist, Dworkin, Arneson, and Cohen may dissent from at least one of the defining ideas.

What is an opportunity?

This book defends equality of a constellation of opportunities. But what is an opportunity? Freedom and opportunity seem similar, but what is the difference between saying, "You are free to buy the house on the corner" and "You have an opportunity to buy the house on the corner"? One difference is that the "opportunity" statement suggests that you have it now but may not have it later – now is the "opportune" time to act (and that is the older meaning of "opportunity"). Another is that the "freedom" statement can be a way of saying that it may be a stupid thing to do, but you are free to do it; the "opportunity" statement suggests that buying the house is a good thing. Opportunities are freedoms to do or attain something thought desirable.

Up to a point, then, an opportunity is like a freedom (call this the "freedom dimension" of opportunity), but in another way it is not. The statement "The students at Lombard School do not have the opportunity to learn a musical instrument" does not mean the same as the statement that they are not free to do so. We speak of greater and lesser opportunities in cases where we would not speak of greater and lesser freedoms: we might say, "The opportunity to attend college has increased over the past half century," and defend this assertion by noting that the number of college students has grown more rapidly than the population. Or we might say, "Job opportunities are fewer now than they were six months ago," citing a growth of the labor force and a decline in the number of positions available. We might say, "You have a better opportunity to be hired by the Post Office this year because they are hiring more than 1,000 new employees" and compare the current employment increase with one a year ago where only a little more than 200 were hired. Here the opportunities one has are related to the *probability* of realizing them. So opportunities are somewhat like probabilities; we can call this the "probability dimension" of opportunity. It is important to keep in mind that in some ways opportunities are like freedoms and in others like probabilities.

The similarity between opportunity and freedom is suggested by Peter Westen's article "The Concept of Equal Opportunity" (1985), which presents an analysis of opportunity that parallels Gerald MacCallum's analysis of freedom in "Negative and Positive Freedom." Westen points out that opportunities are always the opportunities of an *agent or agents* to achieve some *desired state or activity* in light of the consideration of some possible *obstacle* to that achievement. Thus, opportunities involve an implicit or explicit triad – agent, goal, obstacle (almost exactly as MacCallum said about freedom). I have argued that opportunity is not equal and cannot be as long as opportunities for the most desired social positions are limited. These arguments involve seeing social practices and institutions as obstacles to opportunity for some people: ghettoization of black people in the United States, curricula and attitudes of school administrators and teachers in disadvantaged neighborhoods, background of children from families with less formal education, modes of parenting, and shared attitudes that tend to lower aspirations to attain high-status conventionally defined. If we understand these as obstacles, the arguments presented conform to Westen's formula. I have argued that general limits on *quantity* of opportunity to develop and contribute complex abilities are a remediable social obstacle to equal opportunity.

Not everything relevant to our achieving our goals is an obstacle that limits opportunity. At one point Westen writes: "No two people can have an equal opportunity to attain a specified goal by every measure of opportunity [that is, in consideration of every obstacle] unless they are both guaranteed the result of attaining the goal if they so wish" (p. 845). This is wrong. Consider the opportunity to become an electronics technician. Given color-coding of wiring, people with poor color vision are less likely to succeed. That does not mean that they lack the same opportunity. What they lack is ability readily to distinguish color-coded wires. Lacking an opportunity and lacking an ability are not the same. Lack of an ability is internal. An obstacle relevant to opportunity is external to the agent.

Admittedly, if we conceive color-coded wiring as an alterable social convention (wires could be coded with numbers or letters), we may say that this convention deprives those with color deficits an equal opportunity to be electronics technicians. We conceive the convention of color-coding wires as an *external* obstacle for some agents. If we take the convention for granted, then we think of the deficit as internal to the agent, as lack of a relevant ability.

Therefore, not everything relevant to achieving goals is relevant to opportunity. Being of average height affects the likelihood of playing in the National Basketball Association, but not opportunity to play. Only factors which we think of as external to the agent (the effects of racial identification, schools, family, neighborhood culture) are relevant to opportunity, particularly external factors that are social artifacts. Something physically impossible – to win the Olympic 100-meter dash at age 60 – is not something we lack opportunity to do. So opportunity egalitarianism is about the ways *social structures, institutions, policies, or practices* make some achievements less likely or impossible for some people. Opportunity egalitarianism proposes changing social structures which have the consequence that many of us, of necessity, are consigned in our working lives to routine, relatively mindless labor.

Resources, capabilities, and commensurability

A difference between a freedom and an opportunity seemed to be that in calling something an opportunity we imply that it is desirable. But what is desirable? There are two approaches, approximating the two traditions. The more popular, associated with Rawls, is to embrace the moneyist conception of the good, to identify wealth and income as important "all-purpose" goods that can be translated into other goods (Rawls 1999: 54, 79). (There are other all-purpose goods – social bases of self-respect, liberties, and opportunities – but money is particularly important to Rawls because he believes that liberty and opportunity do not vary much; only money and authority vary significantly [pp. 55, 80].) Accepting money as an all-purpose good, liberal political philosophers can appear neutral between particular conceptions of the good (as I will argue, however, they are not really neutral). When people have money, they can spend it as they wish. Emphasizing money as a good, philosophers can respect citizens' conceptions of the good – to be a devout Christian or Muslim, to study philosophy or astrophysics, to maximize wealth or leisure, to end poverty and hunger. Whatever their conception of the good, wealth and income help to achieve it. So apparent neutrality between conceptions of the good is *connected* to the moneyist conception of the good.

We can look at what makes life good in another way, more "objective," more "perfectionist." An alternative conception of the good has been developed by Sen (1992), who proposes that some functionings are central to human life – being adequately nourished and otherwise in good health, adequately clothed and sheltered, and participating in the life of one's community. Governments should secure for their citizens the *capabilities* to engage in these functionings. So everyone should be able to obtain adequate nourishment, even though some may choose to fast.

Nussbaum (2000) has developed this approach most concretely; the central capabilities include being able to live, to have good health, to move about without being assaulted or injured, to be sexually active, to use our senses, imagination, and thought, to have a full emotional life, to reason practically about how to live, to have friends and be respected by others, to play, and to control our material and political environments. Governments are to insure that each citizen has the capability to realize these functionings. But which functionings any one of us realizes depends on how we choose to live. So while being sexually involved with others is a central human functioning, although governments should insure that people are not deprived of that capability, they should not insure that people function sexually.

Neoclassical egalitarians accept that goods are commensurable. For example, Rawls's difference principle says that inequalities are allowable provided they improve the situation of the least advantaged group; to say when the difference principle is satisfied, we have to measure goods. Rawls can compare how well off the least advantaged group would be in one arrangement with how well off the least advantaged group would be in a different arrangement: measure the money the typical member of each group would have to pursue that person's conception of the good. The difference principle (as it strives for perfect justice) tells us to prefer that arrangement where the least advantaged group is better off. Money as an all-purpose good makes these comparisons possible. It also makes it possible to measure equality.

Dworkin's (1981) approach is resourcist, but more similar to than different from Rawls's. Dworkin proposes to make us as equal as possible in resources so that differences in how well we fare are due to our choices, not to brute luck. But when are resources equal? Dworkin proposes starting with an equal initial distribution of *external* resources (goods, things); but when is it equal? Give each person an equal amount of money (he says clamshells) and let them auction and trade until no one prefers the resources others have purchased to her own.[4] Equal money guarantees equality of resources.

But resources include not only external goods but also *internal* resources as varied as health and energy, intelligence, cultural background – powers that we just happen to have (or lack). Equality in initial distribution of external resources has to be supplemented with a way to deal with differences in "internal" resources that affect earnings; insofar as they are the result of "genetic luck," they do not entitle one to be rich while another is poor. So Dworkin proposes an income tax which, like an insurance system, would give the less talented a share of the greater wealth earned by the more talented. (Notice that money is a common measure.) Talents are treated as "quasi-resources;" they are not the same as external wealth and not fully commensurable with it. But, when they lead to wealth, some personal advantages create a duty to compensate others; corresponding disadvantages – poor health, a dull wit, unappealing appearance, or just the absence of talent – make us entitled to compensation for our relative disadvantage. Just as talents are treated as quasi-resources, so the proposal to compensate those with inferior talent treats talent and compensation as "quasi-commensurable." Not everything straightforwardly has a price, but every unchosen disadvantage that affects earnings may be ameliorated by transfer to the disadvantaged of resources of a different sort from the disadvantage. Low-wage or unemployed workers, whose condition may be due to a lack of marketable talents, may be compensated by a negative income tax; the money they receive is not the same sort of thing as the talent or work they lack but is treated as quasi-commensurable with it.

This approach to commensurability raises three related problems. First, Elizabeth Anderson asks us to put ourselves in the position of someone being compensated; it undermines dignity to be told by society that you deserve compensation because your lower earnings are a result of your lack of marketable internal resources (Anderson 1999: 306). Second, when someone's earnings are less than others, it generally is not possible to trace how particular characteristics affected earnings. Third, Dworkin's proposal assumes that it makes sense to lump together "internal" resources and measure their quantity; this is surely wrong. What could it mean, counting such varied things as resources, to say that we have equal resources? How can we measure your smarts against my good looks, my ambition against your cultured family? We have particular defects or virtues that make us different from one another: near-sightedness, susceptibility to arthritis, ability to work at great heights. For each defect or virtue there is an appropriate response to make it possible for someone to contribute and flourish. But it makes no sense to lump these together and judge whether someone's earnings were influenced by inferior resources.

[4] Dworkin endorses money and markets as a device to measure the opportunity costs to others of the resources one seeks. See Dworkin 2000: 66–71, and 2004: 342.

Here, the Sen/Nussbaum approach is superior. If the capability to have adequate nutrition is one that any decent society owes each member, then each should have precisely that capability. Nothing else can compensate for it.[5]

Perfectionism and liberal egalitarianisms

Neoclassicists argue that governments should avoid "perfectionist" commitment to a particular conception of the good (should be neutral between conceptions of the good). In contrast, I propose that we should create universal opportunity to realize a constellation of goods (development of complex abilities contributed to society and social esteem for that contribution); this opportunity is to be made available universally by *sharing* routine labor, including care of children, and complex labor as well.

My proposal seems distinctly *il*liberal. It *requires* that each contribute routine labor in order to make it possible for each to contribute complex abilities. It precludes devoting one's life exclusively to intellectual, artistic, or technological achievements. In insisting that each has the opportunity to contribute complex mastery, the proposal fails to show equal regard for folks who have other conceptions of the good life – or so it seems.

Neither egalitarian liberalism nor egalitarianism of opportunity is neutral. Every society offers some opportunities and forecloses others. It is hard to see this because there is near-consensus in political philosophy on the moneyist conception of the good, on social relations mediated by money, where the means of life are commodities produced for exchange. Money may be sought only as a means, but it is a means that has consequences for how we will live together. When we accept money as a good, we accept that it is good to have money. Then why do some have more than others? Suppose, playing by the social rules, they come to have more. But we accept the social rules; so we accept that they should have more. They deserve it (by the rules). We rationalize their having more. (In chapter 10, I explain this as "the rationalization principle" – if we accept a social order, we rationalize it.) If they deserve the money, they are more worthy in some relevant way. Hence social esteem attaches to wealth. Since wealth is unequal, so is the associated social esteem. Because social esteem attaches to money, money becomes an important *positional* good,

---

[5] Unfortunately, Sen is not clear about this difference between his philosophy and Dworkin's. He criticizes Dworkin's equality of resources for failing to take account of special needs such as pregnancy (Sen 1992: 33). This criticism is incorrect. But it is important *how* Dworkin arrives at meeting this need. For Sen the relationship between the personal characteristic (pregnancy), the relevant capability/ functioning (health), and the solution (additional food and special prenatal supplements, prenatal health care) is simple, direct, and transparent: to insure capability to function, specific needs must be met. For Dworkin (2000: 300), the connection between these works through insurance auctions and markets that ask us to compare things that do not seem commensurable. Dworkin treats pregnancy as an *impairment*; to compensate, impersonal resources should be increased; the response is to impairment not pregnancy. Sen calls for *appropriate* responses to these specific needs.

used to compare our worth (in two senses!) relative to others. Inequality leads to envy, social division, and feelings of superiority and inferiority.[6]

This way of organizing society makes it impossible to live in a good society by standards of the tradition, descended from Marx, where human association is governed by planning for the good of all, where the goodness of a life derives from what we do, not what we have. Although the popularity of this ideal has receded in the last few decades, that is irrelevant. Every proposal creates some possibilities and forecloses others.

It might be argued that in a liberal society the social outcomes are the result of the decisions of individual actors, that liberal societies are less coercive. These ideas are sociologically and historically naive. Markets are a form of freedom that arises from the power of a state to suppress other forms of distribution. In societies with minimal political centralization, property rights do not allow the exclusion of others in need: people do not starve while others eat (Harris 1991: 123). Traditionally, property rights in grain in rural communities in France and England had been qualified by the needs of the local poor. Establishment of the right to exchange freely required exclusive ownership rights that suppressed norms of distribution to the needy. When grain was to be sold on national markets, French peasants seized it, enforcing traditional norms. Only the forcible suppression of these grain seizures by the French state in the seventeenth and eighteenth centuries created a national market for grain. These conceptions of property and exchange could become dominant only by forcibly displacing other conceptions.[7] The "freedom of deciding where to work" was created by abrogating traditional feudal rights, driving English copyholders (tenant farmers) and squatters from their land through enclosures and consolidations; in the United States, "freedom of exchange" was accomplished through the destruction of native societies (and often their peoples).[8] This argument, that capitalist property requires the exercise of state power, will be generalized in chapter 9; there I argue that inequalities that disadvantage the least well off arise only with the centralization of coercion.

We live in the aftermath of processes that created stable capitalist property and markets. Accepting markets is a judgment about what is socially desirable just as much as is the proposal to share labor in order to create unlimited opportunity. I argue in chapter 12 that sharing labor is incompatible with markets and the moneyist conception of the good. So we have to pick our perfectionism.

---

[6] Liberal egalitarianism tries to combine moneyism with equality. In chapter 12, I argue, based on the rationalization principle, that this is an impossible combination: egalitarian norms make no sense – in daily life – to those who accept money, markets and the ways these create inequalities. Part of this argument is a more developed explanation of why prestige attaches to wealth.

[7] On France, see Tilly 1986. On comparable English struggles, see Walter 1980.

[8] On English enclosures in the seventeenth century, see Marx 1867: ch. 27; Hill 1961 and 1972; on the eighteenth and early nineteenth century, see Thompson 1975 and Neeson 1993; on the expropriation of natives in the United States, particularly in relation to the cotton/slave economy, see Takaki 1979.

Why pay the costs of opportunities and provision of other goods?

One advantage of egalitarianism of opportunity is that each has reason to want everyone else to succeed. In meritocratic conceptions of equal opportunity we may, for reasons of efficiency, want the most qualified to succeed: with the most qualified people in the most demanding jobs, we all benefit from better products and services. But competitive opportunity is a "zero-sum game": since opportunities are limited, when one person realizes an opportunity, another person loses opportunity. We want our competitors to lose opportunities. I will explain in chapter 8 how unlimited opportunity gives each of us a reason to want others to develop and contribute abilities.

It is particularly important to explain why we should want others to have opportunities, because opportunities have costs. If everyone is to have opportunity to develop musical talent, to learn philosophy, to master quilt-making, or to become a good writer, there must be resources devoted to their training. In our society, the problem of resources is handled in the following way: most pre-college education is segregated by race and income; in schools where there is more integration, students are tracked into different classes. After that, opportunities depend a great deal on how much money one has. Money rations opportunity. Suppose that in a better society opportunity was not rationed by money. It still costs resources to create opportunity. So we need a reason to devote resources to creating opportunities. We need to explain why we should support equal opportunity.

The same goes for other egalitarianisms. Why should we support equal resources or equality of capability? While these forms of equality seem to make sense intuitively, that does not mean that "on the ground," in daily life, people would have reason to want others to be equal to them. If these ideals are not easily and naturally supported in daily life, there is little chance that they will be realized. In chapter 8, I show why, sharing labor, we each have a natural reason to devote resources to creating opportunities for others. In showing this, I will have answered one of the important questions egalitarians need to answer: Why would ordinary people support egalitarian forms of organization?

Egalitarianism of opportunity and the neoclassical tradition

I described two egalitarian traditions and two issues that distinguish the traditions. One issue is contribution versus distribution. The Aristotelian tradition, particularly in the version defended here, looks to people's life activity to determine whether their lives are good. The central good for which we seek equal opportunity is to develop and contribute complex abilities. The conception of equality is contributive, the opportunity and duty to contribute to society on an equal footing with others. The neoclassical tradition assumes a moneyist conception of the good, for money is the all-purpose means to other goods. It emphasizes distributive equality, who gets how much of the material benefits of social cooperation. For the most part we are passive recipients of justice.

The second issue is commensurability versus incommensurability. The value pluralism of liberal political philosophers requires some way of measuring people's claims on social resources against the claims of others. The standard procedure in the neoclassical egalitarian tradition is to start with an equal distribution of the benefits of social cooperation (showing equal regard for each person regardless of that person's particular conception of the good) and then consider deviations where one would receive more than another. Both equality and deviations from it require a measure, and the standard measure is money – income and wealth – the "all-purpose" good. Egalitarianism of opportunity, like Sen's capabilities approach, would specify the goods needed for a person to flourish and attempt to secure these for each person: adequate nutrition, health care, housing, decent clothing, security, and the opportunity to develop and contribute abilities. It would not treat the various things necessary for a good life as commensurable.

In chapters 12 and 13, we will return to the issue of contribution versus distribution. There, I will give a final defense of egalitarianism of opportunity, show why it is incompatible with market and money relations, and why the required normative relations among us would be supportable by all of us. These arguments together are the beginnings of a theory of contributive justice.

Chapter 5

Can Everyone Be Esteemed?

Opportunities of limited and unlimited supply

Opportunities for wealth and power are limited: not everyone can be rich or more powerful than others. These positions are widely viewed as the "best" – for good reason: the wealthy and powerful have longer and happier lives. Because more aspire to these positions than can attain them, opportunity is competitive. To imagine opportunity that is not competitive, we must imagine opportunity for goods that are not scarce.

Things that we desire can be of either limited or unlimited supply. If a good is of unlimited supply, there is, practically speaking, enough for everyone; your having it has no effect on whether it is available to me. Air is typically of unlimited supply. You breathe, and I breathe. Your breathing does not affect the availability of air to me. We don't compete for goods of unlimited supply.

Most things are of limited supply. Jobs, promotions, political offices, housing, clothing, food, health care services: while some are more plentiful, none is unlimited. So we have ways to decide who gets them and under what conditions. Some of these goods are social in a straightforward sense: jobs are a good only in a society that has jobs (although all societies have labor, not all have jobs). Other goods – food is an example – are more weakly social. Some foods are not produced by people at all – for example, wild honey – and they may be available to anyone who comes upon them. Still, all of these – both the more strongly and the more weakly social – are of limited supply. We can't all have as much honey, wild or domestic, as we might want.

What about opportunities? The goal of an opportunity is a good. As a freedom, opportunity can be in greater supply than the good for which it is an opportunity. Suppose a company promotes employees by competitive examination to district manager. You and I are both eligible and hence have the opportunity to become district manager. Yet there is only one district manager. So the *opportunity* to become district manager is in greater supply (since you and I both have it) than the single position of district manager. This is true in the freedom dimension of opportunity: we are both eligible and free to apply.

But there is only one promotion. After someone is promoted, the opportunity is gone. The promotion is of limited supply. As a result, in its probability dimension each person's opportunity is a function of the opportunity of every competitor; you have a greater opportunity if and only if I have less. While it is true that we are equally free to apply, we do not necessarily have the same opportunity (probability) to be promoted; you may have a better opportunity because, with my pending divorce and child care problems, I do poorly on written examinations. Where the goods we seek are of limited supply, so are the opportunities to attain them.

The issue of *how much* opportunity there is arises in the probability dimension of opportunity. In the United States in the 1970s children from lower-income families had a greater opportunity to attend college than did the corresponding families of the 1930s; college places grew faster than the population, particularly places in low-tuition, public colleges. If the number of college places and the population are unchanged, so is the amount of opportunity. On these assumptions we can increase the opportunities for children in the poorest families only if we decrease opportunities for others.

If we increase the number of college spaces, we can increase the opportunities for the poorest without diminishing opportunities for others. But college spaces are sought largely because they make it possible to gain other advantages. So if the number of college places is increased, are we also to imagine that the number of positions of advantage is increased? Or are we to imagine that access to positions of advantage now requires more than a college degree? The point of these questions is to become clearer about what it means to say that opportunity is limited. As long as the number of relatively desirable positions in society does not increase, neither does opportunity to attain them.

The probability that an aspirant will realize an opportunity is a function of how much opportunity there is. For example, if we double the number of people who train to be a doctor of medicine, then, for each person who aspires to this training, we double the probability that she will receive it. If the quantity of a good matches or exceeds the number who aspire to that good, opportunity has become, practically speaking, of unlimited supply. Physicians generally have higher incomes than others, but opportunity to have a higher income is not increased. It is impossible to increase opportunity for relative wealth. To have a higher income is a *positional* good – its value is in its relation to others.[1] Suppose, in contrast, we seek to be physicians because we want to contribute medical skills; then opportunity can increase, if more health care is provided or if the labor of providing services is shared among a larger pool of providers.

If opportunity is competitive, the opportunity good (the good for which we have an opportunity) is of limited supply. If the good were of unlimited

---

[1] Hirsch (1976) contains a subtle discussion of the economics of positional goods and the limits they create for human well-being.

supply, your getting that good would have no effect on whether I can get it. If opportunity is unlimited, that does not mean that everyone succeeds in attaining the opportunity good. Rather, like the opportunity to become a licensed driver, there is no limit to those who can attain the good, and one person's success has no effect on the likelihood of anyone else succeeding. If the number of desirable positions is unlimited, then so is opportunity. In order to be "unlimited," the number of positions does not have to be infinite. It simply has to be expandable so that it can match the number who aspire to and meet the qualifications for the position. In chapter 7, I will show how sharing both routine and complex labor can create unlimited opportunities to attain the most desirable positions.

Two sources of esteem

Opportunity for wealth will never be unlimited. If opportunity is to be unlimited, the goods have to be ones that can be expanded indefinitely. Luckily, there are important goods with that characteristic: social esteem and self-esteem.

Humans are the most intensely social of primates. We were social before we were human. Articulate speech gives evidence of our sociality: only humans can spend hours entertaining one another with chatter, jokes, teasing, stories, reminiscences, bragging, mocking, argument and dialog, and verbal learning. Because we are so social, a positive self-valuation depends on what others think of us.

We develop an identity, a sense of self, in community with others. That sense of self is defined largely through norms that we learn from others, what it means to be a good person. We want to think well of ourselves, but to do so we must conform to our own understanding of what a good person is and does. We have situated and relational identities: a teacher, a father or mother, a hard worker, a Christian, an anti-racist, Mary's husband. Each identity is defined through norms of behavior that we esteem and disesteem. Perhaps a teacher may embrace a norm never to mock a student and to be patient in the face of difficulties in communicating ideas. Then, for that teacher, to be aware that he lost his composure and embarrassed a student threatens a diminishment of his esteem for himself as a teacher. The same would hold for other identities central to our sense of self. And there are norms that define quite generally what a good *person* does and does not do.

All these identities – from the general one of being a good person to the more particular ones, for example being American or an internationalist – are socially learned. People who embrace the same identity may disagree about its normative content; for example, teachers disagree about what it means to be a good teacher. Still, conformity with norms implicit in an identity and the esteem of like-minded others (who share our idea of good teaching) are central to a positive view of ourselves. Let us call the esteem (positive valuation) derived from conformity with norms implicit in an identity, and esteem derived from others who share our ideas of its normative content, esteem grounded in *norms of identity*.[2] Norms of identity are one kind of *norm of esteem*.

Another kind of social esteem is attached to social positions. As we saw in chapter 3, social positions are statuses within a group defined by rights and responsibilities. So physician, architect, postal clerk, auto assembler, welder, grocery stockman, and secretary are positions, but so are PTA member, choir director at Emmanuel Lutheran, Mexican citizen, poll watcher, and soccer coach. In many societies, social esteem is attached unequally to social positions. The social esteem attached to a position is *prestige*. In contemporary capitalist societies, some positions are loci of much prestige, others of social contempt: so (and these are generalizations about the dominant norms of prestige), greater prestige is attached to the position of electrical engineer than to that of housekeeper, which is a position of contempt (low prestige). Positions of great prestige are also called "high-status" positions and positions of contempt "low-status" positions. Many positions are of middling prestige: auto mechanic and store manager, for example.

People seek positions of higher prestige (usually accompanied by higher income) at least partly because of the social esteem attached to the position – at least, they aspire to these positions when they believe they are available to them. We seek to think well of ourselves. Because self-esteem is reinforced by social esteem, positions of prestige are avenues to self-esteem.

There are, then, two sorts of norms of esteem. There are the norms of esteem associated with an identity as a teacher or parent. We called these "norms of identity." There are also norms that give more prestige to some social positions than to others. Call these "norms of prestige."[3] Both sorts of norms ground social and self-esteem.

We use the same word, "teacher," for both an identity and a position. Being a teacher can ground social esteem in two ways. As an identity, "teacher" is the locus of norms of identity (a good teacher encourages students to question received wisdom) which ground social and self-esteem. As a position, a norm attaches prestige to it, conventionally greater prestige for teachers of young adults (college teachers) than for teachers of young children (pre-school teachers).

Norms of identity apply to positions, regardless of the prestige attached to the position. We esteem people for doing what they do well. So, while "mother" is not a position of high prestige, we esteem a mother who is able to nurture self-confidence in her children while teaching them regard for the feelings of other people; we esteem an auto mechanic who has encyclopedic knowledge of the possible causes of particular problems, is properly modest about what

---

[2] My most developed published explication of norms of identity is Gomberg (1997), but see also Gomberg (n.d.).

[3] I use the word "norms" in the phrases "norms of prestige" and "norms of esteem" even though it has a different meaning from its meaning in the phrase "norms of identity;" generally, I use the word "norm" to refer to shared expectations of conduct, but in the phrases "norms of prestige" and "norms of esteem" it refers to shared understandings of what is a good *position* or a ground of esteem, not what is good conduct.

she knows, and is willing to test alternatives before settling on a diagnosis; a newspaper delivery person who is determined, reliable, meticulous, and organized; a teacher's aid who is patient with students, sensitive to individual differences, and inventive in reaching students who do not respond to ordinary methods; a nursing assistant who is devoted to patient needs and inventive in circumventing bureaucratic obstacles to good care; an auto worker who takes care of his work assignment and defends co-workers against unjust treatment; a licensed driver who is considerate of other drivers and alert to and avoids possible dangers to self and others.

Each social position has norms of identity, an ethic internal to the position that can ground social and self-esteem. In societies with limited positions of prestige, prestige is a positional good in limited supply; in contrast, esteem grounded in norms of identity is not a limited or positional good, for there is no limit to the number who can be esteemed for doing what they do well.

Comparative and competitive

Someone might object that for there to be good driving (of an automobile) there must also be bad driving to contrast it with. So esteem grounded in norms of identity is competitive. But this is to confuse competitive and comparative. Normative evaluation is comparative. Norms are social controls of behavior enforced by according esteem to folks who conform. All stable human societies have norms of nurturing the young; some people in the group have responsibility for caring for particular children and insuring their passage to adulthood. Those who carry out their duties are esteemed for this; those who slight their duties are subject to contempt or punishment. Applying norms is comparative. We are comparing behavior to the standards set by norms. If all behavior met norms perfectly, with never a deviation, we would not need a norm.

Norms are needed because social life contains conflicts. The duties of caring for a child can conflict with the demands of career, a desire to see old friends, or simply the desire for rest and recreation. There is always some tug toward deviation. Because of that tug, conformity will never be perfect; there will always be some unevenness.

Some unevenness does not mean a lot. We can strive toward perfect conformity. And it is because there is no limit to how much better we can become that there is no competition for normative esteem. There is nothing in anyone else's behavior that limits the esteem I can get for being a good father. I only have to be a good father. No one else's success affects my ability to succeed. So the opportunity for esteem for being a good father is of unlimited supply.

Power and other sources of prestige

In societies where there is a division between complex and routine labor, greater prestige attaches to some positions than to others for at least three reasons: some positions are thought to be more socially useful; some are positions of power;

some involve complex tasks. All can be sources of prestige. While connected, they are not the same. In chapter 6 we will see why usefulness and complexity entail prestige. Here, we connect prestige and power.

Corporate executives have prestige because they can give commands and be obeyed, as can doctors and dentists, who often are the bosses of their offices. Similarly, prestige attaches to wealth. In chapter 12, I explain why prestige attaches to wealth (an account of this was also given in chapter 4).

Why should prestige attach to power? The answer is developed most fully in chapter 10; here I anticipate. When some people have the social power to give orders or commands to others, we accustom ourselves to these relationships, in the absence of struggle against them: we rationalize why they may command us; we think it is right (the rationalization principle again – if we accept it, we rationalize it). By according greater prestige to those who have social power, we say they are better in a way that makes it right that they should give orders to us. Thus prestige attaches to power.

Must positions of prestige be of limited supply?

It is a commonplace of sociology that prestige is a positional good, that is, that some hold high-prestige positions only if others have low-prestige positions. Michèle Lamont writes: "Prestige, money, and power are positional goods, resources that are distributed on a zero-sum basis – that is, they exist in finite number and take their value relationally" (2000: 306, n.13). In societies where positions of prestige are limited, where janitors sweep up after mathematicians, prestige is of limited supply. But does it have to be of limited supply in all possible societies?

The same consensus does not exist in anthropology. In his classic work, *The Evolution of Political Society*, Morton Fried defines an egalitarian society as "one in which there are as many positions of prestige in any given age-sex grade as there are persons capable of filling them" (1967: 33). The example Fried gives is the position of a "successful hunter." Gatherer-hunter groups do not limit the number of men who can attain this position. And, as Fried points out, by giving credit for killing game in a variety of ways (the Ju/'hoansi credit the *maker* of the first arrow to strike the animal rather than the hunter; hunters may not be carrying any arrows they made themselves [Lee 1979]), they virtually insure that any sufficiently hard-working and cooperative adult male can attain a position of prestige. Positions of prestige are not limited in number. Your being a successful hunter does not affect my opportunity to become one. A successful hunter will hang back from hunting to give others the opportunity to bring meat into camp.

So under some circumstances prestige may be of unlimited supply. In stratified societies it is a positional good of limited supply. To the extent that our self-esteem depends on holding a position of prestige, we may compete not only for prestige but also for self-esteem. To that extent, where positions of prestige are limited, self-esteem can become a scarce good, and many may lack self-esteem and self-confidence in many social situations. As we will see, however, people try to sustain self-esteem at whatever cost, and the cost is often social unity. The struggle for self-esteem leads to divergent norms of prestige.

This surely is a defect of a society, that it makes it impossible for us to agree on what social positions are worthy of esteem. We can make the opportunity for prestige unlimited by sharing routine and complex labor. Then it would be possible to have shared norms of prestige without diminishing anyone's opportunity for prestige.

Dividing labor and limiting positions of prestige

We need to make connections. The important connection is between the division of complex and routine labor and limiting positions of prestige. When complex and routine labor are divided, positions requiring complex labor are positions of higher prestige, and these are usually very limited in number; most folks do routine labor. Prestige becomes a scarce good. Access to it is often competitive. Positions of complex labor tend to be the positions of prestige because complex skills draw admiration or esteem – both the agent's own esteem for what she has done and the esteem of others (as will be explained in chapter 6); this esteem is associated with positions using more complex talents. These positions are limited and so is the prestige associated with them.

As a result there is a *tendency* for social esteem to be a scarce good. This is only a tendency for three reasons. First, people in low-prestige positions tend to move in different social circles from folks in higher-prestige positions: janitors do not generally go to the same parties as college professors and suffer from comparing the prestige of what they do with that of the professors. Several years ago, I invited one of my students and her husband to my house for dinner. In the course of the evening I asked him what he did. He said, "I'm in business," but did not say what the business was. As I got to know them better, I found that he had a small janitorial service (he and two others that worked with him) and had contracts to clean bathrooms and other public places. He had not wanted to tell me that. This was not a problem for him most of the time. He did not usually socialize with professors. But when he did, it became a source of shame.

If such encounters were common, the socially shared sense of superiority and inferiority would make the low prestige attached to our position apparent and painful. But because of social segregation, people are able to avoid the pain of others looking down on them. People compare themselves in terms of prestige to those like themselves, and so they are esteemed within their circle. A janitor may be respected in a neighborhood of cab drivers, hospital laundry workers, nurses' aides, sales clerks, car wash attendants, and unemployed people.

Second, people may be respected for doing what they do well. Earlier, we noted that a good mother may be esteemed even though "mother" is not a position of high prestige. Someone who does data entry may be esteemed for doing it accurately. This applies generally to positions of low prestige. Thus we may receive social esteem despite the low prestige of our position.

Third, social esteem may derive from yet other sources that have nothing to do with one's position in the organization of labor. One may be a second baseman and cleanup hitter on the company softball team, a deacon in the church, a respected member of a quilt guild, an outstanding "fantasy baseball" player at a local bar, or a neighborhood computer guru helping others set up and maintain their personal computers. Besides esteem for what we do, there is esteem for personal qualities: hair, eyes, skin, a graceful gait. All these can be sources of social esteem entirely independently of esteem derived from the prestige of one's position.

These last three points qualify the tendency for social esteem to be a good of limited supply. Nonetheless, we had better hope that we don't run into an old childhood friend who has become a doctor while we are still working as an X-ray technician, our medical ambitions having been checked by an "F" in organic chemistry. Such encounters can arouse feelings of failure and inferiority, derived, I suggest, from a comparison of the prestige of what we do with that of another; we can't avoid making the comparison, since we grew up together. How important is this consciousness that our social position is one of lesser prestige? Does it constitute a serious deprivation of social esteem, serious enough to have an important influence on self-esteem? The questions are ones of fact. I believe that the harms often can be important.

Tenuous self-esteem seems to be a mass phenomenon. Those of us who are teachers, particularly if we teach students who are not among the elite, know that many students are limited by their own beliefs about what they can do. Students often do not appreciate that learning involves failure. They fail and give up, interpreting the experience of failure as evidence of limited talent, that they are not "smart enough." In contrast, students who learn better have reservoirs of self-confidence and a tolerance for failure, turning repeated failures into challenges and eventual success. The connection between self-esteem and the ability to master difficult material is profound. I am suggesting that the lack of tolerance for failure is related to limited self-esteem and that this lack of self-esteem is a mass phenomenon.

Moreover, if earlier arguments are correct, in societies that limit positions requiring complex abilities people must be persuaded that their failure to attain those positions is their fault. The alternative – the belief that my failure shows that there is something wrong with the social system – tends to destabilize a society. In short, social stability requires not only that children be trained for routine tasks from an early age and that their aspirations be shaped accordingly but also, as part of that process, that they believe that they are not suited, talented, or smart enough to carry out those more challenging tasks. Lack of self-esteem, particularly as it concerns "smartness," becomes a mass phenomenon in societies that divide complex from routine labor and people have limited opportunity to attain positions of prestige. Not everyone with a low-prestige position suffers from diminished social and self-esteem; still, diminished esteem is more common among those in low-prestige positions; it is a harm to them; it is a consequence of the division between complex and routine labor.

Simple egalitarian societies which lack political centralization embrace an egalitarian conception of opportunity. While not all folks are equally esteemed, the opportunity to attain positions of prestige is limited only by age and sex. There is no limit to the number of group members who may attain prestige as a hunter, storyteller, healer, or even group leader (this last is true among acephalous foragers – where leadership in group activities is shifting and contextual). The effect on personality is striking to anthropologists who have lived among such egalitarian peoples: their robust sense of their own worth, of their value to the group, and of their ability to contribute. In these societies, self-esteem is neither diminished nor tenuous.

In contrast, the division between complex and routine labor, by limiting opportunities to attain positions of prestige, limits the esteem available to us. Moreover, the opportunity to attain positions of prestige – a direct avenue to social esteem and self-esteem – will (for reasons given in chapter 3) be unequal, and so will the opportunities for social esteem and self-esteem. Thus the division between complex and routine labor creates unequal opportunities for positions of prestige, for social esteem, and for self-esteem. These are important goods. Having less opportunity to attain them is a serious loss.

The division between complex and routine labor limits positions of prestige, making prestige a scarce good. It exposes people in positions of low prestige to feelings of inferiority – or the fear of being seen as inferior – in many social situations. This is another important harm.

The arguments of the last three paragraphs assume that the dominant norms of prestige are accepted by all as grounding esteem. We will now see how people defend themselves from these consequences and the further problems that these defenses create.

Self-esteem and sub-group norms of esteem

People try to sustain a good opinion of themselves. So how do people sustain self-esteem when they are racially demeaned, in low-status occupations, or unemployed or on public assistance? The answer is universal throughout class societies: those demeaned by dominant conceptions of prestige develop alternative prestige rankings, shared within a group, which elevate some qualities that the dominant norms diminish and diminish some that dominant prestige rankings elevate.

School success can be thought of as "nerdy," "geeky," or "uncool." Ambition can be selfish or disloyal to old friends. Michèle Lamont notes that the French workers she interviewed valued being able to do work that is boring and repetitive (see chapter 3 for the full quote in another context). People who do demeaned physical labor elevate physical strength. The Hallway Hangers (see chapter 3) valued toughness. Some American white workers Lamont interviewed valued working hard, being able to get by on little money, and being more concerned with friends than with material possessions. Black workers she interviewed elevated collectivism and solidarity and disparaged successful people as domineering, exploitative, selfish, unconcerned, and lacking integrity. My readers can supply many more examples of sub-group counter-norms from their experience.

These counter-values elevate what those demeaned by dominant prestige rankings have. (There are problems of whether they are consistent in their valuations. We will return to this in chapter 8 in discussing racism.) How could it be otherwise? We strive to sustain a positive view of ourselves.[4]

Social unity: can social esteem be of unlimited supply?

It is time to draw together the threads of this chapter. We are social creatures who try to sustain a positive opinion of ourselves and need the support of others to do so. Central to that positive opinion are normative identities, defined through shared *norms of identity*. Like all norms, these are subject to disagreement. Still, there is no limit to the number who can be esteemed as a good teacher, parent, Christian, or anti-racist as long as they meet the norms by which they and a relevant reference group define those identities.

The phrase "norms of esteem" can also refer to *norms of prestige*, norms which attach prestige unequally to positions, more to an architect than to a draftsman and less yet to the janitor, more to the plant manager, less to the line supervisor or electrician, less yet to the machine operator, less yet to the porter gang, and least to the unemployed or public aid recipient. These norms of prestige heap contempt on many who do necessary labor and absorb the psycho-social costs of a society with many low-prestige positions and many unemployed. To defend their self-esteem, those subject to contempt by dominant norms erect counter-norms, elevating themselves and diminishing the elite.

There is a price to be paid for limiting positions of prestige. One price is that the strategies of self-defense (building counter-norms to the dominant norms) do not work very well. People are aware of how they are perceived. This awareness can be painful.

The other price is social unity. No society that limits positions of prestige can be united around common norms of prestige. This social division arises from norms of prestige contemptuous of many necessary positions. We need day care workers; we need unskilled construction labor; we need garment workers; we need farm labor; we need car wash attendants; we need stock clerks in grocery stores; and, as the Federal Reserve Board will tell us, we need unemployed

---

[4] We could call this *the ego-defense principle*. When low-status folks erect counter-norms to defend self-esteem, this application of the principle is in *conflict* with the rationalization principle, which accords esteem to those with power and wealth.

people to keep wage inflation under control. Yet these folks are subject to contempt. They defend themselves psychologically. The defense creates social division. This social division has a very nasty edge: it is racism. The division comes from limits on prestige and on opportunity for prestige.

Social unity is possible if norms of prestige hold no worker in contempt. To realize that possibility, we need unlimited positions of prestige and unlimited opportunity for them. In chapter 6, I defend the goods for which there can be equal and unlimited opportunity. In chapter 7, I sketch how a society might be organized to realize these goods and discuss several problems and objections, clarifying the proposal. In chapter 8, I show how the proposal to share routine and complex labor can overcome social divisions.

Chapter 6

Opportunity for What?
Defending the Constellation

What makes life good?

In *The Market Experience*, Robert Lane calls "those whose jobs offer self-direction, substantive complexity, and challenge, variety, little supervision, and intrinsic satisfaction of excellence or self-determination" the "privileged class" among workers. They do "freely and (usually) with social approval and support what they want to do and usually do best." The privileged class seems to be professionals, who report the highest levels of satisfaction with their jobs, education, and living standard; among professionals, urban college professors may rank highest (1991: 302–3).

I could not argue with that. Freed from the distractions of maintaining discipline that many high school teachers face, I have followed a love for a discipline that first captivated me in my youth. When my students grapple with philosophical questions, I enhance their lives. Philosophy is endlessly challenging and difficult, yet engages important questions. I have remarked in class, "I can't believe that I get paid to do this!"

What makes this life so good? While some elements of my pleasure are idiosyncratic, or nearly so, some are also universal, or nearly so: the enjoyment of complexity, of contributing to others, and of being respected for this contribution. This constellation of goods – contributing developed abilities to the good of others and earning esteem for those contributions – is part of the best life.

Egalitarianism of opportunity would make the *opportunity* for those best things unlimited and available to all equally. Here I defend three ideas about what makes life good: (1) that it is good to develop and practice complex abilities; (2) that it is good to contribute abilities to the benefit of others; (3) that it is good to think well of oneself and to be thought well of by others. To defend the constellation of opportunities, I defend three other theses about the *connections* between complexity, contribution, and esteem; (4) that what one "does" – how one contributes to a larger group – is central to our esteem for ourselves and from others; (5) that we are esteemed by others and ourselves more for contribution of complex than for routine abilities; (6) that someone's exercise of complex abilities in daily social labor has important effects on her other activities and sense of well-being generally.

These six ideas suggest that what is good – besides material well-being, love, and security – is a life where we think well of ourselves because we contribute developed abilities to the good of others and are socially esteemed for doing so. I am defending equal opportunity to attain this constellation of important goods. My argument is that these are not just conventionally important goods, relative to time and place; they are universal human goods. While not every *individual* desires them, in all *societies* they are desirable. In egalitarian societies (where opportunities are limited only by age and gender), they are universal grounds of esteem; in stratified societies, where opportunities are unequal, they are considered appropriate goods for advantaged classes.

These goods tell us something about what it means to be part of a human group. Human societies depend on their members to contribute to sustaining the group. Because we evolved using our wits to solve social and subsistence problems – our special strength as a species – exercise of complex abilities for the good of the group is especially esteemed. Because we rely on shared norms of esteem for social control, we normally care greatly what others think of us and seek to think well of ourselves by norms we share with others. I defend the constellation by arguing that these goods are universal in human societies; these are goods for human beings.

Perhaps more important, I defend the constellation by appealing to you the reader: what do *you* believe makes life good? If you agree with the constellation and if those who agree can persuade most of the rest, then we have the social basis for bringing about a society where these goods are available to all.

The good of developing and exercising complex abilities

The typical one-year-old is curious, into everything. This desire to learn, understand, investigate, is not unique to humans, but we take it further than other species. We spend our prolonged infancy mastering bipedal locomotion, spoken language, manual skills (such as tying shoelaces), and, in urban civilizations, written language, mathematics, and knowledge of nature. We master physical abilities: running, wrestling, jumping, and, in urban civilizations, playground games such as basketball and double-dutch jump rope. We develop and master cultural abilities such as singing (including harmony and polyphony), musical instruments, storytelling, skits and mimicry, and painting, jewelry-making, and other decorative arts and crafts. In hunter-gatherer societies we may learn to track animals and to distinguish flora, fauna, and geographical features of our environment.

Most important among cultural abilities is mastery of complex social relations. We learn, apply, and develop norms of interpersonal cooperation, morality, and etiquette. We may master strategic social thinking, how to achieve our ends in complex social situations, particularly how to enhance social harmony when there is stress. Jane Austen's heroines often combine moral integrity with skill at maintaining harmony and regard for the feelings of others.

We enjoy learning, particularly when investigation is self-directed. Mastering a skill or knowledge gives a sense of accomplishment (more on this later in discussion of complex abilities and esteem). We enjoy practicing complex abilities, even when our abilities are stretched to their limits – provided that these more stressful tasks are relieved by periods of relaxation. We enjoy the exercise of thoroughly mastered complexity (Jo Wolff [in correspondence] suggests the example of Picasso sketching a dove). Learning and exercising complex abilities are essential goods. A life without them, a life of routine activities that do not stretch our minds or creativity, is to that extent not a good life.

The good of contributing our abilities to a social group

While studying for the PhD in philosophy, I was given a one-year suspension from graduate school. I was arrested on campus during the occupation of the administration building; I had earlier been put on final warning because of participation in campus anti-war and anti-racist demonstrations. I wrote my father to tell him. Soon I received his reply. "Dear Son," he wrote, "I want to let you know how proud I am of you." He wrote that his friends complained that their children were only interested in making money; they told him that he was lucky to have a son committed to principle. After going on in this way for a page (typed, single-spaced), he closed, "But I hope you haven't harmed your career." Many would like to "do well by doing good," but often we pay a price if we interpret our responsibility to society as protesting injustice. Perceiving a conflict between doing well and doing good, some abandon hope of making a living by doing good. Still, many desire to contribute positively to society.

All societies accept the norm of contributing to the good of others. Among the most egalitarian human groups, acephalous nomadic foragers, norms require the sharing of food and other goods (Leacock and Lee 1982: Introduction). Sedentary egalitarian groups have inequalities of wealth but require redistribution to others in case of need (Harris 1991: 113). In stratified societies, things are complicated, but the *ideal* of contribution to the group is maintained, both through tribute to society's leaders (in state-level society taxes) and through norms of redistribution from leaders to the needy – though these norms may be honored in words only (Gilman 1995: 237–8). In modern, market-oriented economies, gainful employment is typically understood not just as providing for self and family but as contributing to society. We retain the ideal of contributing, at least to the family, household, or extended family. Rulers are honored for their "public service" as if they cared for all of us just as we care for our families.

We are the most intensely social of mammals. It makes sense that our lives go better when we see ourselves as contributing. Research reported by Tim Kasser

(2002) shows that people who are intrinsically motivated, including toward helpfulness to others, are psychologically healthier and have better relationships.

The good of thinking well of ourselves and being thought well of by others

This section returns to some themes of the last chapter: self-esteem and its support by social esteem. Here I argue that self-esteem and the social support of it are universal goods. It is necessary to repeat some of the argument of the last chapter to see how the goods of self-esteem and social esteem are part of the constellation.

Humans are uniquely a normative and normatively self-conscious species. By "normative," I mean this: we use language to develop, dispute, refine, and apply expectations of one another's behavior; the results of this dialog are norms, shared expectations, enforced by at least the opinion of someone's actions. Positive opinions of actions and agents I have called "esteem," negative opinions "disesteem." Much behavior answers to these social expectations of conduct.

We are normatively self-conscious in that we identify ourselves through categories – teacher, parent, American citizen, or simply person – that we understand normatively; we develop expectations of ourselves as, for example, teachers, what a teacher does and does not do, and these norms are central to our self-understanding, to identity. (We called these "norms of identity.") We thus internalize standards of conduct. Normativity and normative self-awareness are universal in human societies.

Norms are enforced by our estimation of conduct. To "esteem" is to think well of; to "disesteem" is to think badly of. Our ethical life does not work unless it is centrally important to us to think well of ourselves and be thought well of by others, not necessarily all others but at least by a "reference group" with which we identify. This also is a human universal (Gomberg 1997).

Regardless of what about us may inspire esteem, it is important to be thought well of by others because that opinion supports a positive view of ourselves. Self-esteem is an absolutely central good, together with the related good of self-confidence. Without a good opinion of ourselves and confidence in that good opinion, it is difficult to undertake new tasks or to approach the tasks of daily life with positive feeling.

While each of the three goods I have discussed is good in itself, it is in the interconnections of these goods that we see most clearly that this constellation is central to a good life.

Why labor is important to self- and social esteem

"What do you do?" we might ask in a friendly way of a new acquaintance, inquiring how someone earns her living. What we "do" is important, for it represents the contribution of labor to others. In market economies, how we earn a living may not always inspire respect from others (imagine someone replying to an inquiry about what he does: "I am an exotic dancer"). This possibility underlines the duality of our labor, as sustaining self and family and as contributing to society. The belief that our labor contributes to a wider group is important to our esteem.

A damaging blow to self- and social esteem for adults (especially males, for reasons related to expectations of men versus women) is unemployment, particularly if it is prolonged. People who remain unemployed are disparaged as lazy or incompetent. While this disparagement is usually unfair, the unemployed lose recognition as economic contributors. This loss can be devastating to dignity and self-esteem – especially because the unemployed themselves accept the value of contributing and hence feel worse about themselves. In the United States for the past 50 years, black people have suffered twice the rate of unemployment as whites. The scars of this assault on people's dignity are deep in many neighborhoods.[1]

Labor connects us positively, as contributors, to a wider social world. Because of this, labor offers opportunities for esteem usually unavailable from leisure activities. This is true even though many positions performing essential tasks are of low or middling prestige. Examples come readily to mind: mother, janitor, street sweeper, refuse collector, newspaper delivery person, letter-carrier, parcel delivery person. Their low or modest prestige is due either to the association of their labor with cleaning up or with the lack of qualifications needed for this labor (or both). But apart from whether labor is useful by standards on which all would agree, subjectively our labor is seen as contributing to society. Hence, whatever the value of leisure activities, they do not seem contributive as labor is, nor do they provide esteem for contributing as labor does.

Why we think more highly of complex than of simple abilities

There is a natural reason why prestige is associated with positions requiring mastery of complexity. Consider our reaction to hearing a clever impersonator or remarkably clear philosopher, seeing a skilled magician, or watching Michael Jordan or Allen Iverson play basketball. We respond with admiration, a form of esteem. The esteem arises naturally from the difficulty, cleverness, grace, beauty, or wisdom of the activity, qualities that are present beyond their ordinary measure in our mundane tasks.

Can this observation about the connection between difficult tasks and admiration be extended to explain why positions requiring complex knowledge and skills such as professor, doctor, dentist, or mathematician are positions of

---

[1]   Baldwin 1949 and Clark 1965 give poignant accounts of this pain.

prestige? Three qualifications have to be made. For reasons related to the rationalization principle – and discussed in chapter 5 – prestige may come from power alone, not from complexity associated with a position. Also, positions requiring complex knowledge and skills may have little prestige attached to them – an experienced auto mechanic skilled in diagnostics, for example. Moreover, there is a gap between the extraordinary achievements of the people mentioned in the previous paragraph and the more ordinary mastery usually associated with positions of prestige.

Nonetheless, think of how we felt as college students about a favorite professor: the admiration, even awe, at her mastery of her discipline. Just as we admire the mastery of a great entertainer, so, at a more modest level, we admire the mastery of a professor, doctor, and skilled mechanic. This esteem inspired by mastery of complexity explains why there is a *tendency* for prestige to be attached to positions requiring complexity. This explanation allows that where getting dirty at work detracts from prestige, we may not accord much prestige to auto mechanics.

When a child first masters a complex skill (relative to its age) – walking, tying shoelaces, shooting a basketball, writing a story, driving a car – these accomplishments draw our esteem. But complexity is relative. So at a certain stage we expect that we can all do these things (or their appropriate counterparts). The opportunities to contribute greater complexities become curtailed for many adults. Our tasks become routine, easily mastered, and cease to inspire esteem from either ourselves or others. Two quotes from auto workers interviewed by Arthur Kornhauser in the 1950s show how a life consumed by routine labor can affect people. Worker 1: "Factory work is so monotonous. You are always being told where to go and what to do. It slows them up; they can't think for themselves; they are like machines or robots. A man does the same thing over and over again so many times he just doesn't care any more. It seems I just don't care any more; I am there and that's all." Worker 2: "It weakens their mind. Many men when they first come here were sharp and alert; after a few years they are not the same; their mind is dull. It sure has weakened me; it has taken the life out of me. Some days I feel I'm 70 years old" (he was actually 43; Kornhauser 1965: 80). Routine, easily mastered labor can undermine self-confidence, self-esteem, and one's will and energy.

Some are able to spend a lifetime in challenging and difficult work. Learning new things and practicing old mastery both make us feel positive about ourselves and inspire esteem from others. In philosophy and physics, in engineering and architecture, and in quilting, gardening, and storytelling, the challenge is endless. We are never "done." Of course, labor of unrelieved difficulty is burdensome. Intensely difficult tasks should alternate with routine ones. While learning a new skill or mastering new material can stretch us to the limit, we also enjoy practicing a thoroughly mastered skill.

A philosopher may enjoy the stress of trying to master John Rawls's theory of justice. But we also enjoy leading a group of students through a discussion of gender roles for the fiftieth time; there is the challenge of introducing ideas to a new group, and each group will raise new issues or old issues in different ways that lead even the instructor to learn something fresh. The rate of learning is not as great as when mastering something new, and the pleasure of leading a discussion in ways one has mastered is a different pleasure from the one of learning to master something new and difficult. We need both pleasures. Both activities – learning something new and practicing a mastered skill – contribute to social and self-esteem. And we need to just relax, to "chill," as well.

How complex, challenging work enhances one's life; how routine labor damages it

Robert Lane writes that people with work that is self-directed, substantively complex, and varied, "gratify their wants, and perhaps needs, in the processes of producing and not of ruling or consuming" (1991: 302). The 10-year longitudinal study of the effects of work experience on life and personality by Melvin Kohn and Carmi Schooler provides evidence that self-directed work contributes to self-esteem (1983: 142, 204). Occupational self-direction (substantive complexity of work, and absence of both routine and close supervision) leads to more challenging leisure pursuits (pp. 81, 239–40). Conversely, as we noted, lack of challenge at work causes people to become intellectually less flexible and open and to pursue less challenging leisure activities. Kohn and Schooler found evidence that "the cognitive capacities, the thinking ability, of those with simple repetitive tasks *deteriorate*" (Lane 1991: 324; emphasis in original. Cf. Kohn and Schooler 1983: 144). These results give empirical support to Adam Smith's speculation about the effect of routine, repetitive labor.

When workers believe that their jobs do not utilize their abilities, it leads them to feel alienated and fatalistic. Kornhauser writes: "[N]onuse of abilities [causes] lowered self-esteem, discouragement, futility, and feelings of failure and inferiority in contrast to a sense of personal growth and self-fulfillment resulting from more varied, responsible, challenging undertakings that afford opportunity to develop and use one's ideas and skills" (1955: 129). Kornhauser's interviews, which prompted workers to talk extensively about their jobs, lives, and how they felt about themselves, give further evidence that our labor affects our personalities and abilities.

Many with routine jobs hate work and cherish time away from work. Years ago, when I was a postal worker, a sign by a time clock read: "Those who believe that the dead do not come back to life should be here at quitting time." Ending their shifts, workers came out the door jubilantly screaming, "Jailbreak!" These same workers had spent their work shifts moving slowly, conserving energy in the event they had to work overtime (this was true at least in my own case).

When we hate our work, we try to find satisfaction in shopping and buying, channeling energy and intelligence into consumerism, or we may engage in hobbies (which often involve consumerism). Tim Kasser (2002) provides evidence that consumerist values are correlated with unhappiness and poor mental health. Moreover, as we have seen, mind-dulling labor can have generalized effects which make leisure less challenging too. People with challenging, complex jobs derive satisfaction from what they do every day. As we noted, challenging labor changes the laborer, making her increasingly more capable and more likely to engage in leisure that develops her abilities.

Complex labor enhances self-esteem because mastery of complexity makes us aware of our own abilities and draws admiration from others. Conversely, routine labor can easily detract from self-esteem, as the quotes from Kornhauser seem to show; people compare what they are with what they might have been, and this can make them sad. On the other hand, people adapt; they change preferences to sustain a sense of their own worth (as we saw in chapter 5). Still, routine, simple labor tends to make us less capable.

A common objection to "meaningful work" proposals is that *leisure* pursuits can promote intellectual development and a sense of accomplishment unavailable at work. Therefore, it is suggested, in a just society people might choose a life of routine, unchallenging labor in exchange for higher income or more leisure time, both of which might enhance leisure pursuits (Arneson 1987). However, as we noted, unchallenging work affects personality, self-esteem, and capability in ways that make less likely the pursuit of complex leisure activities. People who do self-directed, complex work tend to engage in more challenging leisure pursuits. Kohn and Schooler write: "The strong, positive effect of the substantive complexity of both men's and women's work on the intellectuality of their leisure-time activities is powerful evidence that people generalize directly from job experience to the activities they perform in their leisure time" (1983: 239–40). (A more important objection is that Arneson's proposal would undermine equal opportunity; I argue this in chapter 7.)

Consider a life that involves daily tasks that develop our abilities and hence contribute to personal growth, a life that through the exercise of those abilities contributes to the good of others and inspires esteem from others and from ourselves for both the contributions and the complex mastery that they require. This life is good independently of other goods. Other goods cannot replace this constellation. A good society should offer equal opportunity to attain this constellation.

At the end of chapter 5 we saw an important consequence of dividing labor between routine and complex: many spend their working lives in positions of low prestige and are therefore subject to social contempt. This contempt is not an artifact of arbitrary evaluations. The connection between complexity and esteem is a natural one and so, therefore, is the connection between positions requiring complexity and prestige. Workers doing routine labor are subject to social contempt from others. But more: they can (but need not) be haunted by doubts about their own abilities. Workers interviewed by Kornhauser emphasized that "It don't take no Einstein," that you can't use your brain, that anyone off the street can do the job as well (pp. 166, 167, 169). Those who do only routine labor do not receive the natural self-esteem we feel for doing difficult tasks, particularly ones that engage our minds, in their everyday work lives. The costs of separating routine and complex labor include contempt for many who do necessary but routine tasks and an internal cost paid by those folks. So everyone should have the opportunity to contribute complex abilities to society, not on a zero-sum basis, but on a basis where we can all flourish together.

Is this an adequate defense of the constellation?

Is the argument of this chapter strong enough to justify creating equal and unlimited opportunity to attain the constellation? Dick Arneson told me he was unpersuaded. He told of his maternal grandfather who worked a routine job in a paper mill but was a revered patriarch. He wrote to me: "I think it would be very good if society were organized so everyone had a life as good as my grandfather's, so I think sharing complex work is not needed for the sharing of the good life justice demands." Let us develop the example in a way favorable to the objection. Suppose that he gave particularly wise leadership to others in his family, combining a warm heart with grasp of human differences and an ability to help others to develop themselves. He rarely lost his composure when there were difficulties and found ways of helping others to get along. Surely a life such as the patriarch's is possible, perhaps not even uncommon: a person works an unchallenging job but exercises great intelligence in other matters.

It is not enough to show that the patriarch is *possible*. We must ask whether social organization makes the patriarch's intelligence *less likely*. The story of the patriarch does not rebut evidence that routine labor tends to harm the worker by making him less intelligent or the arguments that a person who does exclusively routine labor is deprived of both the important good of contributing complex abilities to a larger group in his work life and an important source of self-esteem and social esteem. Nor does it rebut the argument of chapter 3 that, as long as there are many positions of routine labor, many children will be trained for those positions, thwarting the full development of their potential. These arguments and evidence, I believe, make a strong case for making this opportunity available to everyone non-competitively, so that we can all realize the goods of the constellation together.

In arguing for unlimited *opportunity* to realize the constellation, I leave open the possibility that some may prefer not to develop their abilities. This possibility, like the possibility of celibacy or fasting, must be allowed. But I would expect that in a society where we could all realize the goods of the constellation together, few would choose a life of unrelieved routine labor.

Still, the argument that there should be unlimited opportunity to realize the constellation is provisional. In chapter 7 I develop the proposal to share routine and complex labor in more detail and in chapter 8 I argue that this proposal creates the possibility of transforming social relationships in yet other ways that would make human societies more communal and nurturing of their members.

Chapter 7

Sharing Labor

Sharing routine tasks

Mary and I married in 1965. We had grown up in families where our fathers were "breadwinners," our mothers "homemakers." In the months after the wedding, as I studied for preliminary examinations for the PhD, she supported us working in an anthropology museum. After work she prepared dinner; on weekends she shopped for groceries, washed clothes, and cleaned the apartment. I washed dishes after dinner and studied. After a few months she said to me: "This won't fly," or words to that effect. We agreed that I should help her. Influenced by the Women's Liberation Movement in 1967, we rejected the idea that responsibility for housework was hers (and that I should help her). We agreed on something like an "equal" division of labor, though in time we became more flexible. This division of labor has made it possible for us both to work outside the home.

When I was an undergraduate at the University of California in the early 1960s, many students, including me, lived or boarded at the cooperatives. In the coops, students worked a few hours each week, preparing food, waiting tables, washing dishes, or carrying out other essential chores, labor which reduced the price of room and board. Contributing manual labor for a few hours was consistent with studying philosophy or mathematics.

For my mother, prestige comparisons with my father were painful; as long as she was "just a housewife" she was not considered his equal. After high school she had worked. My father earned a law degree. Determined to have a career of her own, she went to college in her forties and was a very successful student. Black women provided her with "help" as they did to many white women of her generation and status who had or aspired to their own careers.

The coops and my own marriage illustrate a different solution: sharing responsibilities for a household or cooperative makes it possible for people to do other things outside the home or cooperative. This chapter discusses how this norm might be extended to all routine labor.

How a hospital might work

How might a hospital work if routine and complex labor were shared? We will leave aside hospital administration (which has its own division between routine and complex labor). Other tasks include, at the routine end, housekeeping, laundry, food service, messenger service, and nursing assistants; doing more complex labor are licensed nurses, X-ray technicians, and phlebotomists; more complex yet is the labor of respiratory, physical, and other therapists and various lab technicians; greater responsibilities are assigned to registered nurses (who often do record-keeping) and dieticians; yet greater responsibility is given to nurse-practitioners and physician assistants; then there are the MDs: residents and attending physicians. Obviously there is no clear division between routine and complex labor, but some labor is more routine, other labor more complex, and, related to that continuum, there is a continuum of responsibility with some workers under close supervision and others very much self-directing.

The spirit of sharing routine and complex labor is expressed by the idea that everyone, including doctors, cleans up; no one need spend a full work week doing housekeeping. Doctors clean toilets. Doctors and nurses change bed linens. Similarly, no one need spend a full work week in the laundry room or peeling vegetables in the kitchen. Dieticians peel vegetables. Highly trained people share this labor. Sharing routine labor would have two immediate consequences. First, those who now do more routine labor would have time to master complex tasks if they chose. Second, those who have complex abilities would find it difficult, at best, to devote as much time as now to the exercise of those abilities. As a practical matter, the transition to sharing routine labor might not be made "all at once," but phased in as the number of people with complex mastery grows. These details need not concern us. What is important is the goal: to share routine labor *as equally as possible* among all who are capable.

The *opportunities* to learn and practice complex abilities would increase greatly, and more trained people would be needed to serve patient needs. I argued in chapter 6 that learning and contributing such abilities are central human goods and are important paths to social and self-esteem. Given unlimited opportunity, people would seek to make their lives better; many who have labored in food service, housekeeping, and laundry will acquire more complex abilities relevant to health care.

"Do you want a janitor performing brain surgery on you?" That is an obvious challenge. But what we seek is opportunity. People should not do things for which they are untrained or unqualified. If we share routine labor, those now confined to routine tasks will have the opportunity to acquire qualifications and master new knowledge according to their interests. One may learn respiratory therapy, another inoculations, another diet and health, another neurophysiology, another how to diagnose pulmonary pathologies, and another surgical techniques. In order to contribute an ability, one must show that one has mastered it. But "positions" could be broken down into specific abilities that have been mastered and hence could be contributed. Most important, each person who previously did only routine labor would have the opportunity to acquire new abilities.

If opportunity to acquire complex abilities is to be expanded, then each person who has mastered a complex ability would need to help others to master that ability. This is to imagine a very different world from our own. Each worker would have at least four responsibilities: to contribute routine labor, to master new complex abilities, to teach others the complex abilities she has mastered, and to practice those complex abilities.

Three ways of dividing labor

The phrase "division of labor" can mean at least three things. One division of labor is necessary to complex societies; the other two are inessential to complexity but part of class-divided societies. One division of labor arises with science and complex technology. Human social knowledge becomes so vast and complex that it is impossible for anyone to begin to master all of it in either theoretical or practical sciences; inevitably, we have specialists. Some understand one thing, others another. Because we specialize and coordinate our specializations, collectively we can know and do more than any individual could know or do. This organization of knowledge and of the application of knowledge to labor characterizes the production of goods and provision of services in any modern complex society. I have no quarrel with this division of labor.

The second division of labor arises in societies where workers producing food and other essentials create a surplus to support the rest. Routine and complex labor are divided. Some people do tasks that require extensive training and apprenticeship, while others do simple tasks mastered more quickly. This second division of labor arises with and is partly identical with a third: the division between organization and execution; some organize production and others labor under their instructions. These last two divisions of labor overlap because one complex task is to plan the labor process. But they are not identical: enforcing the plan of production on those who labor may not be complex, and much complex work does not involve planning the labor of others.

The division between organization and execution is primarily a division between those who control production and the workers who labor in it; the division between complex and routine labor is primarily a division *within* the working class. Complex labor is more desirable for reasons Robert Lane has given, particularly its being self-directed. There is a connection between labor's being routine and its being closely supervised. When labor is not closely supervised, workers will sometimes need to make decisions. In the last section, we left aside issues of supervision. Here we need to discuss how the division between organizing and supervising tasks on the one hand and executing assigned tasks on the other might be overcome.

A story from my work experience may make clearer the difference between more and less closely supervised labor. After I was denied tenure on my first teaching position I worked both as a manual clerk in the main St Louis mail-processing center and as a letter carrier. The two jobs were strikingly different. A letter carrier is assigned an eight-hour task, and to some degree the carrier decides how the task is executed. At the start of the day, I had several containers full of mail, a wooden sorting case with holdouts for the addresses on the route, a motor vehicle, and a task: by the end of the shift that mail should go from those containers into the mailboxes. There is a method to this: sorting the mail at the case, pulling it down in a way that corresponds to a plan to deliver it, transferring the mail to a vehicle, and then driving and walking the route. Carriers are relatively free of supervision when on the streets. For this reason many carriers prefer this labor to that of a clerk, and some even regard themselves as superior to clerks.

In contrast, a clerk reports to the timekeeper and waits for instructions (I am describing my experience as a manual clerk in the late 1970s). A supervisor tells the clerk to go to a work area and clock in on a particular operation, for example, to sort incoming letters by zip code. A tray of letters in front of her, the clerk distributes those letters to holdouts in a wooden case. When the tray is empty, the clerk gets another tray and repeats the process. For how long? Until the clerk is told to stop doing what she is doing and do something else. This continues for the duration of the eight-hour shift (or ten or eleven hours if overtime is required). You have no reason to think about what you are doing. Many of us hated being powerless over our work; it made us angry and reluctant to work, but if we worked, the time passed.[1]

As a clerk, I least minded working in "pouch rack" (small parcels). At 1.00 a.m. or so the supervisor would send me to the "633" (zip code) area where there were several hand trucks of parcels: "Make the 7.00 a.m. dispatch." Then, as with carrying mail, I was on my own for six hours, free to get that mail sorted into pouches, the pouches onto hand trucks, and the hand trucks to the loading docks by 7.00 a.m. The boss left me alone.

Much work is worse. Workers on an assembly or bottling line may perform the same task or small set of tasks for an eight-hour (or longer) shift – on a bottling line in a vinegar works I used to snap the plastic shaker caps onto bottles of vinegar. The worker's life activity is under the control of others during the work shift. However, unlike the situation of a postal clerk, where a supervisor directly controls a worker's labor, in assembly-line work the line itself, combined with the detailed organization of tasks, imposes control over the pace and organization of labor. Assembly-line work, like manual clerking, represents the extreme of routine labor in that the worker has little room for choice in exercising her energies. Even worse than clerking, it typically involves repetition of a very small set of tasks.

---

[1] Chris Rudd informs me that with the use of Optical Character Readers (OCRs) postal labor has been further deskilled; now clerks load and unload the OCRs.

A hospital housekeeper, while of lower status, may have more control over her own labor than other workers. Like a letter carrier, she may have the responsibility for cleaning a certain number of rooms or polishing floors. But, at the same time, she may have some discretion in figuring out how those tasks are to be completed. So while her tasks are controlled by others over an eight-hour shift, they may not be controlled hour by hour or minute by minute.

The hardest parts of car repair are diagnosing what is wrong and figuring out how to fix it. Then there is the repair itself. The higher-status mechanics perform all three parts of this process: diagnosis, planning the repair, and completing it. Some shops (for example, muffler and brake shops) separate diagnosis and planning the repair from the task of completing the repair. The last task is given to a low-status worker who is paid less than mechanics who perform all the tasks.

These examples show how the two divisions of labor are connected: the separation of organization and execution and the division between routine and complex. Those who command plan the labor process. Both these divisions of labor make one's labor feel alien to the worker. The examples reinforce what Robert Lane has written, that the most oppressive routine labor is closely supervised. Close supervision makes it pointless to think about what one is doing, and this is oppressive.

We can overcome the division between organization and execution if workers make decisions about their own work process, either individually, as now often occurs to a degree, or collectively. At minimum, all should have the *opportunity* to participate in making the organizational plan relevant to their work. This should help to end the alienation that derives from having no control over one's own work.

The phrase "organizational plan" represents a continuum of plans from the specific plan at the point of service or production (where, at one extreme, even the letter carrier in the current division of labor makes some decisions about the precise details) to, at the other extreme, the coordination of production and distribution at the widest scale. To say that "all should have the opportunity to participate in making the organizational plan" is to say that all the relevant plans, from the most specific to the most general, should be up for discussion by everyone. Not everyone need discuss the plan of a letter carrier. But the plans relevant to what each will do need to be discussed.

In the Soviet Union in the 1930s the Stakhanovite movement was initiated when a group of coalminers reorganized the method of cutting the coalface and timbering the newly opened face. By itself, this new method of organizing the labor process is just another method of dividing labor tasks, and its particular virtue – that it eliminated the need for workers to switch tools as they changed tasks – would have been applauded by Adam Smith. Stakhanovism was a positive development to the extent that workers took initiative in reorganizing the labor process, seizing responsibility from management. Their activities began to break down the division between organization and execution.[2]

---

[2] For a more detailed account of Stakhanovism, see Siegelbaum 1988; my interpretation of Stakhanovism is indebted to Anonymous 1979.

The *general* plans that *coordinate* labor must be open for discussion. Workers' control of the immediate labor process is not enough to unite organization and execution. That immediate labor process is part of a larger coordinated social process. The coordination on ever larger scales is the most important labor plan. If this coordination is in the hands of a relatively small group, organization and execution will be divided. Only when those who labor participate in planning the economy on the widest scale can we break down the division between organization and execution.

What I have just written engages issues not only of workplace democracy but also of the extent to which the role of markets in coordinating behavior can be replaced by conscious, collective decision-making. These problems should not be slighted. But to explore them and do them justice is another book – at *least* one.

Can routine and complex labor be separated?

The other division of labor is between routine and complex. If some necessary labor is easy, repetitive, and boring, then we share it. Each can have the opportunity to develop and contribute more complex abilities.

In many necessary tasks it is hard to separate the routine from the complex. One example is childrearing. Women have borne primary responsibility, and mother (or father) is not a position of prestige. Much child care is routine. Sometimes one must simply be sure children do not harm themselves or someone else. Changing diapers, doing laundry, keeping a house tidy, safe, and tolerably clean, dressing an infant, and playing with children of various ages may not stretch the mind. Yet interacting with children makes demands on one's personality. I used to stare off at the wall and think about some philosophical (or other) issue while changing my daughter's diaper until I noticed that she was looking at me; now, it seemed, I had to engage her in a friendly way. The best pre-school teachers show great patience and kindness with children – important qualities if a child is to be secure and self-confident, and qualities also needed in a parent.

Parenting can call for difficult judgments. How much restriction should a child have at each stage of its development? What do you do when a child won't sleep at bedtime: pick her up or let her cry? or when a child says something racist or ridicules students who are disadvantaged or joins a clique that excludes others? Teenagers can drive the sanest parents to counseling. While much parenting is routine, the task of developing a child's self-confidence and her sense of being securely loved makes demands on our personalities; in addition, there are genuinely difficult judgments of how to deal with problems of growing up. Parenting weaves together simple, complex, and emotionally demanding tasks.

Other tasks may make us doubt that we can meaningfully separate routine from complex. Many "complex" activities involve hours of tedious detail work.

Professors may grade simple quizzes or try to offer constructive responses to student compositions. Computer programming may involve not just designing a program to perform a task and then writing code to implement that design, but also hours of debugging code. Theoretical work in the sciences may involve mechanical work obtaining and organizing data. Software engineers write code. Logicians do proofs. Even writing a book such as this, addressing a "theoretical" problem, involves many more hours of editing than actual composition, and the editing can be tedious. The division between routine and complex seems to be *internal* to most tasks rather than a division in the organization of labor.

I disagree. A scientist or philosopher doing detail work is implementing her own labor plan and thinking about details in that context. The programmer debugging her program understands the entire process and how each line of code enables the program to do its task. (My wife, who is a programmer, tells me that debugging *other people's* code is oppressive.) The scientist or philosopher sees the importance of the details to the problem that engages her. Let me give an example from my ventures into carpentry – I am not a carpenter. Recently, I rebuilt the structure underneath my back porch, a 16′ × 24′ addition built in the 1950s; the porch was never built with enough concrete footings and much of the insufficient wooden support had rotted. I dug six 4′ holes into which I poured concrete to form piers, and on them I placed 4′ × 8′ pillars; on the pillars I put 4′ × 8′ cross members which supported the floor joists. I doubled the floor joists from 2′ × 6′ to 4′ × 6′; everything was tied together with construction adhesive, lag screws, carriage bolts, machine bolts, and other screws. I enjoyed the mechanical work partly because the carpentry was not routine for me and partly because I was realizing my own plan, the making of which was also not routine for me.

Like the philosopher/carpenter carrying out his own labor plan, people who have complex mastery often carry out mechanical detail work. They understand the role of the details in the overall project and want the entire thing completed properly. This is fully human labor, uniting mind and body, conception and execution. In contrast, when some organize labor and others execute the plans, detail work involves carrying out others' instructions; workers are not fully human. Their minds are removed from labor. This is routine labor that is oppressive and alienating.

My observations about the interconnectedness of routine and complex labor suggest that scientists and philosophers should continue to work as they have. Moreover, they suggest that rather than scientists sharing assembly-line work or postal labor (as doctors would do housekeeping), such labor should be reorganized so that workers plan and organize the labor process. In *The Moral Economy of Labor* (1993), James Murphy advances this argument.

I agree that workers should organize and plan labor, but that idea is insufficient. Caring for a home involves organizational tasks, but, for many, these do not make that labor engaging. I suspect that this will be true throughout much of the labor process: once major decisions are made about how to organize production, the remaining organizational work is often minimal, the remaining labor overwhelmingly routine. Professors and programmers have to help with it. If they don't, then they will have engaging challenging work, where the routine parts complete a task of their own complex design, while other workers will spend the overwhelming majority of their time in routine, uninteresting labor. Therefore, scientists, philosophers, and others whose projects involve some routine elements must help with this other routine labor. If we do not share these mundane tasks, equal opportunity becomes impossible (as I will make clear shortly).

In the third volume of *Capital*, Marx speculated about a period of history when the tasks of providing for our needs would diminish to a small portion of the day; we could leave the "realm of necessity" to enter the "realm of freedom." Freedom in the realm of necessity consists in workers "govern[ing] the human metabolism with nature in a rational way, bringing it under the collective control instead of being dominated by it as a blind power; accomplishing it with the least expenditure of energy and in conditions most worthy and appropriate for their human nature. . . . The true realm of freedom [is] the development of human powers as an end in itself" (1894: 959). I disagree that necessary labor is an inferior form of freedom. In a passage in the *Grundrisse*, Marx wrote that the key condition of freedom is not whether the labor is needed, but whether the tasks are self-chosen and fully engage human abilities (1858: 611–12). Routine labor – dusting, vacuuming, washing clothes – can be self-chosen. But only when we engage in more difficult tasks do we feel truly human. Making the opportunity for mastering complexity available to all requires sharing routine labor.

What is a complex activity?

"You write as if everyone will be a mathematician or philosopher, but that is not so." Am I stereotyping complex activities and labor? What activities and labor make our lives good?

Gardening, star-gazing and amateur astronomy, bird-watching, juggling, singing or playing an instrument, playing bridge, chess, dominos, or cribbage, developing hybrids of soybeans, and quilting: all are areas where people can develop and exercise complex abilities. I have no prejudice in favor of the theoretical, no presumption in favor of the useful beyond that defended in chapter 6. How people use the time freed by sharing routine labor would be up to them.

Of course, as I argued in chapter 6, all but a few will choose to devote energy to mastering and contributing complex abilities if the opportunities to do so are available non-competitively. Just as routine labor is shared, so is the contribution of complex abilities. But contribution depends on one's mastery: one must be a competent astronomer to contribute to the community.

What counts as a contribution (when is a complex activity *labor*)? I return to this question in chapter 13.

Why conditional opportunities can be of unlimited supply

Repeatedly, I have written that opportunity "to contribute complex abilities to the social group" should be equal and unlimited. Why are unlimited opportunities conditional on the *contribution* of abilities to others?

In liberal egalitarian philosophies (Rawls, Dworkin, and Sen) the question "why contribute?" does not arise; it is assumed that contribution is assured by market relationships. In market societies and money economies, money and race ration opportunity. The present book does not assume markets or a money economy. The development of abilities costs social resources. These are not unlimited. So we must decide how to allocate resources. Equal and unlimited opportunity to develop abilities makes sense if the abilities are devoted to the group. Otherwise, why should the society devote resources to any individual?

But there is a problem with this proposal. If the resources to create opportunities are limited, how can opportunity be unlimited? There can be unlimited opportunity if the devotion of resources to the creation of opportunity leads to a net gain in resources. This can be the case where the opportunity is opportunity to contribute to the social group.

An example will help. The resources available to teach skills of orthopedic surgery are limited by the number qualified to train others. Suppose that the opportunity to learn orthopedic surgery is conditional on a willingness to teach this craft to others. In using teaching-orthopedic-surgery resources to give others the opportunity to learn orthopedic surgery, we increase teaching-orthopedic-surgery resources. The use of limited resources to create opportunity leads to a net gain in resources whenever the opportunity includes the duty to create opportunities for others. So this opportunity can be unlimited. This is the only opportunity likely to be unlimited in a modern society with a complex division of labor. But, because this is opportunity to attain social esteem for one's contribution to others' opportunities, this is an important opportunity to create. In chapter 13 we return to the question of why we are motivated to contribute.

Is sharing labor coercive or unfair?

No one should be excused from routine labor. How much? That would depend on someone's abilities – energy, health, age – not what else (of a more complex nature) she can do. A norm is a shared social expectation of conduct. Everyone who is able should contribute (more or less equally, depending on ability); this would be enforced as a general social expectation.

The labor-sharing norm would not be symmetrical in requiring people to do routine labor and to acquire and contribute complex abilities. Normal people can do routine work, the drudge work we try to avoid. All must do it so that all have the opportunity to acquire more complex abilities. For routine labor, the emphasis is on each *doing* it. For complex labor, the emphasis is on *sharing* it. That is, since it is a source of greater social and self-esteem, people will want to acquire and contribute complex abilities. The problem, I estimate, is not that we will not want to *do* it but that we may not want to *share* that labor with others who have the relevant abilities. For complex abilities, the norm is to teach others what one knows and share the labor (including teaching) with others. With routine labor, the norm is to do it.

Can sharing labor be implemented without coercion? In chapter 9 I argue that coercion was needed to *create* the division between routine and complex labor. I believe that the *transition from* a society that divides routine from complex to one where both are shared will be violent and coercive. Many who avoid routine labor will resist a norm requiring them to do it. The transition to labor-sharing involves issues in political philosophy, some of which are discussed in chapter 9. On the other hand, once established, all would flourish in a social order where we share routine and complex labor; the norm would make sense to us. I argue for this conclusion in chapter 13.

Would requiring the sharing of routine and complex labor be irrational and unfair? Suppose Donald *wants* to spend more than the average time doing routine labor. And suppose Lakeisha is good at teaching mathematics. Suppose Donald volunteers to pick up Lakeisha's share of the routine labor so that she can spend more time teaching math. It seems irrational not to allow this arrangement.

Moreover, someone may object that requiring everyone to do routine labor eliminates an incentive to acquire and contribute complex abilities. As things stand, we acquire complex abilities in order to escape a life of routine labor – we study philosophy so that we don't have to spend our lives sorting mail. On my proposal, there's no escaping routine labor. So – someone might argue – no one will develop abilities that are difficult to acquire. My proposal, if implemented, would lead to a society where only the crudest abilities are developed. This would again make the proposal irrational.

In addition, my proposal seems unfair, unnecessarily limiting of people's freedom. Thus it is likely to be particularly coercive.

In reply: First, people naturally want to acquire complex abilities. They do not need an extra incentive to do so. Second, we want to contribute developed abilities to others. For both of these there are the incentives of social and self-esteem which attach naturally to the development and contribution of these abilities.

But what about Lakeisha, who wants to let Donald clean her classroom so that she can spend more time teaching children math, something she is very good at? There are two ways of understanding this example. First, we could understand it as something that might happen. If Lakeisha devoted herself to teaching math to children and did not share maintenance work while Donald picked up the slack for her, this would violate the norm of sharing labor. She should be reminded that in sharing routine labor she creates opportunity for others to teach math; she should do her share.

Second, we could understand this example as a recognized social possibility. This would lead to a competition inconsistent with equal opportunity. Let me explain. If some can be excused from routine labor by spending more time doing complex labor, we have positions where some do only complex labor. (Lakeisha would occupy one of those positions.) These will be of limited supply because we prefer to contribute complex abilities. Who will do the essential routine labor? Who does the more interesting work? We must have a way of deciding. The obvious solution is to select those who show the most ability and commitment. So we have a competition for these desirable positions. But, as I argued in chapter 3, competitive opportunity will never be equal. Parents with advantages will advantage their children. When positions are of limited supply, people are trained for them in numbers that approximate their availability. Socialization trains some children for routine labor, stunting their potential. So we should reject a norm that would excuse Lakeisha from routine labor.

Equal opportunity requires us to share routine and complex labor. Once this is understood throughout society, once it is understood that only under these conditions do all of us have reason to develop abilities in all children, once we have overcome the resistance of those determined to hang on to relative advantage, this norm can be accepted as fair and sensible.

Another objection: equal outcomes and equal opportunity

One reader of this book has argued that the real cause of unequal opportunity is unequal outcomes and that it is wrong to isolate the division between routine and complex labor as *by itself* causing unequal opportunity. This division of labor causes unequal opportunity only as part of a broader division between positions entailing many advantages – income, prestige, and power, as well as more complex and challenging labor – and those entailing many correlative disadvantages. Hence, it is this broader inequality of outcomes that is responsible for unequal opportunity not the division between routine and complex labor by itself. For, this reader wrote, "we can work up an intuitive idea of packages of reward (interestingness, hardness of work, dangerousness, income, leisure, etc.) which are roughly equal in value, and conceptually at least think that equality of opportunity would be realized if everyone faced roughly similar prospects of reward. Of course, such a society would have roughly equal outcomes, but I think equality of opportunity would also be achieved, rather trivially." Equal opportunity does not require that the division between routine and complex labor be ended, only that outcomes be equally desirable.

In reply: How are we to imagine positions "roughly equal in value"? I assume this means equally valued by all. If so, we must assume that people's preferences are roughly the same. Then they choose between routine labor with more income and leisure or more challenging labor with less leisure, but without a strong preference among these options. Let us grant, for the sake of argument, that this is the initial situation. But are these preferences stable? Would similarity of preferences continue so that each person finds the same features positive (high income, interesting work, much leisure) and negative (low income, routine work, little leisure) and each position roughly equal in value? Or would some be socialized to prefer boring labor and high-income consumption and others interesting labor accompanied by an ascetic lifestyle? The socialization principle (of chapter 3) implies that the second is inevitable. Preferences would evolve so that some children would grow up preferring some social positions and other children preferring others among an array of alternatives that their ancestors might have found equally desirable.

Would this result in unequal opportunity? The question is hard to answer because the problem of achieving equal opportunity assumes a structure of positions where some are more advantaged, by standards nearly everyone recognizes. But we started with a situation where, by hypothesis, no position was more advantaged; then I argued that that situation would change into one where some people were socialized to some positions and others to others. To complete the argument that opportunity would be unequal, I must revisit some ideas of chapters 5 and 6. In all societies complex contributions are naturally esteemed more than simple ones, and labor is our central contribution. Where money mediates social relations and is a reward for work, it is a measure of the value of labor; more esteemed labor is rewarded more than less esteemed labor. Societies where complex and simple labor are divided thus create a structure of more advantaged and less advantaged positions, by the norms that dominate the society. Since some will be socialized for the more advantaged positions and others for less advantaged ones, opportunity is unequal.

The objection was that inequality of outcomes, not the division between routine and complex labor, creates unequal opportunity. This is wrong. That division of labor will be accompanied by a structure of advantage and disadvantage; that conclusion, combined with the socialization principle, is sufficient to show that opportunity will not be equal.

I have now fulfilled two earlier promises. In chapter 6, to the proposal to give people the option of either complex labor or more routine labor combined with more money or more leisure, I objected that it would lead to unequal opportunity. This proposal would lead to training some for more complex and others for more routine labor. In this chapter I objected to the proposal to leave people alone if their complex work involves routine tasks (professors who grade quizzes). Again, we now see why that proposal is incompatible with equal opportunity.

Can we separate occupation from wealth, prestige, and power?

Prestige centers on occupation, but also on power and income, which tend to go with one's occupation. Folks with prestigious occupations have higher incomes and the prestige associated with wealth itself (a separate source of social esteem); they use that wealth to exercise inordinate power, an exercise which further enhances prestige. So, one might argue, what is wrong is that prestige, wealth, and power *converge* in a few hands. If we separate these, if some people gain prestige through occupation, others are wealthy, and yet others are powerful, then prestige, wealth, and power will not converge in the same people. Opportunities will be expanded in a way different from the one I have suggested, not by making opportunity unlimited but by preventing the easy translation of one sort of good (prestige, power, money) into the others (Walzer 1983). Let us consider this proposal as an objection to my argument for sharing labor.

The proposal is sociologically naive. Earlier (chapter 6), I argued that prestige naturally attached to positions requiring complex mastery. In chapter 5 I connected prestige and power. To recall, power and prestige are connected because we accustom ourselves to being commanded by others. Those who have power are able to command others. If we do not see their commanding us as right, we tend to resist, and this resistance destabilizes social relationships. Stable societies rationalize such command–obedience relationships – an instance of the rationalization principle. The most natural rationalization of a command–obedience relationship is to think that those who command have qualities which suit them to give orders to others. Prestige associated with power rationalizes command. In societies with wealth differences, it is good to have more wealth. We either reject such social organization or we accustom ourselves to it. If we accustom ourselves to it, we rationalize why some are wealthy: they must deserve it, have earned it. By the rationalization principle, prestige attaches to wealth. (I return to this argument in chapter 12.) So prestige attaches to both power and wealth.

Power leads to wealth and wealth to power, and both lead to more interesting occupations. In societies that allow differences of wealth, wealth is desirable because it is an all-purpose good giving access to other goods. Power gives one ability to acquire wealth, and the powerful make themselves wealthy. If they cannot mobilize their power to attain the most general all-purpose good, they are not very powerful. Because money is all-purpose, it leads to power. One may, as Walzer suggests, try to block some exchanges – directly buying political office – but it is impossible, in money economies, to prevent wealth from purchasing access to power. Both wealth and power allow access to more interesting and enjoyable work.

Egalitarian liberals try to uphold the market and egalitarianism at the same time. This is an impossible project. Market norms are anti-egalitarian. They are individualist; they imply freedom to pursue self-advancement and individual reward for individual effort. This criticism applies to the pluralist variant of egalitarian liberalism considered here. Norms of prestige rationalize a social order where some have greater wealth and power and more interesting occupations. These goods will be closely associated except by those who reject market economies and their concentration of wealth, power, and interesting occupations in a few hands.

Would sharing labor be efficient?

Consider this objection (from Jo Wolff, in correspondence): "A society which divides routine and complex labor is a stable equilibrium. A society which does not divide labor will tend to evolve into one that does because dividing labor is more efficient. Those who do complex labor best will get even better through concentrating their efforts. As a result we can all consume more." I reply in two ways.

First, efficiency is a relative notion. Efficient for what? The objection assumes that efficiency is productive efficiency, maximum quantity of production (holding quality constant) per unit of labor. Alternatively, the organization of labor could be efficient in maximizing workers' abilities and their wide-spread contribution and be assessed for its efficiency in creating these goods. How important is *productive* efficiency? If people are in danger of dying or suffering malnutrition from insufficient calories, efficiency in producing food is very important. Once productive efficiency reaches a level where needs are met, it may be less important than fulfilling work. Above a certain threshold, greater production and consumption do not make people happier (Hirsch 1976; Layard 2005).

Market economies reward productive efficiency. Providers of commodities and services produce as efficiently as possible. Efficient producers gain market share; inefficient producers are driven out. This requirement of productive efficiency leads to a stable equilibrium around social practices, such as the division between routine and complex labor, which enhance productive efficiency. Whatever is profitable will be produced. Effective demand for goods depends on who has money and what they want. We have Hummers and liposuction alongside malnutrition and epidemic obesity.

Imagine a society without markets and their insistence on productive efficiency. Production may be oriented toward meeting needs, not producing whatever can be sold profitably to those with money. Suppose that shared norms aim at developing abilities in as many people as possible and enabling contribution of developed abilities. A different stable equilibrium would emerge. What emerges as a "stable equilibrium" depends on the norms governing social intercourse.

Second, we should not concede too quickly that we sacrifice productive efficiency when development of abilities is primary. What is productively efficient in one social context may not be so in another. In battles between management and labor over wages and work conditions, it may not be productively efficient to depend upon workers, whose developed skills give them leverage in disputes with management. For example, workers protesting wages can "work to rule [do exactly as told, exercising no initiative and judgment]," disrupting production; workers are irreplaceable when production requires great attention to detail and workers take many years to acquire the relevant powers of observation and judgment.[3]

Management is reluctant to share power with workers. So it may try to replace skilled laborers who can disrupt production with unskilled workers.[4] Deskilling labor shifts power toward capitalists. Dividing labor into the routine and the complex is a stable and efficient equilibrium under circumstances of class struggle. Under other circumstances, when production meets human needs, creating greater opportunities for workers to use complex abilities in the production process might lead to greater productive efficiency. I return to issues of productive efficiency in chapter 12.

Would positions of prestige be of unlimited supply?

If labor is shared, positions of prestige would be of unlimited supply, but the word "position" would not refer to the statuses with which we are familiar. In our system there are few physicians, compared with other workers in medical care, and, of these, many work 60- and 70-hour weeks. If we shared labor, no one would likely work that many hours as a "physician." Complex abilities could be organized into positions in a more fine-grained way, and general statuses such as physician disappear. Someone might be an "abdominal surgeon" based on study and apprenticeship, but have no training in diagnosing skin abnormalities. If we break down positions into more categories of mastery, it would be easier to share complex labor. Positions such as "abdominal surgeon" or "abdominal diagnostician," entailing mastery of complexity, would carry prestige. Positions of prestige could be of unlimited supply. Sharing labor, everyone could occupy one.

If opportunity for prestige is unlimited in this way, is it prestige? As "positions of prestige" become unlimited, as opportunity to contribute complexity expands, they cease to be "positions" so strictly defined by rights and duties. Labor becomes more fluid. As categories for positions become less well defined and fixed, the "prestige" associated with these "positions" also becomes less clear and well defined.

Some object that prestige is necessarily a scarce good, but this objection is wrong. While prestige must attach to positions of accomplishment, societies can be organized so that there is no limit to the number of such positions. Technologically simple societies do not limit the number who may gain prestige as hunters, healers, or storytellers (as we do not limit the number who may be

---

[3] See Painter 1979: 66–74. Hosea Hudson describes his work in a foundry making iron pipe; he was so skilled that he was able to battle the bosses on the shop floor. Hudson was a semi-literate former sharecropper.

[4] See Noble 1986 and Braverman 1974 for some history.

licensed drivers). Not everyone holds a position of prestige, but everyone has the opportunity to do so. By sharing labor, something similar could be accomplished in modern societies.

We will be esteemed for contributing our labor to the good of our community; we will be esteemed for mastery of complexity; and we will be esteemed for doing what we do well. By sharing routine labor and creating unlimited opportunity to develop more complex mastery, the opportunity for prestige and other forms of social esteem becomes unlimited. Social hierarchy is replaced by egalitarianism. Everyone is allowed and encouraged to flourish.

Sharing routine and complex labor makes sense; people could accept norms requiring us to do this. This is the only way to create equal opportunity for social esteem.

Chapter 8

Transforming Relationships

Competitiveness

"Face it, Paul, human nature is competitive. If people are not competing for careers, it is something else. When we can't fight a war, we invent war-like games. If you believe human relationships can be transformed by sharing labor, you are engaged in wishful thinking." This objection raises the question of "human nature."

I am an optimist. Two lines of argument persuade me that it is reasonable to be optimistic that relationships can be predominately nurturing rather than competitive. First, there is evidence that higher levels of egalitarianism and mutual support are possible from studies of nomadic gatherer-hunters such as the Ju/'hoansi of the Kalahari Desert by Lorna Marshall, Richard Lee, and others in the late 1950s and 1960s.[1] There is more evidence from the lives of relatively egalitarian sedentary peoples (some will be cited in chapter 9). People seem capable of both mutual support and competition. Which predominates may depend on cultural adaptations to an environment and how people produce the means of life. Where mutual aid and sharing are required to secure the means of life, we are capable of that.

Second, and this argument is developed in this chapter, familiar social structures encourage competitive relationships, while alternative structures would make nurturing relationships possible or even likely. When opportunity is limited, advancing our interests requires us to compete. We want others to fail, since their failure increases the probability of our success. A personal anecdote illustrates this point.

---

[1]   On the group variously called !Kung, Ju/'hoansi, or bushmen of the Kalahari, see Marshall 1976; Lee 1979, 1982, 1993; Shostak 1983; Wiessner 1982. On Inuit (Eskimo), see Balikci 1970; Briggs 1970, 1982; Freuchen 1961. On Mbuti pygmies, see Turnbull 1961, 1982. Lee and Daly (1999) is a compendium of forager societies with a bibliography and useful analytical essays.

As a college freshman I hoped for a career teaching philosophy. By the time I was a sophomore I was hanging around the philosophy Teaching Assistants' office. Their conversation alarmed me. Graduate students at the University of California at Berkeley talked about the prospects for passing the preliminary examinations for the PhD. It seemed that many were failing or passing only after several attempts. Those who finished their degrees and sought teaching positions had difficulty. Some of these students were my own teachers, whom I admired. It seemed to me that if I wanted to teach philosophy, particularly on the Pacific Coast where I had grown up, it wasn't enough to do well; I had to be the best. The successes of other students became threatening to me.

Competition for social esteem

When prestige is a scarce good, some people may have permanent caste-like inferior status, or, alternatively, people may compete for prestige: you get it only if I don't. The struggle for social recognition occurs among both individuals and groups. As individuals, we compete for positions of prestige. The struggle for those positions can cause those whose ambitions are frustrated to feel like failures. Or, if they accept their status, they may adapt to their social position, but "losers" pay a psychological price.

The struggle takes place at a group level as well. We identify ourselves through categories shared with others – primarily categories of "ethnicity," "race," or nationality, identifying putative social groups that can have group reputations: black folks can be thought undisciplined and violent, Jews stingy, rich people callous and unfeeling, folks on welfare lazy or, more positive stereotypes, Asians can be thought hard-working and studious, workers disciplined and tenacious. Some groups are identified with positions of either high prestige or positions of contempt; for example, Jews may be stereotyped as highly educated professionals; "welfare-dependent inner-city mother" may be code for "poor black woman." As racial or allied categories are linked with positions of high or low prestige, there is a struggle for group status.

Just as individuals seek social recognition, so people who identify with groups have a stake in group reputation; their self-esteem can be bound up with group prestige. People who believe they are "white" or "American" may believe in the "superiority" of these groups to elevate their own self-esteem (Lamont 2000: 35). Similarly, people who identify as "black" can be committed to successful black politicians as enhancing the prestige of "the race" and, vicariously, themselves.[2] These last points are central to the social psychology of racism.

The harms of attitudinal racism are real and tenacious. People in low-prestige positions may suffer contempt when they come into contact with those above them. As noted in chapter 5, low-status people construct counter-values to dominant norms and avoid contact with those above them. But these

[2] For the theory, see Tajfel and Turner 1979.

strategies do not work very well. People "on the bottom" know how others look at them and suffer because of it.

In this chapter I argue that the poisoning of relations among individuals competing for the same goods and the psychological harms of racism are traceable to individual and group contests for social recognition. The contests derive from limits on positions of prestige, limits which make scarce the social esteem derived from prestige, particularly for the working class. So individuals and groups battle for conventional social esteem (or else they erect counter-norms that elevate things demeaned groups are good at and derogate the advantaged). Group battles poison relations among groups just as individual battles can poison those among individuals. The solution to these psycho-social harms is to make positions of prestige of unlimited supply by sharing labor.

Social comparison and self-esteem in Franz Kafka's "The Judgment"

A story by Franz Kafka displays how competition can harm relationships. In Kafka's "The Judgment" Georg Bendemann writes a letter to a friend in St Petersburg inviting his friend to his impending wedding (Kafka 1913). Georg's friend had grown up in the German mercantile town where Georg is in business with his father. The friend had last visited three years earlier. His business in St Petersburg "had flourished to begin with but had long been going downhill." He had little social contact with either Germans or Russians, "so that he was resigning himself to becoming a permanent bachelor."

Georg asks himself, "What could one write to such a man?" Georg had considered inviting him to return home but rejected the idea because it would be telling him that "all his efforts hitherto had miscarried" and that he was "just a big child who should do what his successful and home-keeping friends prescribed." Georg wishes not to humiliate his friend.

Two years earlier, Georg's mother had died. While Georg's father responded to his wife's death by becoming less aggressive in business, Georg had applied himself with "greater determination." Georg reflects: "perhaps it was mostly due to an accidental run of good fortune – which was very probable indeed – but at any rate during those two years the business had developed in a most unexpected way, the staff had had to be doubled, the turnover was five times as great." Georg's friend had invited Georg to relocate to St Petersburg, but the figures he gave for the prospects in Georg's line of trade "were microscopic by comparison with the range of Georg's present operations." Moreover, Georg has just become engaged to "a girl from a well-to-do family."

Georg had not written to his friend either of the business expansion or of his engagement. Georg had dealt with the divergence of their fortunes by writing mostly about trivial events in their home town. He had told his fiancée that he would not invite his friend to his wedding because "he would be hurt, perhaps he would envy me and certainly he'd be discontented and without being able to do anything about his discontent he'd have to go away again alone." Under pressure from her, however, Georg changed his mind and wrote his friend to invite him to the wedding: "I know that there are many reasons why you can't come to see us, but would not my wedding be precisely the right occasion for giving all obstacles the go-by? Still, however that may be, do just as seems good to you without regarding any interests but your own."

Georg takes the letter to his father to tell him of his decision to invite his friend, explaining, "If he's a good friend of mine, I said to myself, my being happily engaged should make him happy too." His father had gone into decline after his wife's death. Georg's father seems to be listening to Georg, but then he confronts Georg with his doubt whether he has a friend in St Petersburg, accusing Georg of "pulling his leg." Georg reminds his father that he had met this friend and is alarmed by his father's apparent deterioration, resolving silently to take better care of him and to have his father come to live with him and his wife. Georg carefully undresses his father and puts him to bed, discovering that his father had not been taking care to wear clean underwear.

At this point his father springs erect in bed and accuses Georg of lying to his friend (whom he now seems to know all too well) and, in business, of "finishing off the deals that I had prepared for [you], bursting with triumphant glee and stalking away from [your] father with the closed face of a respectable business man." He accuses Georg of being seduced by his fiancée, "the nasty creature," and of disgracing his mother's memory. He says he has been writing to Georg's friend telling him the truth and exposing Georg's lies. Georg responds to this litany of accusations by falling increasingly under his father's spell. His father finally says: "So now you know what else there was in the world besides yourself, till now you've known only about yourself! An innocent child, yes, that you were truly, but still more truly have you been a devilish human being! – And therefore take note: I sentence you now to death by drowning!" Georg runs out of the house and jumps off a bridge into the river.

With his friend in St Petersburg, Georg had to decide whether to disclose or conceal his business prosperity and then the good fortune of his engagement. At first he concealed these things for fear of hurting his friend, but then changed his mind and carefully invited his friend to share in the joy of his wedding. With his father there was no concealment. The fears he had concerning his friend's reaction were realized in his father's jealousy of both Georg's marriage and business success. These are particularly painful to his father, who has lost his wife and become less capable as a businessman.

In both cases, Georg, an ideally sensitive and caring person, has destroyed the friendship, either by concealment or by humiliation. By the effects of his actions he has been "a devilish human being." But since the effects occurred despite the best intentions, the judgment could be rendered and executed only by madmen.

Underlying the story is the assumption that Georg, his father, and his friend derive their sense of self-worth from their successes in their business and personal lives. Business success is relational and competitive: it is being superior to others. Success is important for that superiority, not mainly for material needs. Success in one's personal life seems only weakly competitive, but surely it is the case that not everyone can marry into money. The prestige associated with business success and with marrying well is scarce and success threatens the equality associated with many friendships by making a friend painfully conscious of his own relative failure. Georg's friend should be happy for him, but he may feel even worse about himself (as Georg feared he might).

Societies where positions of prestige are attained through competitive success and where people derive much of their social (and self-) esteem from conventional prestige can create problems for friendships. One person's success can threaten a friend's sense of self-worth, particularly when comparison is unavoidable. Friends find themselves competing for social and self-esteem, a competition which can harm the friendship.

Group identities, racism, and the struggle for a sense of self-worth

Many of us are identified with an ethnic, racial, or national group. Groups may be regarded as superior or inferior, as accomplished or lazy. The esteem for a group can affect our own self-esteem. In many situations black people are viewed with suspicion. In a striking essay, "In My Next Life I'll be White," Laurence Thomas describes his experience as a visiting professor at a "Midwestern university." He was reading a bulletin board on campus, "a 150 pound [man], well groomed, tweed jacket, tie and wool slacks," when he found himself surrounded by four campus policemen. He writes, "Four officers! What on earth was I reported as – 10 feet tall in military garb? Or, 'There is a black man . . .'?"

This happened to a conservatively dressed black man on the university campus. For those less fortunate, the identification of black people with criminality has greater and more persistent harms. My students, especially black males, report women clutching handbags when they enter elevators and refusing to accept doors held open for them. My student Terrell Jackson tried to stop people to ask directions when downtown; none of the white people he approached would stop. (I speculate that they saw "black man" and assumed that they were being panhandled.) Young black women have reported that, on public transportation, white people often refuse to sit by them. (This happens even more frequently to black men.) Constant slights and humiliations are wearing and insulting.

Police intimidation is more striking. The following incident was reported to me by a student. She and a male friend had just visited the home of another of her friends and were leaving in his car. It was after 11.00 p.m. As they came to the end of the alley, their path was blocked by an unmarked car. At least four men in plain clothes surrounded their car, demanding that they get out to be searched. My student challenged their right to do so without a search warrant. One man replied that there had been a report of a gunshot and that they could do as they saw fit. The men cursed at the two young people, forced them to lean against the car, and searched them. (She found out that the search of her friend included body cavities.) The plain-clothes men then said that the search of the car had disclosed a bag of "drugs" (which they had planted – it turned out to be a plastic bag filled with cotton). The men threatened to take the two young people to jail. After several minutes of foul language, intimidation, and searching the students and the car, one of them said to my student, "If you stay in school, we'll just forget the whole thing." They then drove off. From surveys of my classes, it seems that most of my students have either experienced incidents such as this or have family or friends who have.

What happened to Laurence Thomas is hardly unusual. It is accepted by society and difficult to protest (there is probably no official police record of the incident with my student, and it is virtually impossible to identify the officers who did it). When no one protests, we are accepting it as normal. This acceptance must have a negative effect on self-esteem. When an individual knows he may be subject to such treatment, it robs him of self-confidence in public spaces.

In the United States, racial identities were consolidated in the first half of the nineteenth century as many people came to think of themselves as white. In nineteenth-century society, individuals increasingly competed for social rewards such as wealth. Competition became group competition. In his book *White Supremacy*, George Fredrickson describes riots in the 1830s by dispossessed white mobs opposed to racial "amalgamation." Fredrickson believes that "the participation of lower-class whites in these disorders was induced to a great extent by the status anxieties generated by a competitive society" (1981: 153).

In July 1863, during the Civil War, after black workers in New York City had broken a strike by Irish longshoremen, Irish workers, themselves dispossessed and marginal, turned their hostility toward the draft system and black people generally. A war to enhance the position of black people threatened their fragile position. More recently, the opposition to busing for integration in Boston in the 1970s, while sponsored by influential local politicians, found its base of support in South Boston, the poorest white area in Boston. Racial identities can lead to conflicts between impoverished groups.

Social goods such as employment, education, and safe neighborhoods are not only desirable in themselves, but represent higher status. Low-status groups are objects of social contempt, experienced by group members as an assault on self-esteem. This may lead low-status groups to protest their condition, both material deprivation and social contempt grounded in their deprivation. Where status is a scarce good, this protest is a threat to other low-status groups. Groups are in competition for status, and those who identify with these groups are in a struggle for self-esteem. Efforts to raise group status, when combined with people's tendency to favor their own groups, threaten to create a social order riven by racial antagonisms and unable to govern itself by common norms. When we conceive ourselves as competing for the same goods, it sustains self-esteem to think we deserve them and others do not. If I have them and you do not, I am likely to think that the system is just and that you do not have them because there is something wrong with you. If you have them and I do not, I am likely to think that you have been unjustly favored. Because black people are, and are known to be, in an inferior position, black and white people tend to develop different views of their social world, differences which entrench racial division (Sigelman and Welch 1991; Kinder and Sanders 1996).

Michèle Lamont's *The Dignity of Working Men* shows how racial contempt is embedded in the philosophies of many working-class men, constructing a sense of self-worth through values that elevate their accomplishments. She interviewed black and white male workers in New Jersey and, for comparison, ethnically French and North African immigrant workers in Paris. Here I focus on American white workers. These workers, none of whom are college graduates and many of whom are in low-status jobs, value devotion to family, hard work, responsibility, economic independence (not depending on government support) and loyalty to neighborhood and friends. Many are strongly conscious of being white and negatively stereotype black people as not living up to their moral standards.

Central to many workers' racism is their belief (shared by some black as well as many white people) that black poverty is due to black people's moral failings. There is also a general tendency to blame poor people for their situation. We should keep this in mind. Attitudinal racism represents an inclination to elevate oneself by derogating those who are more disadvantaged. These workers attribute black poverty to less ambition, lack of discipline, unwillingness to work hard, wanting to have everything handed to you (welfare), and wanting special privileges (affirmative action). One worker told Lamont that, "he wishes [black people] would fight more to survive on their own, just as he himself does against all odds" (2000: 61–2). This attitude gets its force from the difficult circumstances of many workers for whom "'not giving up' is so central to their own senses of self" (p. 62). When they compare themselves to those worse off, many of these workers believe in the American dream – that you can make it through grit and determination – and they regard their own self-sufficiency as proof of that.

Consistent with this attitude one might expect that these workers would regard as deserving those more successful than they are. Indeed, 25 percent of the white men Lamont interviewed had unequivocally favorable views of "those above" them in social standing and income. But 75% of the white men were either ambivalently (27 percent) or unequivocally (47 percent) critical of those above.[3] They lacked integrity, were two-faced, backstabbing, insensitive and superficial, snotty, overly competitive, judgmental, and dishonest, and stepped on others to get ahead (pp. 107–9). The superior economic position of the middle class did not always indicate moral superiority.

---

[3] Two conflicting principles explain the variation. On one hand, the rationalization principle encourages conventional prestige rankings. On the other, defense of self-worth leads people to construct counter-norms contrary to these rankings.

There is both consistency and inconsistency. People consistently elevate themselves. Moreover, the white workers always regarded integrity, discipline, responsibility, and loyalty as values. There is also inconsistency. When considering black people and those worse off, these workers saw the American dream of opportunity and blamed black people or those worse off for moral failures. Yet most of these workers refused to regard those more successful than themselves as having taken better advantage of their opportunities and as being morally deserving. Rather, many emphasized the moral *failures* that, to them, explained success greater than theirs. Anyone above or below them is a moral failure. This inconsistency is important for two reasons.

As a practical matter, for those who wish to fight racism, it may be a useful wedge to get friends or family members to reject racism: "If you can see that you were disadvantaged in relation to those who had educational opportunities handed to them, why can't you see that others have had even fewer advantages than you?" These questions, particularly when raised in the context of an ongoing relationship, may be useful in encouraging anti-racist thought and action.

More to the point of this book, these inconsistencies arise from group contests for prestige. People try to sustain a sense of their own worth. When people see themselves as belonging to a group, they elevate the group they identify with. Where group prestige is scarce because positions of prestige that determine group prestige are themselves scarce, I elevate the prestige of my group by derogating other groups. This is the heart of the social psychology of racism. It, or allied phenomena based on other group categories, is inevitable in competitive societies that limit positions of prestige. Our desire to live in a society without racism gives us another reason to share labor.

Amour-propre in Rousseau

Jean-Jacques Rousseau's second Discourse (*On the Origin of Inequality*) contains a classic exposition of contests for social esteem. Rousseau uses the phrase *amour-propre* (which "leads each individual to make more of himself than of any other") for a sentiment that arises as men come to live in larger groups. When people "assemble[d] before their huts around a large tree," they began to "consider the rest" and "wish to be considered in turn" as they danced and sang, "and thus a value came to be attached to public esteem. Whoever sang or danced best, whoever was the handsomest, the strongest, the most dexterous, or the most eloquent came to be of most consideration; and this was the first step toward inequality, and at the same time toward vice" (1755: 400). Rousseau writes that after the invention of property and the arts of metallurgy and agriculture: "Behold, then, all the human faculties developed, memory and imagination in full play, *amour-propre* interested, reason active, and the mind almost at the highest point of its perfection. Behold . . . [every man's] wit, beauty, strength or skill, merit or talents: and *these being the only qualities capable of commanding respect*, it soon became necessary to possess or to affect them" (emphasis added). In these circumstances, "Insatiable ambition, the thirst of raising their respective fortunes, not so much from real want as from the desire to surpass others, inspired all men with a vile propensity to injure one another" (p. 403). The evil of inequality includes this propensity to seek social esteem at the expense of others.

Though Rousseau's description may be exaggerated, there is truth to it. I offer the following analysis, an alternative to Rousseau's, of competition for social esteem. In societies where there is a division between routine and complex, self-directed labor, many positions are loci of low prestige. This is true for two reasons. First, where there is such a division, routine labor is generally under the direction of others, and, for reasons deriving from the rationalization principle, when one person is under the direction or control of another, greater prestige attaches to the one in control, less to the subordinate. Second, routine labor deprives those who do it of feelings of self-worth because their tasks are so simple (as we noted in chapter 6). The social esteem that attaches to positions requiring complex mastery does not attach to these positions. For both reasons, prestige is a scarce good.

If holding a position of prestige is important to social and self-esteem, then we compete for a scarce good (esteem) central to well-being. To become an academic philosopher, we compete for admission to graduate school, compete within graduate school for grades and recommendations of professors, and then compete as a young academic for recognition within the profession. We may desire the good of a position of prestige, but to attain that position we have to be, or lead others to believe we are, better than others. The competition for social esteem that Rousseau describes seems to be a consequence of social structures where we compete for limited positions of prestige.

This conflict of interests arises from limits on opportunity: I will be able to spend my life in engaging labor (teaching and writing philosophy) only if someone else does not, for there are limited positions that allow a person to do this. While there are limitations to this point – consider folks who live well despite frustration of their youthful ambitions – the point is sound.

Some facts limit the force of Rousseau's argument. Those denied social esteem by dominant measures of prestige construct self-esteem in other ways, often supported by like-minded others. Nevertheless, those in low-status positions are aware of this denial of conventional social esteem, and many resent it. And people pay a price: while they assure themselves of their worth as Christians, as good providers and parents, and as champions of their bowling league, many retain a feeling that they are not too bright.

Esteem and respect

In "The Natural Goodness of Humanity," Joshua Cohen develops a solution to competition for social esteem, inspired by Rousseau's solution. Here I explain why Cohen's solution is inadequate. Cohen emphasizes that, for Rousseau, the realm of citizenship and membership in a political community can provide recognition of the equal worth of each person, thus replacing a rivalrous conception of worth with an egalitarian one: "[W]hen individuals have the public status of equal citizen in the society of the general will . . . [they] can reasonably be expected to acquire an understanding of one another as equals. . . . [B]y establishing citizenship rights and taking the interests of each into account," these political arrangements "confirm our sense of our own worth." Reciprocity helps this process: others "uphold my sense of self-worth, generating a disposition to reply in kind and uphold their sense of their own worth" (1997: 127).

> Given public conditions of equality – both in the rights associated with the status of equal citizen and in the content of the general will – I come to see myself an equal; others, therefore, affirm my worth when they treat me as an equal. Because of that affirmation, the society of the general will discourages the inflamed form of self-love. . . . [T]he existence of a general will . . . provides a way to affirm the equal worth of each even in the face of the inevitable differences in the social and economic circumstances of different citizens. (p. 129)

Thus, on Cohen's sympathetic interpretation, political equality can ground a non-competitive sense of self-worth despite limited economic inequality.

Equality of citizenship is like other equality under norms. What I mean is this: norms are general, and implicit in that generality is to treat relevantly similar cases alike. As a result, the accusation, "You slighted me," is universal in human communities; it expresses the complaint of not being treated as others under the general norm. Equal citizenship – the rights of citizenship belong to all alike – is a form of equality under norms. If the laws are not applied to me as to others, I am deprived of equal respect.

It is a separate – more abstract and political – issue whether the norms themselves show equal regard for all. In defending the difference principle Rawls argues that the norms show regard for the least advantaged by maximizing resources available to advance their conception of the good. Cohen emphasizes how the political norms that Rousseau defends show regard even for the least of us; participatory citizenship "brings citizens together under manifestly equal conditions: [quoting Rousseau] 'the person of the humblest citizen is as sacred and inviolable as that of the first magistrate; because where the represented person is, there is no longer any representative'" (p. 129). The arguments Cohen defends ground self-worth in political equality. In both forms just defended (applying norms impartially to all and the norms showing equal regard for all) political equality applies to all equally and *indifferently*; whatever treatment one deserves merely in virtue of one's status as citizen (honoring one's right to participate in the political process, treating one as equal before the law) has nothing to do with what makes one different from others. This solution does not affirm our worth in the right way. Equal citizenship provides the respect due a citizen, not the esteem we seek for accomplishments and virtues of character, mind, and body.[4] Our need for esteem is a need for assurance that our particular characteristics and accomplishments are worthy. Esteem may fall to someone for having a beautiful face, or, more commonly, be earned by one's moral integrity and personal responsibility, mastery of quadratic equations or the flute, contributions to family harmony, commitment to political equality and opposition to racism, devotion to one's students, or planting flowers that enliven the neighborhood. But esteem is for something particular about oneself. The respect due a citizen cannot satisfy this need for a sense of self-worth.

Individuals who strive for a sense of self-worth through achieving positions of prestige come to view others in a hostile way as their competitors. In Kafka's story, unequal success destroyed friendships; Georg's father's *amour-propre* could not tolerate Georg's success when compared with his own decline. The successes of competitors can humiliate or shame us.

Where self-worth depends on individual or group prestige, it is of limited supply and subject to social competition. Many struggles for self-worth play out through group categories; these struggles give the more advantaged an interest in affirming their superiority to folks in an inferior social position. This leads to the psycho-social harms of racism; social division by racial and other categories arises from the need to affirm our worth. As long as positions of prestige are limited, some will be subject to social contempt because they hold positions of low prestige. Individuals identified with groups disproportionately in low-prestige positions are subject to the same contempt. The opportunities to win esteem for our accomplishments are limited by the division between routine and complex labor: some do labor that is so simple that it deprives them of self- and social esteem – or they are unemployed.

Moreover, people who are disesteemed are often, on that account, disrespected. Terrell Jackson (socially identified as "black"), who could not get white people to give him directions in downtown Chicago, was not shown minimal decency owed between people in public spaces. Being "black," my student is stereotyped as personally dangerous or at least annoying. The disesteem for the group ("a black man is likely to be a panhandler") leads to disrespect for the individual. Official representatives of the state such as police also deny black people equal respect. While I (perceived as "white male professor") was apprised, nothing more, by campus security (with powers of state police) that my registration validation sticker was missing from my license plate, one student reported repeated tickets for the same violation. Contempt leads to disrespect.

The Rousseau–Rawls–Cohen solution – to develop norms of equal citizenship and accord equal respect under these norms – does not deal with problems of unequal and limited prestige attached to social positions. There is a need for assurance of self-worth, for esteem derived from one's own qualities, actions, or accomplishments, that equal respect as citizens does not satisfy.

---

[4] This point comes from Fred Neuhouser (2002), who, criticizing Cohen, pointed out that esteem is for what makes us different from others and that we need to be esteemed, not just respected.

From competition to harmony

Do the proposals of chapter 7, the sharing of routine and complex labor, provide a solution to these problems of social esteem and self-worth? There are certainly limits to the solution. Sharing routine and complex labor cannot prevent someone from feeling like a failure for not having found a mate; it cannot prevent envy of others who are happily married while we are lonely. It cannot prevent our feeling that we have not succeeded as well as others at the complex tasks we have tried to master. Nor can it prevent some being esteemed more than others for their mastery.

Moreover, absolute equality of esteem or prestige makes no sense. The esteem we earn for conformity with norms is necessarily measured by our virtues; it is appropriate to what people are or have done. The same is true for the esteem we give to people for their wit or beauty. It is accorded for something specific to the person, and we will never all be equal in those regards. The esteem we win for mastery of complexity will never be equal because our mastery will not be equal. The prestige associated with a position of great skill or accomplishment depends on someone having attained the skill or accomplishment appropriate to the position. Different positions require different levels of accomplishment; so prestige will never be absolutely equal. This will be true even if positions requiring complex mastery are of unlimited supply.

Still, sharing routine and complex labor would make a difference. When positions of prestige are of unlimited supply, we eliminate the basis of *amour-propre*. Sharing labor removes most of the self-interested reason for wishing others to fail: someone else's accomplishments do not detract from my own opportunities. Sharing labor does not remove all possible sting from social comparisons. It does not eliminate the possibility of my being shamed by the accomplishments of others or of feeling inferior or envious. But we are no longer rivals for scarce social esteem associated with positions of prestige.

By making unlimited the opportunities to develop and contribute complex abilities and for social esteem and prestige, we transform the relationships between people. Now imagine, as in an ideal household where routine chores are fairly shared, that routine labor of sustaining a complex modern economy is shared. No one spends an entire lifetime in routine labor unless by choice. The routine labor in maintaining and improving public spaces, in producing the necessities and conveniences, and in keeping records of these activities is shared by all capable of it. How would such a society create mathematics, science, philosophy, architecture, landscape design, engineering, art, medicine, and all other more complex activities that enrich our lives? There would be as much mathematics or philosophy as there were people who chose to develop these abilities and share their accomplishments socially. The same would be true of engineering, art, architecture, and medicine. And it would be true of music, all the visual arts, and the many crafts and practical skills such as gardening.

Now look at opportunity from the point of view of any individual. Each of us has a reason to want others to develop their abilities. The accomplishments of others do not detract from the opportunities available to each, but enhance the quality of our lives, enriching them with science, architecture, landscaping, art, and medicine.

There can be a revolution in how we relate to other people and intuitively perceive them. Now we often see others as dangers partly for reasons I detailed, but also, generally, because in societies of limited opportunity resentful "losers" may strike out and endanger the rest. If labor is shared, other people enrich my life. When opportunity is limited, we often view others doing the same work as competitors for limited esteem. When esteem and opportunity are of unlimited supply, I can view others as making me better at what I do. Instead of feeling threatened by others' accomplishments, a philosopher can enjoy the ways in which a large community of philosophers helps us all. The more accomplished philosophers there are, the more people there are to help each other to become better. Pharmaceutical researchers can help one another; brain surgeons can help brain surgeons. Many people sharing a similar mastery can elevate everyone's work (Terry Rudd has been trying to get me to see this point – I finally got it).

Viewing others with suspicion starts in school (if not sooner), and schools too can be transformed. As it is now, we compete for grades, often fearing that if our grades are not higher than others', we will not accomplish our goals. Students become grade-grubbers rather than learners. Teachers use grades to coerce students into subservience. Grades – at worst, the normal bell-shaped curve – are the epitome of limited opportunity. If a grade curve is a valid measure, then ability must also follow a curve; so it is assumed from the beginning that ability is limited in a way that corresponds to opportunity. Teachers see themselves as discovering talent, not nurturing talent. Where the goal is to develop *everyone's* abilities (because there are no limits on opportunity), teachers and students can nurture the talent of each of us, not divide us into "bluebirds" and "robins" based on reading level or post the walls with charts with stars comparing student achievement. The nastiness of the schools, where academic "losers" form their own cliques based on looks, athletics, drugs, music, tattoos or body-piercing, and so on, can be replaced by a flowering of many talents and mutual enrichment. Students can be optimistic that they will be able to contribute the talents they develop and therefore approach learning with confidence in a spirit of mutual support.

To see others in this way is a revolution in our values and in our relationships. But that revolution is made possible by making opportunity unlimited, removing the objective basis of the jealousies and envy that poison relationships now.

A society so imagined fleshes out Marx's idea of a world where "the free development of each is a condition for the free development of all," or Rawls's idea of a social union of social unions, where our diversity of developed abilities enriches the lives of all and where people doing similar work cooperate to make all better. I am arguing that the key to the sort of harmony postulated by these utopian thinkers (Marx and Rawls, at some moments) is to share labor. The result is that each individual has the opportunity to develop complex abilities – but not only that. Each would have the encouragement of a community of others who have reason to want each of us to develop and flourish. Each has a reason to wish each child to reach her fullest potential; the accomplishments of your children no longer threaten my children's opportunities. Only unlimited opportunity (of the sort I have described here) can create this social environment for each of us, particularly children. Limited opportunity, competitive opportunity whether equal or not, will only frustrate the development of many of us and make us stingy in our praise for and encouragement of others.

Optimism revisited

Can we be optimistic about the possibility of a modern society where competitiveness is replaced by mutual support in developing and contributing our abilities? I have argued that such mutual support is possible if the norms are ones we have reason to accept and support. I cannot prove that such a society is possible. It cannot be proved until its creation is in the past. Yet it seems plausible that competitiveness arises from social structures that set our interests in conflict. Other social structures could create greater convergence of interest. That is what I have tried to show in this chapter. In the next chapter I will review some evidence about how and why egalitarian relations were replaced by stratified ones that limited positions of prestige. In chapter 13, I will sketch a conception of contributive justice and argue that its norms are supportable by all.

Chapter 9

Is Inequality Necessary?

Near the end of the last chapter I pointed out that esteem, whether for wit or beauty or for conduct, will not be equal because we will never be equally beautiful, smart, or good. Inequalities of esteem are compatible with unlimited opportunity to be esteemed within a social group. Opportunity for esteem can be unlimited if labor is shared. There could be unlimited opportunity to attain positions of prestige. Moreover, as I just argued, each has reason to encourage others to develop and contribute complex abilities and thus to earn esteem for those contributions. By contributing developed abilities, we can gain social and self-esteem. While some inequality in esteem is inevitable, that inequality can be brought to a minimum.

Why egalitarianism of opportunity is incompatible with Rawls's egalitarianism

John Rawls believed that profound social inequality is inevitable. Important social goods are of limited supply. He writes about the basic structure of society:

> [T]his structure contains various social positions and . . . men born into different positions have different expectations of life determined, in part, by the political system as well as by economic and social circumstances. In this way the institutions of society favor certain starting places over others. These are especially deep inequalities. Not only are they pervasive, but they affect men's initial chances in life; yet they cannot possibly be justified by an appeal to the notions of merit or desert. It is these inequalities, presumably inevitable in the basic structure of any society, to which the principles of social justice must in the first instance apply. (1999: 7; cf. Rawls 2001: 55)

In this chapter I explore whether such inequalities of "economic and social circumstances" are inevitable. Rawls, you may recall, advances the difference principle – that inequalities are just only if, by allowing some to have greater wealth or authority, everyone benefits, including those with least wealth and authority. But why wouldn't each be better off under conditions of equality?

Rawls believes equality is inefficient. A distribution of benefits is efficient when it is impossible to improve the situation of any person without harming the situation of another. Many efficient distributions are not just, and some just distributions – specifically equal distribution – are not efficient. A "viable human community" must be efficient (1999: 5). A just but inefficient distribution is not "perfectly just," and equality, which is not efficient, is "irrational" (1999: 69; 2001: 151). While not entailed by justice itself, efficiency is assumed in a just society. We can improve the situation of everyone, including those least advantaged, by allowing some inequality.[1]

Wouldn't inequality take away from some in order to give to others? Yes, if the benefits are fixed; no, if they are not fixed. Rawls believes that if some are allowed to acquire more, they will create more wealth. He writes:

> Supposedly . . . the greater expectations allowed to entrepreneurs encourages them to do things which raise the long-term prospects of laboring class [*sic*]. Their better prospects act as incentives so that the economic process is more efficient, innovation proceeds at a faster pace, and so on. I shall not consider how far these things are true. The point is that something of this kind must be argued if these inequalities are to satisfy the difference principle. (1999: 68)

Do not be misled by Rawls's use of "supposedly," and his saying "I shall not consider how far these things are true." Rawls believes that some inequalities provide talented people with an incentive to exercise their talents in a way that benefits the least advantaged. As we saw, he believes such inequalities are inevitable in a modern society.

The word "efficient" can have different meanings. In chapter 7, I distinguished between *productive* efficiency (efficiency in maximizing the quantity and quality of goods produced) and other conceptions of efficiency. And "productive efficiency" is itself open to more than one interpretation. Rawls seems to intend *motivational* productive efficiency: people are motivated to produce more if there is inequality than if there is equality. A narrow interpretation of productive efficiency might limit claims about what is efficient to particular circumstances; for example, in chapter 7, I argued that contests between capital and labor in market economies – strikes, slowdowns, sick-outs, working to rule – might make it more efficient to replace skilled workers with unskilled. But if a society does not separate planning production from the execution of the labor plan, using skilled labor might be more efficient. Rawls seems to have a general

---

[1] The issue here is a general sociological claim. G. A. Cohen (2000) has raised a different issue: whether the motivational assumptions of the difference principle are inconsistent with the moral commitment of each citizen to justice. That is, Cohen is raising a question about the *internal* consistency of Rawls's view. We turn to this question in chapter 12.

view that equality is inefficient because it defeats productive incentives in *all* circumstances.

The difference principle (literally "the supposition that the difference principle has an application") enjoins that some positions or offices should entail greater income and authority than others. Positions of advantage will be limited; some will hold them, others not. The difference principle builds unequal rewards into the *structure* of society.

Egalitarianism of opportunity sets no limit to opportunities for social esteem, including positions of prestige. If another is esteemed or holds a position of prestige, this has no effect on my opportunity. Inequalities are not a harm to those who have less; there are no social barriers to attaining the same goods. Moreover, since each has reason to want others to develop and exercise their abilities and to attain the associated rewards, each has the support of others in attaining positions of prestige.

Income greater than others and authority over others are intrinsically positional and hence in limited supply. Not everyone can have these goods. Those who have greater wealth and authority have greater prestige for reasons related to the rationalization principle (see the discussion in chapters 4 and 7 and the one to come in chapter 10). So wealth, authority, and prestige are limited in societies based on the difference principle. In contrast, when labor is shared, opportunity to attain positions of prestige (whose duties require complex mastery) is unlimited. So there is a clear contrast between the unlimited opportunity advocated here and the limited opportunity of Rawls's theory of justice.

The difference principle and the functional theory of stratification

Rawls believed that some inequalities improve the conditions of all. But on what evidence? In 1945, the year before Rawls entered graduate school at Princeton, Kingsley Davis and Wilbert E. Moore, two professors there, published their influential paper "Some Principles of Stratification" in the *American Sociological Review*. The functional theory of stratification they developed asserts that any society has some positions requiring either scarce "inherent capacity" or prolonged training. When these positions are important to the welfare of society, social rewards must be attached to them. These rewards are necessary either to attract scarce native talent or to induce people to undergo the rigors of the training; in addition, they secure the conscientious performance of the position's duties. These greater rewards are functional: they benefit everyone.

I don't know whether Rawls was directly influenced by the Davis/Moore theory; I know of nowhere that he refers to it explicitly. He does not emphasize rigorous training as grounding different rewards, but he thought some were "more talented" than others. Are some material inequalities necessary incentives that benefit everyone?

Natural lottery of talents?

The functional theory of stratification, particularly in its Rawlsian application, should give pause to anyone with egalitarian sympathies. How are we to justify the belief in an unequal distribution of natural assets? While we are different from one another in a variety of obvious ways, the belief in *natural* differences in talent required by the functional theory is not easy to defend.

Anyone who would use the phrases "distribution of natural assets" or "natural lottery of talent" has created an epistemic burden. How would we know what people's *natural* assets are? The point is developed by John Stuart Mill in *The Subjection of Women* (1869). He argues there that talk of the "nature" of woman is specious as long as women are held in a subordinate position. The same applies to supposed "natural" inequalities of talent, asserted in a society where there is a division between complex and routine labor. If we lived in a world of perfect equality of opportunity, we might have a better idea how people would develop if there were no social forces channeling their energies in one direction or another. But in our society, some people do routine, others complex labor; children are trained accordingly for the positions that await them as adults. In these circumstances, we will never know how children might develop in the absence of social forces that shape some of them differently from others because the opportunities that exist for some do not exist for others. We return to the question of inequality of talent in the next chapter.

What motivates us?

Just as the functional theory of stratification and the difference principle imply a "natural lottery" of talents, so they also imply that the "more talented" will not develop and exercise complex abilities absent personal advantage: either more material goods or greater authority than others. The advantaged are motivated by these greater rewards more than they would be by equal rewards. This idea needs some justification. Since all benefit materially from the contributions of each, why must those who contribute more have greater material benefit? Might they not be satisfied with an equal share of the general benefit or with sharing the benefit according to the needs of each?

Egalitarianism of opportunity assumes that we want to think well of ourselves and that we need (some) others to think well of us. There are other needs – for food, shelter, love and security, and goods (telephones, automobiles) required in a particular society. But beyond these, and often more than these, what motivates is profoundly moral and social. Sometimes people are willing to sacrifice material well-being and even their lives when required by norms with which they agree. This can be a mass phenomenon. A generation of Soviet youth went to war against the armies of the Axis even though they knew that for many of them this would mean the end of their lives (Werth

1964: 693–6). It is wrong to think that we can only be motivated by receiving more than others.

How would egalitarianism of opportunity deal with socially important tasks that no one wanted to do or that not enough people wanted to do? I defend sharing routine and complex labor. I assume that not enough people want to do the necessary routine labor (this is nearly the opposite of the Rawlsian/functionalist assumption). Where not enough people want to do a task, we share it as an obligation. When too many want to do the same thing, we share the task as a matter of sharing opportunity. If we agree on these norms, plenty of us will be appropriately motivated. It is not necessary to assign artificially greater rewards to some tasks than to others.

We might interpret Rawls's endorsement of the difference principle as implying only that such motivation is necessary in society as we know it, not that it is necessary and universal. We might desire greater income or wealth to secure our futures or those of our children. But that desire assumes that these are not secure without that greater wealth. Rawls cites the costs of training as justifying greater income and wealth for those who train their abilities (1999: 136). But the need to compensate for the cost of training does not justify higher pay unless it is justified that people be charged for undergoing training for necessary positions. Perhaps greater rewards are necessary because those with scarce abilities – or some of them – do not enjoy the responsibilities of the more advantaged positions. But the evidence points in the other direction: people find jobs of greater responsibility and difficulty more enjoyable, not less (Lane 1991). Abilities would have to be scarce indeed for the occasional individual with an aversion to this labor (for example, teaching philosophy) to determine the rewards necessary to motivate effort. The motivational assumption of the difference principle is that people want greater rewards than others for their own sake. It is not obvious that this is true.

Rawls does not really defend the implied assumption about motivation. He calls the virtue exemplified in the difference principle reciprocity (everyone advancing self-interest in a way that advances the needs of others, including those least advantaged) and contrasts it with impartiality (everyone advancing the general good) and with mutual advantage (free markets, parties bargaining to advance both parties' interests); he says it lies in between these two extremes (1993: 16–17). But why isn't either "impartiality" (really just a different interpretation of reciprocity) or equality enough? Why are contributions not sufficiently motivated by psycho-social rewards (that is, social esteem) that correspond to our contributions but need not be greater than the rewards others receive?

This is especially puzzling given some things Rawls says about what makes life good. He himself regards the development and exercise of complex talents as good in themselves (1999: 372–80). He also believes (as do I) that meaningful contributions to a social collective are one of life's great goods. He says that, without fair equality of opportunity, some would be unjustly deprived of the opportunity to contribute their developed skills to a social collective (p. 73). Since this contribution is an important good, we don't need additional rewards to be motivated to make it. The Aristotelian view of the human good, particularly in its non-elitist Marxist variant where the good is rational social activity, provides a better account of what makes life good and what can motivate us than does the functional theory of stratification.

It may seem that I have conceded the central idea of the functional theory: those who offer outstanding service to the social group are rewarded by greater social esteem. This assertion, by itself, falls short of the functional theory. We can all agree that social esteem, including prestige, is a powerful motivator and an important good for those who have it. But the functional theory makes the connection between contribution and esteem artificial. It assumes that there is a motivational problem: people are reluctant to train for and execute demanding social tasks. This problem is solved by the social artifice of rewarding some positions with greater material goods and prestige. In contrast, I have argued that we are naturally motivated to contribute to social groups with which we identify. Moreover, the connection between greater contributions and greater social esteem is *natural*: it is impossible to imagine that people would contribute to a common social project and not be esteemed for, and in proportion to, those contributions. Most important, the functional theory assumes that *inequality* of rewards is necessary for motivation, while I believe that the reward of social esteem can be of unlimited supply.

The natural history of stratification

Morton Fried distinguished between rank and stratified societies. Rank societies limit positions of prestige; stratified groups combine rank with unequal "access to the basic resources that sustain life" (1967: 109, 186). In the discussion that follows, I consider egalitarian and rank societies together and contrast them with stratified ones.

We can strengthen the criticism of the functional theory of stratification if we review the natural history of stratification. In egalitarian groups people are motivated to contribute to group good without the inequalities of stratified societies. Although these societies do not divide labor into complex and routine, individuals often engage in tasks requiring immense skill, effort, and courage without receiving greater material reward. In their cultural life, egalitarian peoples develop and employ skills for the joy of it, to be of use to the group, and because of the social and self-esteem a person receives from doing what everyone expects and admires. Moreover, if the functional theory of stratification were true, stratification should arise without coercion since it benefits all. But stratification arises only with the concentration of coercion in a few hands and with exploitation and command.

Marxist orientations are probably more prevalent among anthropologists than among other social scientists. Although theory in sociology and anthropology overlaps, anthropologists look at a wider range of data. Ethnographers have studied societies that are not modern and capitalist; archeologists trace from evidence in the soil how cultural and social complexity arises in a particular area. Thus anthropologists can better identify how and why stratification develops.

The Ju/'hoansi (sometimes called bushmen or !Kung) of the northwestern Kalahari Desert are an acephalous egalitarian people. There is no limit to how many men can be successful hunters or to how many adults can be healers, storytellers, or musicians. Successful hunters will hang back from hunting to enable others to get the credit for bringing meat into camp, a practice somewhat comparable to sharing complex labor. Successful hunting often requires skill, hard work, and courage: in his *Children of the Forest* (1985), Kevin Duffy recounts the story of how an Mbuti pygmy killed an elephant by sneaking under it while it slept and driving a spear into its vitals.

Nomadic foragers have only the most rudimentary division of labor among adults, primarily according to gender. Other egalitarian peoples do have a degree of political and economic centralization (their societies are "rank" by Fried's definitions). A village leader may pool resources for later distribution according to need, social insurance against illness and bad luck. This would be a test of the functional theory of stratification; the group leader has special responsibilities and carries out a crucial task requiring considerable skill. Marvin Harris characterizes the redistributor as one "who works harder than anyone else producing the items to be given away, who takes the smallest portion or none at all, and who, after it is all over, possesses no greater material wealth than anyone else" (1991: 113). Edwin Denig describes a "chief" of the Assiniboin of the upper Missouri Valley: "A chief must give away all to preserve his popularity and is always the poorest in the band" (quoted in Sahlins 1972: 254). In the early nineteenth century John Hunter described Kansa-Osage leadership as follows: "The chiefs and candidates for public preferment render themselves popular by their disinterestedness and poverty. . . . [they] pride themselves in being esteemed the poorest man in the community" (Sahlins 1972: 254–5). Many groups define the responsibility of the group leader as being to distribute more than he receives as tribute. Egalitarian redistribution ranges from "chiefs" who are the poorest in the group to leaders who have no more than others.[2] Their job is to insure that everyone has enough. Those groups with fixed leadership do limit positions of prestige, but prestige is accompanied by poverty, not wealth.

Even groups with highly developed political hierarchies may maintain egalitarian norms. Bruce Trigger marshals archeological and ethno-historical evidence (particularly the reports of early Jesuit missionaries) to reconstruct traditional social organization of the Iroquois during the sixteenth and early seventeenth centuries.

---

[2]   These are not chiefdoms as the term is currently used (hence the scare quotes). For current usage of "chiefdom," see Earle 1991.

While the political organization into positions of leadership such as peace chiefs implies limited positions of prestige and hence unequal prestige, these inequalities are not translated into economic inequality. Men sought prestige by working hard at hunting, fishing, and other essential economic activities, as well as by public speaking and sponsoring feasts; success as a warrior was the primary avenue to prestige. Still, Trigger writes, the "material benefits of chiefly office were more than counterbalanced by its expenses." Chiefs' houses were larger but "not more lavishly constructed or furnished than other ones and served as community meeting places" (1990: 133). When peace chiefs obtained exotic goods through trade, "they were required to dispense these goods generously to other members of their community" (p. 134). "[G]oods were accumulated in Iroquoian society either for routine family use or for redistribution" (p. 135). How was this economic egalitarianism enforced? "Repeated anti-social behavior, including selfishness of any sort, was interpreted as a lack of concern for community welfare" and viewed as a sign of witchcraft, which could lead to the death of the accused. So hoarding is dangerous, while liberal distribution of exotic goods is rewarded with prestige. The Iroquoian case is important because it shows that a society can develop elaborate political institutions while remaining economically egalitarian.

Not all groups are egalitarian and not all "redistributors" are poor. In some human societies, wealth, not poverty, is esteemed. These societies vary greatly in their degrees of political centralization. At the more centralized extreme (leaving aside societies that are at the state level of organization) are what are now called "chiefdoms;" their "chiefs" are men who centralize not only group resources but a certain amount of coercion, usually in the form of armed retainers supported off the chief's stores. These chiefs (pre-contact Hawaii can be considered a paradigm) engage in ostentatious displays of their wealth to impress and intimidate commoners. A greater share of the product of the commoners can be obtained by a chief surrounded by his retainers. Chiefs give commands and expect to be obeyed. While in chiefdoms the ideal of reciprocity is honored in words, Antonio Gilman writes: "In good years peasants, to the extent that they lack power, pay rent; in bad years, peasants, to the extent that they lack power, have no claim on surplus" (1995: 238; see also Earle 1991; Sahlins 1972).

Only when the coercion is fully centralized in the formation of the state is the division between complex and routine labor organized into fixed positions. The state coerces from producers of subsistence enough surplus to support non-subsistence specialists: artists and artisans who make elaborate pottery and statuary, architects and engineers who design and supervise the building of temples, pyramids, and other grand public buildings (as well as others who do the back work), astronomers who chart the sky and trace the seasons, full-time religious specialists, a bureaucracy to administer and coordinate these activities, and the military force at the center of the state (Haas 1982).

Alongside the division of labor, great material inequalities emerge: some live in palaces, others in hovels. The centralization of coercion and the development of full-time military specialists in state-level societies enable the consolidation of exploitation: there is a large increase in productive surplus coerced from the laboring classes. Inequalities of prestige are signaled in prestige goods belonging to (and buried with) the elite (Gomberg 1997; Haas 1982).

State-level societies consolidate command/obedience relationships. The division of labor between organizational and command functions on the one hand and the execution of command on the other becomes central to labor organization on plantations, in mines, and in the political centers. Alongside that division of labor arises the division between routine and complex labor, essentially a division between the most oppressed workers and those with greater skill and autonomy in the labor process. We noted both sorts of division of labor in chapters 1 and 6.

Modern societies harbor a division of labor even more complex than that of early states, as well as large inequalities of material goods and prestige. Capitalist markets, no less than earlier state-level societies, depend upon the centralization of coercion to establish and sustain norms creating national or international markets and capitalist property relations. (We noted evidence for this in chapter 4.) These societies too depend on centralization of coercion to maintain social order. The greatest wealth and prestige lie with the political ruling class or those allied with the ruling class.

Stratification – unequal access to necessary goods – requires the centralization of coercion, leading to inequality of power between commoners and their social superiors in politically centralized societies. Defenders of stratification propose that, in stratified groups with a complex division of labor, even the lowest strata have greater opportunity to live as they wish than members of simple societies. Adam Smith expresses this idea (1776, vol. 1: 16). If the functional theory of stratification were true, we would expect greater rewards for more complex knowledge and skills to arise without coercion (since all benefit). But the division between complex and routine labor with greater material rewards for complex labor becomes consolidated only with centralization of coercion.

Is inequality necessary?

Is inequality necessary? I have argued that, for the most part, it is not. The exception is the residual inequality of esteem implied in rewarding those who contribute to the common good and who exercise complex abilities in making those contributions. Inequality of the sort Rawls defends does not benefit all. It is not required in order to motivate people. It arises because those who centralize control of force can create and maintain inequality; they can use their control of force to control wealth.

Chapter 10

Are Some Born Smarter Than Others?

For if something is capable of rational foresight, it is a natural ruler and master, whereas whatever can use its body to labor is ruled and is a natural slave.

Aristotle

Without in any sense arguing that the less gifted must be slaves or judged as having less than full worth in a group, both the Darwinian and the Aristotelian can agree that nature has made some people leaders and other hewers of wood and drawers of water.

Michael Ruse

I have assumed so far that the distribution of natural assets is a fact of nature and that no attempt is made to change it, or even to take it into account. But to some extent this distribution is bound to be affected by the social system. . . . In the original position, then, the parties want to insure for their descendants the best genetic endowment (assuming their own to be fixed). The pursuit of reasonable policies in this regard is something that earlier generations owe to later ones, this being a question that arises between generations.

John Rawls[1]

This chapter is about the idea that people are naturally suited to their social roles. Lots of people believe it. For example, in a popular psychology text used in the 1970s, we find:

> We wish to know in what ways men differ, the extent of their differences, and how to judge the differences. . . . This is not a task of idle curiosity, for our society requires individuals to be appraised, classified, and given responsibilities on the assumption that they differ and that their differences will suit them better for one social role than for another. We decide by examination who should be admitted to college and who should be granted scholarship aid. . . . In industry and government adults are tested in order to place them in the jobs best suited to them. (Hilgard and co-authors 1971: 356)

---

[1] The Aristotle epigraph is from his *Politics* at 1152a 32–5, but the same idea appears throughout the *Politics*. The second epigraph is from Ruse 1990: 80. The third is from Rawls 1999: 92.

While this passage is preceded by a discussion of how environment as well as heredity produces differences, it is followed by an argument that heredity plays a large role in intelligence differences. The belief that people are naturally suited to what they do is widespread and very ancient, as the epigraph from Aristotle testifies. Plato's *Republic* proposes a similar congruence between people's social roles and their natures.

This book calls for sharing both routine and complex labor. If some people are naturally suited to routine labor and others to complex labor, then sharing labor would have us doing work for which we are not suited.

The idea that we are suited by nature for either routine or complex labor is ideology. Ideology makes social organization which is not rational seem rational. My argument has two parts. First, there is a tendency in all human societies to believe that people are naturally suited to what they do; hence the way labor is organized seems rational. Second, in the societies we know there is no reason to believe we are naturally suited to what we do; hence it is not rational to believe that we are.

Social structure, ideology, and the rationalization principle

Observing his society, Aristotle found masters who organized and supervised production and slaves who carried out their masters' instructions. He believed that people were naturally suited to these tasks. Today we observe a largely similar organization of labor. Some organize and oversee our shops, bus barns, factories, offices, and schools; others carry out specific tasks within the organization of labor, some requiring specialized training, many requiring only mastery of simple skills. Like Aristotle, many view the occupants of these social positions as naturally suited to them.

This sense that people are suited by nature to their jobs may be expressed by saying that some are born smarter than others or, less crudely, that some have a natural aptitude for mathematics or music. These ideas are ideology. Following the historian Barbara Jeanne Fields, we can define "ideology" as categories that *structure* our relations with others but *mislead* us about those relations (Fields 1990). These categories guide interactions with others who mentally organize relationships in the same way. We "make sense" of our social world through them, but they mislead us about that world. While Fields, an historian of the early South, studied race and racism, our concern is the idea of mental superiority and inferiority. The idea that some are naturally superior arises from the division of labor; it structures, as ideology, how we relate to one another.

Several times in this book I have referred to the rationalization principle as one that makes accepted practices seem rational. This principle governs how we *understand* our social world. In stable societies the possibility of change tends to be invisible. Seeing no possibility of change, we accustom ourselves to our society. Part of accustoming ourselves is that we rationalize the social order. The rationalization principle is that in every social order, particularly stable ones, there arise categories and ideas that make sense of the social world to the people who live in it.

Belief in superiority and inferiority of talents grows out of labor organization where routine tasks are done by some, and organizational, technical, and religious tasks carried out by others. This belief is not present in societies where necessary tasks are shared among competent adults. We wish to make sense of our social order. In class societies the ruling class or classes construct rationalizations which they tend to favor, and these rationalizations have disproportionate influence since these classes also have disproportionate control over the dissemination of culture (in seventeenth-century England through control of the pulpit; in the United States today through the media). Class societies construct ideologies that commoners and their rulers or slaves and their masters have different natures.

Ideological categories make social relations seem "natural" and inevitable, even though those relations arise from contingent historical events. Ideology distorts history, obscuring the processes that created categories such as "black" and "white" or "bright" and "slow." It makes it hard to see the possibility of social change, especially social change that abolishes the categories that we use.

Fields's essay "Slavery, Race and Ideology in the United States of America" is about racial categories. Where we perceive one another through racial categories, we act according to norms of "racially" permissible and impermissible behavior. In the United States, many black people follow a norm that allows the use of the word "nigger" in a "black" social context but not in "interracial" social situations; or if the word is used in those situations, it carries additional import. Many white people who tolerate an anti-black joke in a "white" social situation regard telling of the same joke in an "interracial" situation as offensive. Such norms – and there are many – structure social interactions between people who are thought of and think of themselves as "white" and "black." We follow the norms but are usually not conscious of how categories influence behavior.

Categories of "superior" and "inferior" also structure social interactions. If we are not persuaded of our equality with others, we will not engage them in dialog as equals. My student Judy Lawson relates an incident where, having arrived considerably prior to the time of the service at a church she was attending for the first time, she engaged the church janitor in joking repartee. Later, when the service started, she realized that the "janitor," now dressed in a suit, was the pastor; she felt embarrassed, that she had behaved inappropriately. There was, she reports, one norm of appropriate behavior with a janitor, her equal, and another with the pastor, owed greater respect for his position. The ideology of superior and inferior (though perhaps not "natural" superiority) is normatively structuring interpersonal behavior.

What Fields says about racial categories will be useful here, particularly since racial categories always connoted superiority and inferiority. She writes, "People are more readily perceived as inferior by nature when they are already seen as oppressed." The idea that black people were inferior arose, she says, from "the incorporation of Africans and their descendants into a polity and society in which they lacked rights." She continues:

> All human societies, whether tacitly or overtly, assume that nature has ordained their social arrangements. [A statement of the rationalization principle!] Or, to put it another way, part of what human beings understand by the word "nature" is the sense of inevitability that gradually becomes attached to a predictable, repetitive social routine: "custom, so immemorial that it looks like nature", as Nathaniel Hawthorne wrote. The feudal nobility of the early Middle Ages consisted of people more powerful than their fellows through possession of arms or property or both. No one at that time . . . considered them superior by blood or birth; indeed, that would have been heresy. But the nobleman's habit of commanding others, ingrained in day-to-day routine and thus bequeathed to heirs and descendants, eventually bred a conviction that the nobility was superior by nature, and ruled by right over innately inferior beings. By the end of the fifteenth century, what would have been heresy to an earlier age had become practically an article of faith.[2] The peasants did not fall under the dominion of the nobility by virtue of being perceived as innately inferior. On the contrary, they came to be perceived as innately inferior by virtue of having fallen under the nobility's dominion. (1990: 106)

On Fields's view the customary relationship between those who commanded and those who obeyed spawned an understanding, an ideology, that made these social relationships seem natural and inevitable rather than historical and contingent.

Apply the passage from Fields to belief that people are naturally suited to their social tasks: we live in societies where some think and command and others do as they are told. How should we understand this? Aristotle proposes that nature has divided us into natural masters and natural slaves or, in Ruse's phrase, that "nature has made some people leaders and others hewers of wood and drawers of water."

This phrase emphasizes the command aspect of the division of labor. But among workers, labor is divided into some tasks requiring development of complex skills and other tasks easily mastered: between worker-professionals and skilled workers and the semi-skilled and unskilled laborers. Phrases such as "the distribution of natural assets," "the natural lottery of talents," "the gifts or geniuses that people have," and, more specifically, "having a gift for languages," "mechanical aptitude," or "a natural talent for mathematics" grow from this organization of labor. In using them, we rationalize it to ourselves, making it seem "natural" and "inevitable."

---

[2] Here, Fields has a footnote to Blum 1982: 34–6.

Are some born smarter than others?

Can the belief be justified that some of us are naturally suited to routine, others to complex labor? If it can, this defeats the suggestion that it is ideology. Belief in naturally superior and inferior mental talents is grounded in three ideas which, as so used, cannot withstand scrutiny: ideas of nature, of talents, and of the inequality of talents.

Nature

As the sciences developed, we have come to understand "nature" as their subject matter. Since the sciences are well defined (this is a sociological observation – there is a general social agreement on what they are), so is our conception of nature. Does the idea that there is a distribution of natural assets derive from natural science? Some psychologists assert that intellectual abilities as measured by standard IQ tests are (more or less) fixed by our heredity. But this trend hardly could count as part of that undisputed territory we could call natural science. While IQ psychology has influenced folk sociology, there are other sources of the belief in differences of talent. When most folks say that some have natural talents that others lack, they believe themselves to be saying what is just obvious. Here Fields's account is on the mark. What is "just obvious" to us grows out of how we understand our social environment, some doing mathematics, others sweeping up behind them. In using the word "natural," we express a sense that the social order around us (or at least this aspect of it) seems inevitable.

Talents or natural aptitudes

The idea of "talent" already entails that of "nature," since "talents" are what we came by naturally, while skills are acquired through hard work. We speak of "inborn talents" even for mathematics. But babies can't do math. What is meant is an inborn *potential* to *learn* mathematics. But does that distinguish one of us from another? Perhaps what is meant is not just the potential to learn mathematics, but to learn to do it at the level of a research mathematician; "surely, not everyone has *that* potential."

   Here, ideology masks our ignorance. We have a few positions for research mathematicians. Some children develop into adults who do this work. *This* we know. We don't know the "inborn potential" of those who are not research mathematicians. What evidence is relevant? Behavioral tests tell what we have learned, not what we might (or might not) have learned. So "talent" is no better off than "nature" as a well-understood concept (unless it refers to developed abilities, the things people actually do).

One reader responded to this as follows: "We see all the time, for instance, how different children respond to education and training. Put 20 children in a class, give them all exactly the same teaching in math, and we soon see that some can handle mathematical concepts easily while others struggle. My three children have all had the same course of piano lessons, but one has turned into a talented pianist while another one is never going to get far beyond Chopsticks. It's impossible to explain this except on the basis that the first had a natural aptitude that the second lacked." Thus, this reader argued, there *is* evidence all around us to support belief in natural differences in talent.

If this reader is right, then my argument fails that belief in differences of talent is ideology. Consider the second example. One child plays the piano well, while another does not. Is it "impossible to explain this except on the basis that the first child had a natural aptitude that the second lacked"? Assume that there is no competing explanation. Then, it seems, we have an explanation that makes sense and no competing explanation; it is reasonable to accept the explanation – natural aptitude – that makes sense of it.

But a "natural aptitude for music" no more explains why one child readily learns music than the "dormitive virtue" explains why opium puts us to sleep, to quote from Molière's *The Imaginary Invalid*. We *already know* that opium induces sleep; we seek to understand why. We already know that one child learns music more readily than another. Does "natural aptitude" explain why? How well correlated is the aptitude with the behavior? We don't know because the "aptitude" just *is* the behavior renamed. The renaming masks our ignorance of the causes of the behavior. In this context, this is not an *explanation* at all.

Am I being unfair? Consider what we know. Call one child A and the other B. When A is given piano instruction, something about A causes A to respond to the instruction by playing well. When B is given the same instruction, something about B causes B to respond by not playing well. Let's suppose this is an accurate account. (I have reservations: it seems too mechanical; even as instruction begins, developmental processes are occurring and continue throughout instruction.) Let us call the something about A that causes A to learn piano A's natural aptitude for piano. But what is that? We don't know what causes A to learn. So the phrase "natural aptitude" masks our ignorance of the cause and redescribes the behavior: given the same instruction, something about A caused A to learn piano while B did not. That makes this explanation parallel to the explanation of the power of opium to put us to sleep as due to its "dormitive virtue."

Developmental processes are complex. Identical twins have different fingerprints. Why? We don't know. We don't understand embryonic and fetal development well enough to explain this. Because they are identical twins, we are less inclined to say that the reason for the difference is a natural difference between the two. (In fact, since they have the same genes, we are less inclined to say that there is "something about" each that causes each to develop the fingerprints she does.) The difference may be due to "noise" or randomness in developmental processes.[3]

If we don't understand the development of fingerprints, how well do we understand how children learn complex behaviors such as mathematics or playing the piano? We understand them no better. If there is noise and contingency in the development of fingerprints, how much more noise and contingency might there be in development of musical ability?

The example of differences in how children in the same class learn mathematics is exactly parallel. Children learn math differently. We don't know why. It does not, as my reader asserted it did, *have* to be natural aptitude. "Natural aptitude" explains nothing.

But, one might reply, "Much behavioral difference is grounded in natural differences. Studies of the heritability of IQ show that people who share more genes have more similar IQs. Estimates of the heritability of IQ indicate that as much as 60–80 percent of IQ differences are due to genetic differences. The fact that we don't know what genes are involved and *how* they explain IQ differences doesn't mean that we will not some day understand the process" (cf. Herrnstein and Murray 1994). This reply seems to show that citing a "natural aptitude" is not vacuous.

Heritability analysis generates estimates of how much observed variation in a trait is associated with genetic and how much with environmental variation. Heritability estimates concern only variations in a trait in an environment, not what causes a trait. A trait can be completely heritable without genes being the cause of the trait. Ned Block (1995) has given the example of the wearing of earrings by adults in the United States in the 1950s (specifying the relevant trait); all the variation (or nearly all) was associated with being male or female. But the genetic differences between men and women did not cause women to wear them and men not (except in a perverse sense). The relevant explanation was a norm about men and women wearing earrings.

Consider IQ differences between people classified as "black" and those classified as "white" in the United States. These could be highly heritable without genes causing IQ differences. Given racial segregation of neighborhoods and schools, the heritability of these IQ variations could be quite high; genes for producing melanin in the skin might be strongly correlated with IQ scores. But do differences in the genes for melanin cause differences in scores? If the cause is racism – segregation of neighborhoods, schools, voluntary associations (such as churches), and the treatment of people identified as black – then a high heritability of black–white IQ variation, like the variation of earring-wearing behavior in the 1950s, does not mean genes are causing IQ differences. Genes for melanin affect appearance, which, in

---

[3] On development, see Moore 2002. The fingerprint example is from Floyd Banks.

a racist society, affects development of "high IQ behavior." Only in that perverse sense do the genes for melanin explain IQ (Block 1995).

While the last paragraph addresses racial (and implicitly other group) differences, it says nothing about *individual* differences. But these are equally problematic. Heritability, despite the word, says nothing about what causes differences, only that difference is correlated with genetic relatedness in a particular "environment." When environments are measured more carefully, some differences associated with "genes" in an "environment" disappear. For example, when additional environmental variables such as segregation of neighborhood, mother's values and participation in formal organizations, and intact family were factored in, group differences in IQs of Latinos and non-Latinos disappeared (Marks 2005: 218, citing Mercer 1988). So, depending how environments are measured, individual differences in IQ may also disappear.

Most important, in a non-competitive environment ability might develop differently. If competitive environments reward people who are intellectually aggressive and competitive, then development of ability might be caused by these traits. So even if there are genes which influence development of ability in competitive environments, in non-competitive environments these same genes might not influence development of ability. This would be true if there are genes that influence self-confidence or resilience in the face of social discouragement.[4] Similarly, if there are genes that influence IQ in competitive environments, they might not influence IQ in non-competitive environments.

Moreover, heritability arguments have been based on forged data (Kamin 1974). Segregationists fund much of the research; Marks (2005) and sources cited there show how data are corrupted. None of this should be taken to *deny* individual difference, biological and behavioral, or genetic influence on difference. I am arguing for epistemic *modesty* about the causes of behavioral difference. As I stressed, developmental processes are complex and poorly under-stood. What we do know suggests that developmental processes are not "genetic" in any straightforward way (Moore 2002).

Heritability analyses cannot rescue "natural aptitudes." Natural aptitudes explain nothing because they cannot be identified independently of the behavior they are to explain. Philosophical literature is permeated with "folk political psychology." The references to natural differences in Aristotle, Ruse, and Rawls are just that.

Many think they know what they don't know; that fact itself requires explana-tion. "Natural aptitude," "it must be genetic" – these phrases are ideology.

---

[4] See Bowles et al. 2005 for heritability analysis suggesting that there are genetic influences on income independent of the influence of IQ on income; they don't consider how any genetic influences on IQ might have their effect through personality and might be different in non-competitive environ-ments. For another philosophical critique of the use of IQ to explain class inequality, see Barry 2005: chs. 8 and 9.

We see differences. These phrases make the differences seem inevitable but do not help us to understand why some learn piano or mathematics and others not. Still, they are important. The phrases orient us to our social world, making it seem "right" to us. Children show great skill at math or piano. They are "naturals." This can seem harmless, but the dangers are revealed when we consider large-scale social organizations. There, masking our ignorance of why children develop as they do with ideas of "natural aptitudes" does harm. It makes a social order where labor is divided and children are tracked for routine or complex labor seem "right."[5]

Inequalities of talents: measuring abilities

The division between complex and routine labor is more than just an assignment of different tasks; it is bound up with value and status, better and worse, superior and inferior, and with a metric of these. It is not just that some have *different* talents from others, but that they have *superior* talents that justify additional income and status. That the abilities are *rare* won't do; many abilities are rare (the ability to work in the open air at great heights, as high-rise ironworkers can do), but intellectual labor is regarded as a superior ability, justifying additional prestige.

"Inequality" suggests a *metric* of "superior talent." In the United States, IQ tests were to provide such a metric, but they do not. Their history shows the problems. On the original Stanford-Binet, published in 1916, females scored ten points below males. The prevailing cultural belief came to be that women were not intellectually inferior. So in 1937 the Stanford-Binet was restandardized: questions on which females did better were added; questions on which males did better were taken out; the scoring was adjusted so that the average IQs of males and females were the same. Do women and men have, on average, *equal* intelligence? To answer the question we need a metric. But in designing our metric, we need to assume something about whether the intelligence of men and women is equal. There is no way around this problem (Gomberg 1974).

The developers of the IQ test, particularly in the United States, believed that the ruling classes were morally and intellectually superior (Kamin 1974: ch. 1). They designed a metric reflecting this belief. Could class differences in IQ be eliminated as sex differences were? Why not? "But the resulting measure would have no use; it would not correspond with school performance or future achievement." That's right. The content of the test picks out cultural differences correlated with class differences. These differences are then used to rationalize the division between complex and routine labor.

---

[5]   This chapter does not discuss sociobiology or evolutionary psychology, which are more recent biodeterminist trends but less relevant to my themes. For a helpful discussion of the former, see Kitcher 1985; of the latter, see Buller 2005.

Race and the division of labor

I have argued that the way we think about individual and group differences grows out of how we live. I have been influenced by a trend in the historiography of the English-American colonies (and of later periods) that emphasized that the deed preceded its justification. Winthrop Jordan had argued that traditional color tropes – associating darkness with evil, lightness with good – revealed European attitudes that influenced perceptions of Africans, perceptions which in turn caused European mistreatment of Africans (Jordan 1968). These historians disagreed. Not just Barbara Fields (1990), but also Theodore Allen (1997) and Edmund S. Morgan (1975) have deepened our understanding of the origins of slavery and of the relationships between legal and social forms and their rationalization. Studying a later period, Alexander Saxton (1990) and Ronald Takaki (1979) have shown how nineteenth-century culture adapted to slavery and its successor institutions in the South. Saxton has called this historiographical trend "ideology" theory because it sees ideas and culture as growing out of the practices of daily life.

Intellectuals and theoreticians undoubtedly influenced folk political psychology. As people of African descent were marked for slavery in Virginia (a process that took time, since the English had lacked an institution of slavery), the question arose, why *they* should be slaves? One early understanding was pre-racial, that Africans were descendants of Ham, cursed by Noah to serve others because Ham looked upon Noah naked in a drunken stupor (while his brothers averted their eyes from Noah's shame) (Smedley 1993). However, "cursed" is not "inferior" and lacks the same sting. It is bad luck to be born a descendant of Ham rather than his brothers; you live out Noah's curse, but you are no less, intellectually or physically, than others, just cursed.

Racism as a full-blown intellectual construct arises only after developments in late seventeenth- and eighteenth-century science. While European theoreticians disagreed about which race was the least able, they agreed that Europeans – or "Caucasians" as they came to be called following Johann Blumenbach, who thought that Europeans originated in the Caucasus – were the superior race. These ideas arise with European expansion.

Their application to social organization *within* a society was consolidated by American intellectuals. Thomas Jefferson's *Notes on the State of Virginia* (1787, Query XIV), written more than 100 years after Bacon's Rebellion and the turn toward African slave labor in Virginia, expresses a nasty view of Africans, physically and intellectually. Physically, Jefferson believed, the difference in skin color was "the foundation of the greater or lesser share of beauty in the two races." White people could express their passions by "greater or lesser suffusions of color," which is "preferable to that eternal monotony, which reigns in the countenances, that immovable veil of black which covers the emotions" of black people. Jefferson thought that black people appear "to participate more of sensation than reflection." He wrote: "it appears to me that in memory [black people] are equal to whites; in reason much inferior, as I think one could scarcely be found capable of tracing and comprehending the investigations of Euclid." Though Jefferson qualified these reflections as needing further investigation before one could be certain, his "suspicion" was that "Homo sapiens Europaeus" was, in all ways, the superior race (Takaki 1979: 47–58). Jefferson's views are the full intellectual construction of racism. They incorporate ideas of superiority and inferiority and combine them with the scientific view of humanity divided into distinct biological races. These ideas rationalized the social organization Jefferson observed in late eighteenth-century Virginia, though he himself expressed reservations about slavery.

Popularization of the intellectuals' ideas of race and racial inferiority was a nineteenth-century "achievement." White males, increasingly part of the polity, had to be rendered politically safe. Laws were passed extending the suffrage to poor white males; at the same time, laws narrowed the suffrage rights of black men in the North. Pogroms (racist mob attacks against the black population of a city or town) in the 1830s and later must have accelerated the process of regarding black people as inferior and dangerous (Fredrickson 1981; Takaki 1979). Anti-black stereotypes became increasingly popular in the North, where labor was overwhelmingly non-black. Why? Black people were stereotyped as lazy, drunken, sex-obsessed, and undisciplined. The popularization of such stereotypes was used to discipline the northern working class: black people represented everything the worker should strive *not* to be. The "white" ideal of the industrious, sober, and disciplined worker was useful to owners of capital (Takaki 1979). Popular culture, particularly minstrelsy, took up racial stereotypes and extended their popular appeal (Saxton 1990).

After Darwin, racism was given another twist, culminating in the eugenics movement of the late nineteenth and early twentieth centuries. This movement was inseparable from the development of the American version of the IQ test by Lewis Terman at Stanford, the instrument by which the inferiority of black people and others could be demonstrated. Terman writes:

[IQ scores in the '70s are] very, very common among Spanish-Indian and Mexican families of the Southwest and also among negroes. Their dullness seems to be racial, or at least inherent in the family stocks from which they come . . . the whole question of racial differences in mental traits will have to be taken up anew and by experimental methods. The writer predicts that when this is done there will be discovered enormously significant racial differences in general intelligence, differences which cannot be wiped out by any scheme of mental culture.

   Children of this group should be segregated in special classes. . . . They cannot master abstractions, but *they can be made efficient workers*. . . . There is no possibility at present of convincing society that they should not be allowed to reproduce, although from a eugenic point of view they constitute a grave problem because of their unusually prolific breeding. (Kamin 1974: 6; citing Terman 1916: 91–2; my emphasis)

Terman believes that black and other racial minorities are suited to routine labor and should be trained accordingly. As segregated schools were consolidated in the nineteenth-century South, similar ideas about the sort of labor suitable for black people governed the curriculum. The eugenicists' fire was also directed against immigrants from southern and eastern Europe and culminated, legally, in the Immigration Act of 1924, which set quotas for immigrants based on the 1890 (not the 1920) census. Many states passed anti-miscegenation laws and laws authorizing the sterilization of the "feeble-minded." All this legislation was grounded in eugenicist thought.

These ideas went into decline in the United States as they were embraced in Nazi Germany. They made a comeback in the late 1960s and early 1970s with widely publicized writings by Arthur Jensen and Richard Herrnstein. They are still widespread.

Such intellectualizations of racial and class differences fortify the effects of the ideology that grows from everyday life. Because our economy is arranged around the divisions between organization and command and the execution of labor and between complex and routine labor, the ideas of our "suited-ness" to our tasks will (by the rationalization principle) arise as long as these ways of organizing labor are not opposed. This sense of our suitedness, spontaneously expressed as the idea of "natural aptitudes," is then developed by intellectuals into a more elaborate "scientific" rationale. This story of the history of racist thought in the United States should help to explain why I believe that racism displays in blatant form the harms of these divisions of labor.

Rejecting ideology and rejecting the division of labor

The concepts of nature, talent, and inequality (applied to racial and class differences) do not withstand critical scrutiny. It can seem obvious that some are born smarter than others (that there is a "natural lottery" of talent), but this is unreflective belief. The belief is ideology that grows out of the division between complex and routine labor and makes it seem natural and inevitable. It structures, mostly unconsciously, how we interact with others, not directly through categories such as "naturally smarter," but indirectly through the norms of appropriate behavior toward those who occupy positions such as pastor, mathematics professor, or executive, to whom, we feel, a certain deference is owed, and toward workers, to whom we do not show the same deference.

The division of labor deprives a significant portion of us (really the majority) of the opportunity to develop complex knowledge and skills and to exercise these skills in contributions to the general good. How could a social structure that so deprives so many of us be justified? It might be justified by a stunning argument that many are incapable of developing such complex skills. I have argued in this chapter that such an argument is not available to those who believe in the "natural lottery of talent." Since there is neither strong evidence for relevant differences nor any reliable way of identifying those who are lacking, we should give all as equal an opportunity as possible to develop talents and use them for the good of all. That is, there is an important good for all of us that seems to require us to abolish the division between complex and routine labor.

Chapter 11

Race and Political Philosophy

Bringing issues of race and racism to the center of political philosophy

Some 30 years ago I took an interest in the definition of "test bias" as applied to tests of ability. The standard definitions of "racial bias" all referred to some failure of test scores to correlate with another measure, the "criterion" (typically, grades in school for tests of academic ability or supervisor's ratings for employment aptitude tests), in the same way for minorities as for the majority. Suppose they did correlate in the same way for both minorities and the majority. Couldn't this be caused by their sharing the same or parallel racial bias? How could these definitions be defended unless that possibility was ruled out? The issue had been raised by black psychologists who had formed their own organization, the Association of Black Psychologists, independent of the American Psychological Association. Their arguments were ignored. The mainstream continued to use the term "test bias" as if the problem of bias affecting the criterion did not exist.

I thought, "Well, at least philosophy is not divided in the same way psychology is." That was a naive thought. Rawls's milestone writings on justice and Robert Nozick's libertarian response gave new life to the field of political philosophy. But where do these works address racial inequality and the way in which race affects a person's opportunities? There were too few black philosophers for them to assert a voice that could be heard within the discipline; at least I was not hearing it. Today the situation is different. Philosophers writing on race have tried to push that issue onto the agenda for political philosophy.[1] Unfortunately, race still remains at the periphery.

[1] The pioneers of race and political philosophy include Bernard Boxill (1984) and Howard McGary (1999) as well as Charles Mills, whom I discuss in detail below. These are voices in the "analytic" tradition, which I know better, but many others have contributed and are contributing. I apologize for not acknowledging all who deserve honor for their efforts. I discuss Mills because his views provide a sharp, clear contrast with my own on the question whether racism is continuous with other oppression.

This book continues earlier efforts to put race on political philosophy's agenda. In this chapter I argue that Sen's capabilities approach can be revised to state problems of racism and their solutions. Putting racism at the center of political philosophy transforms the capabilities approach: because racial inequality deprives many of the opportunity to contribute – particularly complex abilities – contribution should be a central capability. A theory of justice should include norms of contribution.

Race, unequal opportunity, and the division of labor

When labor is divided between the routine and the complex, many children in each generation must be trained for lives of routine labor. Because categories of race (and allied categories in countries besides the United States) organize unequal opportunity, complex labor is skewed away from black people, and black children have diminished educational opportunity. Racism is an injustice that can reveal something deeper: if black people don't do a major share of the routine labor, then who should do it? If black children are not socialized for routine labor, then who should be?

The vast majority of poor black people in United States cities are ghettoized. Residential segregation leads to segregated schools and social life and limits opportunity. How can we address inequality of opportunity? This question is given urgency by the lower life expectancy and higher rate of incarceration of black people compared with white. But racism must be understood in its economic and social context. Specifically, where routine labor is set apart from complex labor and from tasks of organizing production, it is necessary that some do that routine labor. Some workers must suffer the brunt of unemployment. Society is divided into groups of more esteemed and less esteemed workers. Someone has to be at the bottom of this structure.

Since someone has to be at the bottom, the ordinary ways in which parents try to insure a future for their children will make it likely that "being on the bottom" is somewhat self-perpetuating. Now add to this the long history of slavery, sharecropping, Jim Crow, and other forms of racism and the continuing segregation of neighborhoods, schools, and churches. Then there are government actions. Schools are divided into academic and vocational tracks. Education is organized "rationally" to produce suitable employees. Stories in chapter 1 about concentrating on high-performing students and about zero tolerance show the schools do not aim at educating all children. Highways and public housing projects have been built to maintain racially segregated neighborhoods (Hirsch 1983). Unemployment is sustained at high levels through government action.[2] Legislation affects wage levels by squeezing the "social

---

[2]   The Federal Reserve regards high unemployment as a signal to lower or not raise further interest rates; conversely, low unemployment is a signal of an "overheated" economy and leads to higher interest rates that slow the economy and increase unemployment. How does this work? Businessmen make

safety net" so that workers have no attractive alternative to low-wage employment. Government actions maintain or extend segregation and unequal opportunity as they constrict opportunity.

Although education is central to the organization of unequal opportunity, opportunity need not be organized as it is in the United States, where racial segregation amplifies economic segregation. In some small northern European countries the schools are not as bad for most children. There, immigrant labor plays the same role as black labor in the United States. (In larger industrial countries – Britain, France, Germany, Italy, Russia – the schools train most children for labor of limited complexity. This training is amplified by quasi-racism where immigrants or racial or ethnic minorities are at the low end of the working class.) So if schools must train some children for routine labor (as a rule, at least), then these small northern European countries are "the exception that proves the rule." If children are given more adequate skills, immigrants do the routine work.

While racism is an important part of the story of how opportunity is organized, many non-minorities are caught in the same situation, if not to the same degree. Many racist harms – crowded schools more about discipline than developing ability, depressed neighborhoods, unemployment, and jobs that require mindless obedience – are experienced by many who are not black. Sharing labor, we can transform relationships and eliminate racial conflict within the working class. These are the harms of unequal opportunity that I have addressed and the solution I have proposed. Bringing race and racism to the center of social and political philosophy, we can transform that discipline.

Capabilities and functionings

Of the mainstream egalitarian philosophies, that of Amartya Sen (1992, 1999) seems best suited for articulating problems of racism. Sen identifies ways in which we should be able to function, for example, to live and be healthy. Corresponding to each functioning is a capability to have that functioning. Sen points out that although black people in the US are much wealthier than people in the poor Indian state of Kerala, their life expectancy is lower because they have not experienced the social and cultural reforms that have taken place in Kerala (1999: 22). They have less capability to live.

In chapter 4, I distinguished philosophical conceptions of the good life as activity – those of Aristotle and Marx – from approaches, influenced by neoclassical economics, that conceived the good as something we (passively) experience or receive and justice as concerned more with how goods are *distributed* than with what people *do*. The capabilities approach is Aristotelian

---

decisions whether to expand production partly based on the cost of borrowing (interest rates); higher interest rates make it harder to make a profit and lead to decisions not to expand production. The result is a "cooler" economy and higher unemployment.

insofar as it emphasizes functionings. But in providing capabilities, a society is distributing resources. Still, capabilities are important to justice because of what they enable us to do.

The distinction between capabilities and functionings is used in two ways. First, there are elementary functionings, the things that nearly all normal human beings seek, such as food, shelter, and sex. Still, people may choose to fast, live outdoors, or become celibate and should not be forced to eat, live indoors, or have sex if they prefer not to. Nevertheless, to evaluate whether a *society* provides a decent life, we look at functionings: if people are malnourished, unsheltered, or not sexually involved, something is wrong with that society. *Elementary* functionings are central to life. Any society where many do not function in these ways is defective.

The second reason for the distinction between capabilities and functionings arises from the variety of ways that potential may develop. Imagine that children are provided with the basics of reading, mathematical knowledge, singing and other forms of music, exposure to the visual arts, training in sports and fitness, understanding of society, and knowledge of the natural world. Which functioning the child develops and takes beyond the basic level is up to her. No one's genius develops in all areas simultaneously and evenly. Moreover, much scientific knowledge is specialized, and it is difficult to become expert in several areas. In assessing a *society*, we must look at functionings. A society might have great music but less science – or vice versa. But a society in which no one develops any of these abilities is defective.

Granted, these functionings have a historical and geographical component. In societies of foragers, people do not read, write, do math, or understand modern natural science. Yet people show great skills in hunting, knowledge of nature, storytelling, music, and negotiating the social terrain, cooperating and resolving conflict without central authority and command. They seem to lead good lives. Scientific knowledge is a contingent historical good. Still, the complex division of intellectual labor among the sciences is part of the good life for us now. A modern society without written language, mathematics, and the natural sciences is lacking things that are important.

In *Inequality Reexamined*, Sen mentions "taking part in the life of the community" as a "complex" functioning (as opposed to the elementary functionings, life and health). Let us amend Sen's idea and propose a "general" complex functioning of participating in economic life in a way that confers dignity. The unemployed are denied esteem for participating in productive life. (Nussbaum includes only a right to *seek* employment, not the right to be employed [2000: 80].) A society with high unemployment deprives many of the capability for this functioning.

Most important, we should amend the capabilities approach as follows: a good society should *distribute widely* the contribution of complex abilities. A complex functioning such as composing classical music may not be spread among a large group. But if we allow as a general complex functioning "contributing complex skill and knowledge," then I have argued that this functioning should be distributed very widely. If this functioning is confined to a small group, if most spend their lives in routine labor under close supervision obeying the commands of others, the society does not provide its members with the capability for a good life.

Racism, opportunities, and capabilities

We can use the capabilities approach to assess the racism of a society. Consider the simple functionings of living and having good health. In the United States black people on average have shorter lives and poorer health. These are effects of hypersegregation and generally of being racially identified as black. A comparison between black and white life expectancy and morbidity displays the racism of United States society.

I proposed a complex functioning of participation in the economic life of one's society in a way that confers dignity. In the United States, the unemployment rate of black people has been double that of white people for the past half-century, thus displaying the racism of US society. Interpreted as including such a complex functioning, the capabilities approach further clarifies the harms of racism. Consider now the prestige of social contributions. If low-caste people in India are allowed to participate only in ways that are despised by many, this robs them of dignity. The same holds for anti-black racism in the United States; many black people, and immigrants as well, participate in economic life in jobs that are despised or at best thought undesirable. People are deprived of an important functioning – contributing in a way that draws social esteem for one's contributions, contributing complex abilities – and of the corresponding capability. Jobs requiring complex abilities are skewed away from black people; jobs requiring routine labor under close supervision are skewed toward them. Suitably amended, the capabilities approach can articulate this racism.

The capabilities approach can also describe the solutions. Racism affecting health and life expectancy is ended when racial disparities are ended. Racist unemployment is ended when the unemployment rate for black people is no higher than for white people. Racism in distribution of work requiring complex abilities is ended when it is not skewed away from black workers.

These amendments to the capabilities approach bring race and racism to the center of political philosophy in two ways. First, the capabilities/functionings approach can give natural and appropriate articulations of and solutions to problems of racism; second, focusing on issues of racism *revises* that approach. The second point is the more important. Egalitarians should attend to inequality in their own societies. Inequality in the United States is racist. It makes people's lives worse in ways Sen has noted – lower life expectancy and poorer health. But it also deprives people of equal dignity through unemployment and demeaned labor. To address these forms of racism, we need to revise the capabilities approach, and these revisions benefit political philosophy.

Racism and other oppression

Racism starkly displays harms that are more general. We should eliminate these harms as they affect black people *and as they affect all others*. Revising the capabilities approach not only brings these harms into focus; it sets a project of providing for all the capability of contributing complex abilities. When we focus on racism, when we put opposition to racism at the center of political philosophy, we can see the harms that a good society should eliminate.

This use of issues of race and racism is different from that of most. For contrast, I discuss two writings of Charles Mills. *The Racial Contract* (1997) points out that the central figures of the philosophical tradition emerging from the Enlightenment – Hume, Kant, Mill – adhered to racist thought. They believed that the disadvantaged situations of people of color were due to natural or cultural deficits. For Mills, this fact creates a challenge to mainstream political philosophy: what would the project of finding a fair basis of social cooperation look like if it did not assume that people of color were subhuman, if they had to be included in the polity as equals?

To highlight the inequality, Mills (2004) has developed the notion of racial exploitation. Racial exploitation need not assume that races are biologically real, only that they function as sources of advantage and disadvantage for those identified with them. The difference that race makes to income, wealth, education, and job opportunities constitutes a huge transfer of resources from black people (and other minorities) to white people. All white people benefit from this transfer, although not equally.

I agree with Mills that political philosophy must engage issues of race and that these issues are central to that discipline. In raising these points Mills has performed an important service. I disagree with Mills on both the history of racism and on the reality of racial exploitation.

Mills stresses the conceptual reduction of non-Europeans to a subhuman category. We need to be reminded of this. But he rejects attempts to conceive racism as the most blatant and vicious form of class oppression. Did Englishmen also conceive of their poor as subhuman? The answer is "yes." By the seventeenth century the English were struck by the prosperity of the Dutch and many concluded that the English had failed to take full advantage of their poor. England's problem was, quoting Edmund S. Morgan's *American Slavery–American Freedom*, "the perversity, the stubborn, immoral idleness of England's poor." Morgan goes on:

> Virginia's conversion to slave labor and the use of slaves in other American colonies must be viewed in the context of contemporary English attitudes toward the poor and schemes for putting them to work. According to the men who wrestled with the problem of England's poor, half the English population consisted of wage earners, and all of them would rather drink than eat and rather starve than work. . . . The English poor were "vicious, idle, dissolute." They were addicted to "Laziness, Drunkenness, Debauches, and almost every Kind of Vice," to "mutinous

and indecent Discourses." They were "Miserable, Diseased, Ignorant, Idle, Seditious and (otherwise) vicious." (1975: 320; Morgan's sources omitted)

As in Virginia, the problem in England was how to force the poor to work. Workhouses were proposed as educational institutions where children of the poor would be trained to work at an early age. The philosopher John Locke proposed the age of 3. Enslaving the poor was considered – Bishop George Berkeley proposed that "sturdy beggars . . . be seized and made slaves to the public for a term of years," while Francis Hutcheson "thought that perpetual slavery should be 'the ordinary punishment of such idle vagrants as, after proper admonitions and tryals of temporary servitude cannot be engaged to support themselves and their families by any useful labours' " – but the English poor escaped that fate (pp. 322–5).

Mills points out that non-Europeans came to be thought of as subhuman. But the English poor were thought of as "the vile and brutish part of mankind." In Morgan's words, "In the eyes of unpoor Englishmen the poor bore many of the marks of an alien race." A 1697 Act of Parliament required recipients of poor relief

> to wear a prominent red or blue "P" on the right-hand shoulder. And since they were not only troublesome but also "nauseous to the Beholders," they could be segregated along with other vicious, insane, diseased, or impotent persons within the walls of the workhouses, hospitals, prisons, and asylums constructed to enclose them – the ghettos of the poor – or else they could be shipped to the plantations. (pp. 326–7; Morgan's sources omitted)

In the late seventeenth century the treatment of and attitudes toward Africans and poor English were different but not sharply so. The prevailing view was that humanity was divided into higher and lower orders and that it was natural that the lower orders should serve their betters.

In (what became) the United States, sharp differences in treatment of black and white labor emerged in the late seventeenth and eighteenth centuries and particularly in the nineteenth after the invention of the cotton gin in 1793. With the Declaration of Independence and the founding of the republic came the belief that citizens were equal. Still, slavery continued, and full citizenship was restricted to white men with property (Fields 1990). Racism emerges full-blown in the third and fourth decades of the nineteenth century with universal manhood suffrage. Democracy and equal rights for white men were disasters for black people. The idea that most white people were born to serve their betters was largely abandoned. Now it was necessary, as it had not been earlier, to tell a story why *black* people may be enslaved. Anti-black pogroms made some white workers active participants in racism. Cotton became hugely profitable; immense wealth was extracted from black labor. Slavery – and after the Civil War the sharecropping system and Jim Crow – was justified by the ideology of racial inferiority. The fates of poor white and black people diverged (Takaki 1979).

Jacqueline Jones's *The Dispossessed* chronicles the lives of black and white southern workers as sharecroppers, lumber or textile mill workers, cannery workers, and miners after the Civil War into the late twentieth century. Racism affected the options people had (white sharecroppers could sometimes escape to textile mills where black workers were excluded – 1992: 108), but where they sharecropped on the same plantation or worked in factories, mines, and mills together, black and white shared oppression and exploitation: long hours, low pay, and tedious, closely supervised, and often strenuous or dangerous labor. In northern cities, both before and after the Civil War, wealth was built on the degraded labor of native born and immigrant workers, including women and children. Work in factories and meatpacking plants of cities in the North and Midwest was little better and (in the case of meatpacking) sometimes worse than southern labor. As black workers increasingly migrated to the North and joined white and immigrant workers, there was similar oppression at work, but opportunities for black people were constricted by segregation, inferior schools, and racial profiling. This pattern continues.

Today the United States combines formal legal citizenship rights (for those without felony convictions) with degradation at work. Explore the term "wage slavery," used by nineteenth-century socialists. A slave is a body under the will of another; the slave's will is impotent. A chattel slave is a slave all the time. A wage slave is a slave for a period of hours. While on the clock, a worker does as she is told. Not to do so risks termination of employment. Recall my account of my experiences as a postal worker. Close supervision reminded me constantly that my will was irrelevant. In contrast, working pouch rack or carrying mail left me feeling in control. Of course, I was on a very short leash. But the illusion was important to me and, I believe, to most workers. To be constantly reminded of our (wage) slavery made us feel less than fully human.

Union organization occasionally made it possible for workers to feel like agents. During World War II Karl Lundberg, who had worked at Swift, moved to Ford, where he built armored trucks. He compared his experience in the Packinghouse Workers Organizing Committee with his experience at Ford under the United Auto Workers: "In the packinghouse, if you had a problem with the boss, it got taken care of right then and there. Over at Ford, well you filled out a piece of paper and you waited" (Halpern 1997: 201). Lundberg was paying tribute to the shop floor militancy of the PWOC, which stopped production if management did not deal satisfactorily with grievances. The militancy in the packinghouses gave the workers a sense of dignity. Gertie Kamarczyk said that she "felt like a human being with real rights, a real whole person for the first time in my life" (p. 166). The union's shop floor power made workers feel less like slaves.

Being a "subordinate" carries over to the rest of our lives. Children are trained with emphasis on following orders. (This may be less true of "middle-class" children; see Lareau 2003.) Many difficulties in our intimate lives derive from not knowing how to get along when we move from relations of superordination/subordination to egalitarian relations where differences must be worked out when no one is boss. Many accustom themselves to subordination in relations with others.

Mills points out that in the Racial Contract black people are less than human, don't fully count. But what black people experience is a severe and generalized version of what many workers of all "races" experience at work every day. Subordinate workers at work are not full persons. You doubt it? Try disobeying instructions. Racial identification and ghettoization make it worse: diminished opportunity to do anything but routine, closely supervised labor that reminds us of our "subhumanity;" exposure to police actions based on skin color; humiliation in public places (recall my student asking for directions in downtown Chicago – see chapter 8).

An ideology of inferiority is used to justify the subordination of workers. White workers are stereotyped as authoritarian, beer-drinking, and dumb. In the early twentieth century, Cyril Burt used measures of "intelligence" to "prove" the superiority of the upper classes (Gould 1981). The point is not to deny the reality of racism but to keep two thoughts in mind simultaneously: (1) workers are, for the most part, treated like crap and held in contempt; (2) however bad it is for white workers, it is generally worse for minorities, particularly black folks. Many see one side but not the other. Racism is part of, but an extreme form of, the maltreatment and contempt for workers generally. It is extreme and especially vile because grounded in the perception of the black body. This perception places a brand of inferiority on a group of workers, but one that cannot be removed in the way that one could remove the letter "P."

The rhetoric surrounding the 1996 Welfare Reform Act is a recent example of how racism is confounded with class oppression. Welfare was said to reduce the incentive to work, to encourage dependency, idleness, and moral corruption. Poor folks' moral salvation was in low-wage labor. While racial stereotyping was crucial to winning public acceptance of the law, the majority of those affected were white. Mills's writings on race err in not stressing this connection between racism and class stereotyping and class oppression.

Mills also defends the idea of racial exploitation – that white people benefit from black folks' disadvantages. The word "benefit" has rhetorical impact, suggesting images of white people raking in money from black poverty. But what does the word mean? One group's condition is compared with another's. But what is the comparison? It could just be an alternative description of racism: black people suffer material harms by being identified as black; white people, not being so identified, are subject to these harms to a lesser degree.

Saying that white people benefit suggests something stronger: not just that they are not as badly off as black people but that, absent racism, they would be worse off than now. That is, on this interpretation of "benefit," we are to compare the condition of white people not with black people, but with what the condition of white people would be under conditions of racial equality.

How are we to imagine a society of racial equality (not just one where there is *less* racial inequality here or there)? Mills allows that on one possible scenario the end to "racial exploitation" would lead to *improvements* for most or all white people. But if so, then racism *harms* white people. The claim that white people benefit from racial exploitation seems to imply that in a society of racial equality white people would be worse off. The most important question is how we understand a society without racism.

Racism is not discontinuous with other forms of oppression but is the extreme case that enables us to see other cases as milder forms of the same thing: lives that are shorter and unhealthier and deprived of dignity by the dominant norms of esteem. Societies that limit opportunity have ways of deciding who attains positions of advantage and who toils in routine labor, works part-time jobs, or is unemployed. Race is important in determining those outcomes, but many identified as white share similar oppression.

I have argued that, suitably amended, the capabilities/functionings approach helps to articulate problems of racism and their solution. While that approach provides a criterion for deciding when these specific forms of racism would not exist, it does not tell us how to end them. That question leads to the ideas of this essay: if it is wrong for black people to suffer from higher unemployment, why is it better for others to suffer from unemployment and the concomitant loss of status? If it is wrong for the routine jobs to be skewed toward black workers, why is it better if someone else must work those jobs? Equality requires sharing labor.

This last argument assumes that we accept the constellation I defended in chapter 6 as an important human functioning. The omission of the constellation from the writings of Sen and Nussbaum is an important defect. The needs for life, health, and security must be met. But the opportunity to contribute to the social group in which one is embedded – particularly the opportunity to develop and contribute complex abilities – is an opportunity to meet a basic need too. This opportunity existed for every Ju/'hoansi in a traditional group and probably for humans in classless societies throughout human history. The constellation represents an important functioning, and the opportunity to contribute complex abilities should be included as part of the capabilities approach.

Including the constellation among the important functionings, we ask, "How is the corresponding capability to be made available to all on an equal basis?" The answer is by sharing routine and complex labor, as I explained in chapter 7. Now we have a practical way to address racism without replacing the racist oppression of black people with a similar oppression of someone else.

Race, contribution, and political philosophy

At the beginning of this chapter I recalled the situation in psychology 30 years ago when the issues raised by black psychologists about the definition of "test bias" were ushered to the back of the bus. Philosophers such as Mills have argued that modern political philosophy, from its origins, assumed that non-Europeans were subhuman, children, or in some other way not part of the social contract or the citizenry for whom philosophers sought equal regard. The issues raised by philosophers of race are given the "multicultural" treatment. Articles on "black" topics are published in mainstream journals, as are articles taking feminist points of view. But mainstream discussions of justice – this is a sociological observation – leave questions of racism to the side. The work of Mills and others is thought of as "black philosophy;" mainstream writers have little to say about it. Issues of race and racism become "ghettoized."

Some of the ghettoization can be due to content. If someone writes an article about the foundation of black solidarity, it may seem presumptuous for someone identified as "white" to engage the issue. Other issues – reparations, for example – may not break new theoretical ground but ask how accepted principles apply to a particular historical injustice; these issues may be regarded as "applied philosophy" and ignored by mainstream theories of justice.

Theories of justice need to attend to racism. Educational and other differences – particularly those affected by racial segregation – create unequal opportunities to attain limited positions of advantage. Committed to equal opportunity, we ask, "*How* can opportunity be made equal? How is it to be decided who is to be educated to advantaged positions? Should all be educated to such positions even though only a few will attain them? Should opportunity be unlimited?" When we consider issues of race and racism, we must ask how a society should determine the *amount* of opportunity available. Issues of race and racism raise the most profound questions of social and political philosophy.

Moreover, focusing on race and racism leads us to rethink our conception of social justice. Sen has used data on survival rates to highlight how in the United States the percentage of black people who have survived at various ages is lower not only than the percentage of white people but even than the percentage of Keralans and, for men, Chinese. These data highlight not only the poor infant mortality rates for black babies but also the continued health problems that affect survival even into people's sixties and seventies. These data seem to raise questions of distributive justice: are black women getting adequate pre-natal care? Do black families have adequate access to health care? Traditional theories of justice, whether those of Rawls, Dworkin, or Sen, may speak adequately to these problems of what people *receive*. But race and racism – particularly unemployment and the skewing of black workers toward low-wage, routine, closely supervised labor – also raise questions about opportunities people have to *contribute*. This, I believe, is the most important difference made by bringing issues of race and racism to the center of political philosophy: we need a theory of justice which is more focused on opportunities and duties to contribute and to attain the esteem that comes from these contributions.

Chapter 12

Justice and Markets

"Paul, no one will listen to your ideas about sharing labor. You reject markets as a way of organizing social cooperation, but non-market social experiments have proven disastrous in the Soviet Union and Eastern Europe. China long ago embraced markets and profits. Proposals to organize economies without money and markets cannot be taken seriously." This book does indeed defend ideas that are not fashionable. I believe it is not obvious what is "proven" by earlier social experiments (although I will not explore Soviet and Chinese history here). In this and the next chapter I defend a conception of justice inconsistent with market norms.

The governing idea is this: markets are normative, implying their own conceptions of right and wrong, permissible and impermissible, justice and injustice. The implied values are individualist, not egalitarian. Liberal egalitarianism tries to marry market norms with egalitarianism, but the union will not take. In this chapter I explain why. In the next I develop a non-market conception of contributive justice.

The conflict between the moral powers

In this section I explore the tensions between market norms and equal opportunity. My purpose is to show that market relationships create a conflict between our conception of the good and the demands of egalitarian justice.

In a series of articles and then in his book *If You're an Egalitarian, How Come You're So Rich?* G. A. Cohen has argued that John Rawls promotes a divided consciousness. Citing the slogan that "the personal is political," Cohen asks how someone who endorses the difference principle can try to advance individual self-interest by seeking rewards greater than those of others. To remind the reader, the difference principle asserts that economic inequalities are just only if they improve the prospects of the least advantaged.

More precisely, in a comparison of possible schemes of social cooperation a scheme can be perfectly just only if the position of the least advantaged group is as good or better than the position of the least advantaged group in any alternative scheme of cooperation (assuming that these schemes provide equal basic liberties and fair equality of opportunity).

Cohen reminds us that in a well-ordered just society, all endorse the principles of justice, including the difference principle. Everyone agrees that inequalities are just only if they benefit the least advantaged. Consider someone who can command a higher income because she can contribute more to production; suppose that all will benefit even at the highest income she can bargain for. Will she bargain for that highest income? If she contributes her skills for less than the highest pay, there will be even greater benefit to the least advantaged. She endorses the principle that inequalities are just only if they benefit the least advantaged. Will that endorsement make her deliberation process different from that of someone who would not endorse it? Cohen finds it implausible to suppose that one can endorse the difference principle and bargain for an income higher than others have.

Cohen seems to be pointing to a conflict between two points of view, the one we take as self-interested economic agents and the one we take in endorsing principles of justice. I will develop what I take to be the philosophical lesson of Cohen's argument.

Rawls postulates two moral powers. In agreeing to the difference principle, we look at society from every social point of view including that of the least advantaged; a society is perfectly just only if the least advantaged in that society are at least as well off as the least advantaged would be in any alternative. We assume this point of view as citizens, seeking terms of social cooperation that can be seen to be fair from every social point of view; we seek fair terms of cooperation that could be endorsed by like-minded fellow citizens and form the basis for an "overlapping consensus" among people with different conceptions of the good. This is the point of view of justice.

As everyday people, going to work, caring for our families, participating in a church or soccer club, and promoting the agenda of the National Organization for Women, we look at the world differently: we seek our own good or the good of groups for which we feel special affinity or whose programs, agendas, and philosophies we wish to promote. This is the point of view of our own conception of the good.

The two points of view – our concern, on one hand, to cooperate with others on fair terms and, on the other, to advance our own good – come from two moral powers. We have the ability (power) to develop both a sense of justice and a conception of the good. Neither moral power is "prior" to the other. They play different roles in our lives. We plan our lives based on our conception of our own good; it gives life meaning. The sense of justice is a political conception governing interactions with others. Because it has to be acceptable to all, regardless of each person's particular conception of the good, it cannot depend upon any one such conception. The sense of justice arises to address the problem of how people with different ideas of what is good can live together.

The issue Cohen raises is akin to, but different from, a problem raised in chapter 9. There I asked why Rawls thought inequality was necessary to motivate those with scarce abilities to exercise their abilities so as to benefit all, including the least advantaged. It was not clear why only our being better off than others would motivate us. That issue was raised by Rawls's claim that equality is not perfectly just because it is not Pareto efficient.[1] Is that claim correct? That issue is *external* to Rawls's theory of justice as a political conception postulating two moral powers.

Cohen's argument raises issues *internal* to Rawls's conception of moral powers: it highlights the diversity contained within Rawls's phrase "conception of the good." Part of what Rawls means by a conception of the good is stressed in his Introduction to *Political Liberalism* – namely, religious or philosophical views (which, Rawls believed, had sparked religious wars in Europe). But, more broadly, our conception of the good includes devotion to our own well-being, to the well-being of our families and friends, and to projects or commitments integral to our self-conception. In modern capitalist societies, we use money to advance this good.

Rawls takes market economies for granted. Norms internal to such economies imply their own ideas of right. Norms associated with money and markets *conflict* with concern for egalitarian justice. Writers such as Cohen (and I) wish to bring to a minimum the conflict between self-interest and the good of the social group in which our lives are embedded. Rawls underestimates the extent to which – because of money and markets – our own good conflicts with justice.

Markets tend to set our own good at war with concern for fairness, especially equal opportunity. Income and wealth are, as Rawls says, all-purpose goods in societies where social needs are mediated by money. Money can be used to buy anything, unless law intervenes to prohibit certain transactions (special favors from public officials). Because money is fungible in this way, it sets the good of the individual in opposition to equal opportunity. We don't love all children equally; we have greater love and concern for our own. We are concerned for their futures. Moreover, as parents we undertake a moral responsibility to provide for their development. For most of us, it is part of our conception of the good to enable our children to develop their abilities. We will devote resources to that. Money, as a fungible good, is necessarily in limited supply.

As Rawls imagines it, we exchange our contributions to society for money. The freedom to make or refuse an exchange is a norm implicit in market exchanges. We make the bargain only on conditions that suit us. We decide according to our conceptions of the good, that is, in a broadly self-interested

---

[1] A distribution is said to be Pareto efficient when no one's situation can be improved without making someone else's worse (so all changes are "win–lose"). A distribution is not Pareto efficient if we can improve the situation of some without making anyone else's worse ("win–win" changes are possible).

way. If others can dictate the terms on which we contribute our labor, liberty of the person is violated.

What is my conception of the good? If I have children, it is to provide for their future. They, like me, will exchange labor for money. The greater their training, the greater their ability to bargain for advantage and realize their own conception of the good. So if I am able, I purchase schooling – or housing that entails superior schools. I enrich their childhood through organized sports, cultural or language training, math or science camp. I may work fewer hours in order to mentor them. I encourage a sense of entitlement to advantage (Lareau 2003). To do these things, I may seek the best bargain I can for my own labor – not necessarily the highest pay but perhaps the highest combination of pay with free time. My conception of the good leads me to try to increase resources for my children's advantage. Similar considerations apply to securing my own future in retirement or to securing resources to advance causes, such as anti-racism, peace, or women's equality, which may be central to my self-conception and sense of the purpose of my life. These are typical considerations that we may have in seeking to advance our own good within a money economy.

In a labor market, demand for scarce abilities gives bargaining advantage to those who have them. Wages will be unequal. Some will have more resources to advance the good of their children. They will do so. Opportunity will be unequal. (This argument assumes that *prospects* are unequal; we will consider this assumption shortly.)

Markets have created a conflict between the moral powers. Considerations of justice require equal opportunity. Parental responsibilities – typically central to someone's conception of the good – require us to advance our children's opportunities. The division between routine and complex labor turns opportunity into a good of limited supply. These two moral points of view are in conflict, a conflict of the moral powers. The conflict is not universal and necessary in human societies. It comes from the organization of labor and my market freedom to advance my good by bargaining for the sale of my labor.

One crucial difference between Rawls's view and my own is that I do not assume money and the exchange of anything – labor or education – for money. A money economy where we bargain for income creates a war between our conception of the good – particularly our moral responsibility to our children – and egalitarian concern for all. Egalitarians should try to reduce this conflict between individual and collective good.

Market efficiency and justice

At one point Rawls wrote that markets would lead to equally good jobs for all. If jobs are equally good, then so are life prospects, and opportunity is equal, by anyone's definition of equal opportunity. In that case parents have no reason to favor or be concerned about their children's opportunities, and, contrary to the argument in the last section, the two moral powers are not in conflict.

Rawls writes: "Consider the case of wages in a perfectly competitive economy surrounded by a just basic structure" (1999: 268). He proposes that "[i]n equilibrium the relative attractiveness of different jobs will be equal, all things considered" because "jobs which involve uncertain or unstable employment, or which are performed under hazardous and unpleasantly strenuous conditions, tend to receive more pay. Otherwise men cannot be found to fill them" (p. 269). This is a very radical egalitarianism (and similar to a proposal discussed briefly in chapter 7).

This vision of how a market economy might create equality in a society with a just basic structure contradicts many fundamental ideas contained in Rawls's *Theory of Justice*. It envisions unlimited opportunity. No positions are more advantaged than any others. Moreover, Rawls's examples suggest the very opposite of the difference principle: working-class positions that are unstable, dirty, dangerous, boring, or arduous, not positions requiring superior abilities, require extra material rewards in order to be filled. If the relative attractiveness of positions were equal, then initial starting positions would not be affecting people's life prospects – contradicting what Rawls says about the basic structure of any modern society (1999: 7; 2001: 55). Moreover, the argument that jobs would be equally attractive is incompatible with Rawls's belief that there are scarce abilities that require extra compensation for people who have those abilities (Krouse and McPherson 1988: 93).

The argument says that "the relative attractiveness of different jobs will be equal." If this means that, subjectively, each worker would find each position equally attractive, it makes no sense. Attractiveness would be equal if we all had the same preferences – if not, I don't see how we could find all jobs equally attractive. In no society will people develop the same preferences; we enjoy different things and enjoy the same things differently. Moreover (here I repeat a point made in chapter 7), where jobs are different, we will be socialized some for one job, others for another. So, by the socialization principle, preferences will be different.

Still, Rawls's argument might be stated in another way. Given an objective and neutral way of deciding the relative value of positions, we could ask, "Would markets create positions that were equally good?" In chapter 6, I argued that development and contribution of complex abilities and earning esteem for those contributions were essential goods. So let us suppose that these exhaust what make positions desirable (which they do not) and ask whether markets would create positions that combined routine and complex labor in such a way that each worker, in her labor, had equal opportunity to contribute complex abilities and earn esteem thereby.

This seems unlikely. Markets are good at productive efficiency because efficient producers drive less efficient ones from the market. Sharing labor is not productively efficient; its priority is development and contribution of ability, not producing as much as possible with as little labor as possible. Development of abilities requires resources; markets will train abilities only to the extent that training is productively efficient. Deskilling labor is often more efficient.

Whenever workers are unequal, markets reward producers who take advantage of that inequality to make production more efficient. If workers are in oversupply, producers will reduce wages to the lowest at which they can obtain workers. For example, low-wage black workers in Mississippi delta catfish processors were replaced with even lower-wage undocumented workers; producers then forced black workers to accept pay levels at the same rate as the undocumented workers.[2] Since inequalities enhance productive efficiency by lowering wages, markets tend to create "relative surplus population;" one-third of the world's urban population lives in slums.[3] These "surplus" workers, desperate for work, depress wages. Markets will not create conditions where positions and workers are equal.

Moreover, according to the socialization principle, people are socialized for available labor. Socialization for positions is productively efficient. It is wasteful to train people for labor that they will not perform. Therefore, productive efficiency will tend both to deskill labor and to train workers minimally, only as is necessary for deskilled positions.

From the point of view of market morality egalitarianism is unjust

However, these arguments that markets will not create jobs that are equally good ignore Rawlsian justice, particularly equality of opportunity (a principle Rawls stresses when arguing that jobs would be equally attractive). So suppose that there is the fullest equal opportunity and that all children are encouraged to develop complex abilities. And, *reversing the socialization principle*, suppose that positions must allow contribution of complex and routine abilities so that the positions will correspond to what children have been socialized to do. To rebut the arguments about efficiency we must imagine that producers and providers of services in the just society, where children are encouraged to develop complex abilities and where positions are organized to allow all to contribute such abilities, are not competing with less just and more efficient producers and providers. Now haven't we imagined that a market society could be just?

We have imagined a just market society, but it is unlikely to exist; if it existed, it would not be stable. Markets are normatively individualist. Their norms exaggerate the separateness of persons and underestimate our interconnectedness.

---

[2]   *Chicago Tribune*, 6/11/06; on how businessmen in price-sensitive markets make wage decisions, see also Shipler 2004: 80–9.

[3]   Estimate by Anna Tibaijuka, executive director of UN Habitat; see <http://news.bbc.co.uk/1/hi/world/5078654.stm>. On depeasantization and migration to cities, see McMichael 1996: 95, 179–80; also Mingione and Pugliese 1994: 52–68. The term "relative surplus population" is from Marx 1867: ch. 25. See Gomberg 2002 for more evidence and analysis.

The moral powers are at war because market norms are at war with norms of egalitarian justice.

Markets are normatively individualist; a central norm is that each makes her own way economically by her own efforts. (Market *socialism* does not abolish this norm but shifts the locus of responsibility from the individual to the worker-run firm.) She either starts her own business or seeks advancement in existing social structures through education or other training or through grit. Market norms emphasize that we are responsible for ourselves and free to succeed or fail by our own efforts. Injustices, by market norms, are primarily dishonesty in contractual dealings: fraud, deceit, failure to live up to agreements. We succeed by a combination of grit, hard work, skill, talent, and luck; regardless of the balance of these, people deserve what they achieve. Markets emphasize a number of freedoms: to own property, to transfer it to others according to terms mutually agreeable, freedom of occupation and freedom of travel. These freedoms assume one has the cash to do these things. We are free to own property but have no right to it without acquiring it legally. Even freedom of expression is often a property right: the owners of the means of disseminating culture can use those means as they see fit. (It protects the right of the owners of the *New York Times* to publish what they wish in the paper, not the right of the *Times'* employees to publish what they wish.) Market norms are centrally about rights and freedoms of individuals. They emphasize the individualist ethic that it is up to you what you make of your life.

Individualist values are *necessarily* implied in market societies. Market-based social relations presuppose and reinforce individual economic incentive; pursuit of economic self-interest is thereby accepted as good. If the institutions are accepted, then success in those institutions is good. Rewards fairly earned are deserved. When we endorse markets, we endorse the values entailed by market relations.

To understand better why the connection between values and market social relations is a necessary one, recall the rationalization principle. The rationalization principle states that in any stable society we accustom ourselves to the social practices of daily life and part of how we accustom ourselves is that we rationalize that things are as they should be. (This reduces psychological dissonance arising from the thought that social arrangements are wrong but that we are unable to change them.) We associate virtue with market success. Those who have disproportionate wealth and power are deserving and, because wealth and power are goods, they are superior (in a way relevant to having wealth and power). Prestige and the sanction of morality attach to economic success. So markets *necessarily* spawn individualist values as fundamental morality.

"But, Paul, if this is so, why are European societies so much less individualist than the United States? You seem to be assuming that American individualism is a universal value in market societies." Because of the influence of large working-class socialist and communist parties, there has been less individualism in Europe. Such parties defeat the effect of the rationalization principle by making capitalism less stable. I estimate that as those parties renounce their revolutionary vision, individualist values will become stronger in Europe as well.

Egalitarian conceptions of justice arise from awareness of how our fates are connected. Market norms and values wrongly see us as more separate than we are. We believe that we have achieved our positions by our own efforts. (More advantaged children are, in Annette Lareau's phrase, "born on third base but believe they hit a triple" [2003: 13].) In contrast, egalitarian arguments based on the socialization principle *connect* the academic success of New Trier High School students (in greater Chicago's affluent North Shore area – 99 percent graduation rate; of graduates, 98 percent enrolled in college, 95 percent in four-year colleges) to the 54 percent graduation rate for Chicago public high school students (39 percent for black males, 51 percent for hispanic males) as preparations for different positions in the labor force.[4] The successes of New Trier students *limit* opportunities for Chicago public school students. Other egalitarian arguments (such as those of chapter 8) connect our concern for our own interests to the jealousies we feel for the successes of others; they connect group identities and group rivalries to the social psychology of racism. Seeing these problems, egalitarians propose an *alternative social organization* where all can have good lives.

For folks whose morality is grounded in market relations, egalitarianism is *unjust*. Suppose a law required all jobs to combine complex with routine labor; a businessman would regard the law as unjust infringement on his freedom to run his own business. Robert Nozick's *Anarchy, State, and Utopia* has wide appeal not because its arguments are clever (they are clever enough) but because it harmonizes with what people intuitively believe about justice. Those beliefs come from the morality of markets. Rawls in particular and liberal egalitarianism in general seek to combine egalitarian justice and markets. This union will not work. We have to choose: egalitarian justice or markets, not both.

This is not a "knock-down" argument that it is impossible in a market economy to have all jobs combine routine and complex labor. Epidemiologist Michael Marmot has written about the effect that stress and lack of control of one's life can have on health and longevity; he has recommendations about how to improve health, particularly for the socially disadvantaged:

> What you and I want for ourselves we should want for everyone in society: work that is characterized by a degree of control over the way we manage the job. . . . We also want appropriate rewards for the efforts we expend – be those rewards money, self-esteem, or status in the eyes of the world. . . . We also want not to feel insecure about losing the job. The old style of managing by fear should be long gone. It is bad for employees and, therefore, probably bad for business.

---

[4] On New Trier High see <www.newtrier.k12.il.us/information/pub/ntprofile05_06.pdf> and <www.newtrier.k12.il.us/information/pub/2005reportcard.pdf>. On Chicago public schools, see <www.issuelab.com/downloads/8341p75mini.pdf>.

Marmot favors jobs where workers have control in the workplace. He continues: "[T]here should be no trade-off between a healthy workplace and a wealthy one. It is likely that paying attention to the working conditions that lead to better health will lead to more productivity. Everyone stands to benefit. It is a virtuous circle" (2004: 252–3, 256).

If Marmot is right, then markets can lead to jobs that combine routine and complex labor, give workers more control over their jobs, and train children accordingly. I have argued that this combination will not occur; the push of markets is toward efficiencies that give workers less control and deskill labor. (Some of this tendency can be masked by the international organization of labor, where many deskilled jobs are in less wealthy countries.) Most important, markets reinforce individualist values incompatible with egalitarian justice.

Markets without material incentives?

In his provocative, original, and subtle *Equality, Moral Incentives, and the Market* (1981), Joseph Carens develops a utopian vision combining equality with market-based incentives. His proposal cuts the tie between incentives to contribute and distribution. Distribution for consumption would be equal or according to need. Incentives to contribute are market-based and moral. Each person has a moral duty to contribute as much as possible, as measured by her pre-tax income (a tax system would insure that after-tax income was equal or was adjusted to consumption needs). Social esteem would depend on whether contribution, as measured by pre-tax income, was maximal. However, esteem would not be strictly based on the amount one earned, but on that amount as a percentage of earning potential. So an unskilled worker could earn as much (or more) social esteem as an architect or industrial magnate provided his pre-tax earnings were as high (or higher) a percentage of his earning potential as an unskilled worker.

Carens is aware that if he did not make social approval (what I have called "social esteem") relative to earning power, his proposal would be open to the following objection. If social approval is determined by pre-tax earnings and is the central motivation for market contributions, then social approval has become a pure positional good for which we compete. Such a system where social esteem (for contributions) is in limited supply and is measured by pre-tax income earned threatens very nasty consequences for the social and self-esteem of low earners. My own proposal is to share labor, thus making the esteem earned by the contribution of complex abilities of unlimited supply. Carens's proposal would also make it of unlimited supply but only by comparing actual with potential earnings.

This idea seems dubious for the following reasons. First, there is a natural basis for esteeming contributions of complex skills and knowledge, as I argued in chapter 6; complex abilities naturally draw our admiration. This is not a matter of social convention and cannot be abrogated by a social norm (though, as I argue in the next chapter, it can be strengthened by one). The esteem for a good data-entry clerk will not match that for a mediocre architect; no norm can change this fact.[5] Satisfactions from contributing complex abilities would be available only to some. Feelings of a lack of self-worth derived from doing labor that is too routine would persist (recall the auto workers interviewed by Kornhauser, quoted in chapter 6). It is not enough to be esteemed for doing what you do well if what you do is too easy.

Second, if we base esteem on comparing earnings with earnings potential, we demean people with compliments comparable to, "That's good – for a girl." We say to people that they are contributing a lot in comparison to their capabilities, but it demeans us to be told that we are not capable of much (though, unfortunately, many of us believe that about ourselves). Third, people could have low earning potential either because they lack potential to train and develop complex abilities or because they have (or had) the potential but did not develop it. If we say the first, the previous criticism applies, but if we say the second, we are criticizing people morally for failing to develop their potential. Either way, making social approval relative to earnings potential threatens to demean people for being deficient in either potential or virtue.

Carens embraces markets and their efficiencies, but among these is the division between complex and routine labor. This division gives bargaining advantages to capitalists as they deskill labor, create surplus populations, and lower wages. In his last chapter, Carens allows that, through legislation, the government may set other goals and direct market activity in particular directions that are deemed for the general good. Nevertheless, the division between routine and complex labor is central to productive efficiency. Carens's proposal is focused on preserving that efficiency. He addresses neither mind-numbing labor nor socialization of children for lives of such labor.

Carens still works within the limits of the distributive paradigm. He breaks the connection between contribution and distribution by proposing moral incentives for contribution. Still, by retaining markets and grounding moral incentives in market success, he elevates as the primary economic good the production of things and services. For Carens, labor serves the production of things. Instead, the production of things should serve a life of contribution. We need a conception of contributive justice.

---

[5] Carens allows that prestige would be distributed as in capitalist societies: some positions would carry prestige and others contempt. See Carens 1981: 239, note 98.

Chapter 13

Contributive Justice

> In place of the old bourgeois society, with its classes and class antagonisms, we shall have an association in which the free development of each is the condition for the free development of all.
>
> Karl Marx and Friedrich Engels

Preamble to contributive justice

Black folks in the United States are subject to social contempt. Many black children attend largely segregated schools, often with few educational opportunities.[1] Many adults work for low wages in health care, city or state government, factories, and stores. Many (not all) racist harms are *positional*; in a society where someone has to be on the bottom, black people are disproportionately there. This is widely known to be true. If we accept this social order, we blame black people, not the society.

What harms black people harms most others – though often not as much. Above the level of wealth that relieves destitution, when a *society* becomes wealthier, its members do not become happier (Hirsch 1976; Layard 2005). Individuals seek more money partly to raise their position, but when everyone has more money, just as many are positionally inferior. Similarly, we seek material goods partly for positional reasons – a better handling car, a house with another bathroom, a home theater system. We acquire them, then make new status comparisons and need something else. We buy and buy, and we don't get happier (Schor 1998). Fred Hirsch (1976) compares it to standing on tiptoes in a crowd to see better: when everyone stands on tiptoes, no one sees better. People seek more formal schooling in order to advance, but because many others do the same and the employment hierarchy remains, there are just as many positional "losers."

Because we buy stuff to enhance relative position, there is an "excessive creation and absorption of commodities" in pursuit of status (Hirsch 1976: 84).[2]

---

[1] More than a third (36.5 percent) of black students attend schools that are at least 90 percent minority, schools where 87.7 percent of the students are poor; 70 percent attend schools at least 50 percent minority (Orfield 2001: 35–8).

[2] Slade (2006) details the history of how corporate leaders and advertisers used status competition to create a culture of obsolescence; the culture leads to huge waste.

Collectively, this pursuit is in vain. It creates trash and other pollution that despoil the earth and poison us (Rogers 2005; Grossman 2006).

Tim Kasser (2002) shows that materialistic values encouraged by market economies – wealth, fame, possessions – are associated with depression, anxiety, lack of autonomy, and low self-esteem and well-being. (People who value relationships and helpfulness do better psychologically.) Materialistic values and consumerism are reinforced by jobs that allow little creativity, control, or autonomy. So we seek these at the mall. But spending money doesn't compensate for work we hate. When work uses our abilities and is useful to others, we naturally value ourselves. When work is mindless and seems pointless, we may seek self-esteem positionally, through consumerism and competitive connoisseurship, but the effort doesn't work very well.

The moneyist conception of the good invites positional comparison; if it is good to have money, it is better to have more. But money is of limited supply and positional, a reflection of what we have made of our lives. Poor people are subject to contempt.

Distributive conceptions of justice are part of the problem; *distributive* justice cannot erase the pain of positional comparisons or the need to show that we are as good or better than others. Distributive justice emphasizes what we have rather than what we do. As long as what is important to us is what we own and have the power to acquire, we will never find a solution to racism or to endless and fruitless competition for status.

To have a society without racism or contempt for the poor, we must reconceive what makes life good. Contribution has value *non-positionally*; it makes our lives and the lives of others go better. When we share labor, opportunities to contribute and earn esteem for contributions are unlimited. The most important goods are not positional. This could be a world without racism.

In this chapter I sketch a conception of contributive justice.

Justice is about contribution

Most people think social justice is about the benefits folks receive: who gets what. Suppose that, reversing the relative importance of contribution versus distribution, we conceive justice as primarily about what we give to society.

By "contribution," I mean labor that sustains a social group. Two views of social labor have dominated modern thought. The better known – found in Adam Smith and often assumed in neoclassical economic thought which has influenced philosophy (recently as rational choice theory) – views social labor as a burden. Smith argues that value cannot be measured by a commodity because it "is itself continually varying in its own value." Labor, by contrast, can be a measure of value, for "equal quantities of labour" are always of "equal value to the labourer" because "he must always lay down the same portion of his ease, his liberty, and his happiness" (Smith 1776, vol. 1, ch. V: 37). For Smith, labor is a negative thing, a loss of liberty. Others often tacitly assume the same (see Gomberg 1989 for examples).

In the *Grundrisse* Karl Marx alludes to the above passage from Smith and writes that Smith conceives of labor as a curse: " 'Rest' appears to him to be the fitting state of things, and identical with 'liberty' and 'happiness'." In laboring we must overcome obstacles, but "the overcoming of such obstacles may itself constitute an exercise in liberty, and . . . these external purposes lose their character of mere natural necessities and are established as purposes which the individual himself fixes. The result is the self-realization and objectification of the subject, therefore real freedom, whose activity is precisely labour" (Marx 1858: 368).

Distributive conceptions of justice may tacitly assume that labor is a burden. John Rawls writes:

> [A]lthough a society is a cooperative venture for mutual advantage, it is typ-ically marked by a conflict as well as by an identity of interests. There is an identity of interests since social cooperation makes possible a better life for all than any would have if each were to live solely by his own efforts. There is a conflict of interests since persons are not indifferent as to how the greater benefits produced by their collaboration are distributed, for in order to pursue their ends, they each prefer a larger to a lesser share. A set of principles is required for choosing among various social arrangements which determine this division of advantages and for underwriting an agreement on the proper distributive shares. These principles are the principles of social justice: they provide a way of assigning rights and duties in the basic institutions of society and they define the appropriate distribution of the benefits and burdens of social cooperation. (1999: 4)

Rawls here describes the role of a theory of justice. That description is wrong. The second sentence asserts that "social cooperation makes possible a better life for all than any would have if each were to live solely by his own efforts." What Rawls has in mind is that, because of cooperation, each of us will obtain a "distributive share" of the benefits of cooperation "in order to pursue [our] ends;" that share will include more goods than any would obtain "if each were to live solely by his own efforts." The benefits of cooperation are what you get. The primacy of distribution is assumed.

Rawls here assumes that the "greater benefits" and "our ends" are *not ident-ical with* the acts whereby we produce the means of life, implicitly assum-ing with Smith that labor is a burden not a benefit. At other moments Rawls takes a view closer to Marx's. Explaining why, minimally, equal oppor-tunity requires that careers be open to talents, Rawls writes that "a skillful and devoted exercise of social duties" leads to a "realization of self" which is "one of the main forms of the human good" (p. 73). Later, explaining the idea of a social union, Rawls writes that people "value their common institutions and activities as good in themselves. We need one another as partners in ways of life that are engaged in for their own sake, and the successes and enjoyments of others are necessary for and complementary to our own good" (p. 458). Rawls has social labor – as well as other activities – in mind, for he writes, "The division of labor is overcome . . . by willing and meaningful work within a just social union of social unions in which all can freely participate as they so incline" (p. 464).[3] Marx could embrace this vision.

Marx asserted that labor itself can be, in the right social conditions, "a vital need" (1891: 347). Egalitarian forager societies give evidence that when people work for self and community under conditions of equality, labor is not regarded as oppressive, as a mere means for pursuing "our conception of the good" in our leisure time (Lee 1979).

There are two plausible ways of conceiving what justice is about, either primarily about what we get or primarily about duties and opportunities to contribute. There is no simple argument for the primacy of either. One might argue that without contribution there is nothing to distribute. But it is equally true that if we do not have the food, shelter, clothing, and security we need, we cannot contribute. And one might argue that to develop a theory of justice based on the view that contribution to a social group is an important human good is to assume a particular view of the good life, an inappropriate assumption for a political conception of justice. But, one can equally argue, if justice is about how the cooperative surplus is distributed, then the good life is the acquisition and possession of wealth and the things that wealth can buy; this is just as much a parochial conception of the primary good as conceiving the primary good as self-chosen labor. Or, suppose we argue that contribution is good because it is contribution to *others* and increases what they get; in that case, distribution is primary. On the other hand, we can argue that contributing to others is a good primarily because it enables *them* to contribute; in that case, contribution is still primary. To repeat, there is no simple argument for the primacy of either conception of what justice is about.

However, we can argue that contribution is primary by articulating an ethical ideal of humanity as active, creative, and contributive, as we did in chapter 6. We are a socially intelligent species; our intelligence develops through mastery of language. It is a good for us to contribute to others, and because we are capable of and enjoy mastery of complexity and because such mastery naturally inspires esteem, it is particularly a good for us to contribute complex mastery. Contribution to a social group with which we identify is central to our well-being.

This ethical ideal of humans as social contributors grounds a conception of justice. On the view developed in this chapter, justice is about contribution, and contribution is motivated by the sense of justice. Opportunities to contribute

---

[3] Rawls later came to reject passages such as these as inappropriate to a theory of justice because they represent a particular conception of the good. See Rawls 1993.

should be equal and duties to contribute universal. Distribution of material needs to individuals should advance opportunities and duties to contribute. This conception of contributive justice is fully supportable.

A conception of contributive justice

Four norms – duties and equal opportunity to contribute labor, and duties and equal opportunity to participate in social decisions – are the core of contributive justice.

A duty to contribute

Contribution is both a necessity and a good. As a necessity, contribution is a duty. As a good, it is an opportunity: it is both. Let us start with norms of contributive duties.

Why do we work? We do it in order to pay our bills. This idea is not rejected by liberal egalitarianism. But the sense of justice can and should motivate our working each day. We should work because we seek to live on just terms of cooperation. Working is doing our part in a cooperative venture from which we all benefit. The benefits are both the contributions we make and what we receive. The sense of justice applies in the first instance to what we contribute to the social group in which our lives are embedded. The social group cannot continue and provide for its members unless they contribute labor. This is the first duty of contributive justice. Instead of working for self, we work out of a sense of what just relations with others require. Contribution is cut free from individual material reward and the implied coercion – work or live in poverty – which may move us. While the principle still holds that without labor contribution there will be no food, shelter, or any other goods, it applies to us collectively, not individually. It is part of the reason why we each have a duty to contribute.[4]

The duty to contribute labor implies related duties. Since contribution requires that we have abilities to contribute, we have a responsibility to develop our abilities so that these may be contributed. Since all have a duty to contribute, we should encourage and aid others in developing their abilities so that these too may be contributed.

Equal opportunity to contribute

Contribution to a social group is an important good. We value ourselves and are valued by others for our contributions. So no society treats its members

[4] Contribution from "moral incentives" was widely discussed in the 1960s, particularly in response to ideas popularized in the Cultural Revolution in China. Joseph Carens (1981) develops a theory of contribution from moral incentives but says his ideas were inspired by Cuban society. I am most indebted to the Progressive Labor Party's (1982) defense of contribution from political incentives.

as equals unless it provides equal opportunity to contribute. Equal opportunity must be unlimited opportunity: when opportunity is for goods of limited supply, it will be competitive; children will be socialized for different social positions, and opportunity will not be equal. These opportunities to develop and contribute complex abilities can be made unlimited by sharing labor. If all routine labor needed to produce and maintain food, housing, clothing, transportation, and public spaces is shared by all who are able, then no one's life is consumed with routine labor. Each has time and opportunity (as equal as possible) to develop more complex abilities in the sciences, arts, literature, or practical arts such as landscape design. To create this opportunity, we must share routine labor. We also have a duty of justice to share the contribution of complex mastery with others who have similar mastery. And we have a duty of justice to teach others in order to create opportunity for them.

Duties and opportunities for participation in social decisions

There are two overlapping divisions of labor, between plan and execution and between routine and complex. I have focused on the second division because overcoming the division between plan and execution raises difficult issues of democratic theory, workplace democracy, and non-market decision-making. Still, we should note that there should be both duties and opportunities to contribute to decisions about the organization of society and about production in particular. Depending on how we understand democratic decision-making, we may conceive these duties differently. Many believe that there is a duty to vote. But suppose we think of democracy as addressing the *epistemic* problem of discovering how to advance the good of all simultaneously. Democratic decision-making then requires extensive and widespread discussion in order to obtain information, evaluate proposals, and gauge what people are willing to do. We might not believe that the extensive time required for full discussion would be as rigorously obligatory as contribution of labor to produce necessities. Perhaps not all would be expected to devote a lot of time to these discussions. In contrast, the *opportunity* to participate in collective discussion should be universal. So too should the encouragement of participation and the duty to make *some* contribution to collective decisions – the wider the discussion, the greater the probability that we will come to the best possible decision.

Together, these four norms – duties and equal opportunity to contribute labor and duties and equal opportunity to participate in social decisions – sketch a conception of contributive justice. This conception raises questions about contribution and distribution.

Contribution and distribution of social esteem

We naturally admire and esteem those who contribute to groups and projects with which we identify, and extraordinary contributions naturally inspire greater esteem. In a society governed by a conception of contributive justice, that natural connection between contribution and esteem becomes normative and necessary. Suppose we share a norm of contributive justice requiring us to contribute to the common needs and projects of our society. Then there is a necessary connection between contribution and social esteem. Shared norms are the grounds on which we esteem conduct: when we believe that people should contribute, we esteem those who contribute and disesteem those who take without contributing. Therefore, those known to contribute will receive social esteem.

In a society governed by contributive justice, contribution and distribution of esteem are necessarily connected. Reward for contribution – social esteem – is necessary and moral. It is necessary because in any society with a shared norm that each should contribute, the norm is enforced by according esteem to those known to contribute. The connection between contribution and the distribution of social esteem is moral because it comes from the shared conception of contributive justice.

Contribution and distribution: against individual material rewards

Contribution from a sense of justice is incompatible with individual material reward – income, wealth, or other material goods – being contingent on individual contribution. We need food, clothing, shelter, security, and other good things. Suppose that whether someone receives essential needs is contingent on her contribution of labor. If she does not contribute, she does not eat, nor does she receive health care, shelter, transportation, or decent clothing. The threat of being deprived of needs generates strong contributive motives focused narrowly on personal or family well-being. These motives are likely to overwhelm motives of justice. The narrow focus created by individual material reward for contribution tends to defeat a broader focus of working from a sense of our obligation to the social group. Thus individual material reward for contribution undermines the norm of contributing as a duty of justice.

Moreover, if reward is contingent on contribution, greater contribution will earn greater reward. We will compete for greater material rewards, with the winners able to give their children more advantages. This leads to unequal opportunity as each generation competes for material rewards at least in part to advantage their children in the next round of the competition. Thus individual material reward would undermine equal opportunity. So material needs should be met independently of individual contribution.

Distribution of material needs should serve contribution

Distribution should serve contributive justice. Everyone has a duty to contribute; everyone should have an opportunity to contribute. What norm of distribution would strengthen these norms of contribution? If material needs are unmet, we cannot fulfill our duty to contribute, nor can we realize an opportunity to contribute. So meeting material needs serves the norms of having both duties and opportunities to contribute, making it possible for each to contribute over the course of a lifetime.

The norm of receiving what we need because we need it also enhances contribution from the sense of justice. Now we return to the argument for the first principle: that we owe contribution as a duty of justice since our society has provided us with what we need and since the provision of our needs depends on the contribution of labor. Therefore, normatively, we can reasonably expect that each should contribute. So a norm of distributing the necessities – food, clothing, shelter, transportation, health care – to each makes sense because it provides each with the opportunity to contribute and it should strengthen the motive to contribute as a duty of justice.

Obviously this proposal has implications for privacy and other matters. If now we get what we want because we have the resources to obtain it (and those without resources or social entitlements often get nothing, regardless of need), we can satisfy wants and needs without consulting or justifying our needs to others. If distribution is to be based on need, we would sometimes have to discuss collectively how to allocate what we have to those who may be in need. This discussion could change matters which are now private (for the more affluent) into public issues. This is, it seems to me, an inevitable consequence of finding norms of social justice which are more directly and naturally connected to our dependence on one another for creating the means of life.

These four norms and three ideas outlined above about contribution and distribution form the basis of a conception of contributive justice. They begin to explain why, if we say that people should contribute from a sense of justice and not from self-interest, norms of distribution would derive from norms of contribution. The way things are distributed should strengthen contributive duties and opportunities.

Can contribution be normatively motivated?

Generally, philosophers assume that production and distribution are organized primarily through prices of commodities and labor. Rawls's *A Theory of Justice* contains a brief discussion of socially motivated contribution. He writes: "Some socialists have objected to all market institutions as inherently degrading, and they have hoped to set up an economy in which men are moved largely by social and altruistic concerns." To this he objects that a bureaucracy "would be bound to develop" to control economic activity and that its control would likely be no more just than control by prices. He praises prices as means of coordination and as not implying "a lack of reasonable human autonomy," but otherwise says nothing against non-market motivations except the following: "The theory of justice assumes a definite limit on the strength of social and altruistic motivation. It supposes that individuals and groups put forward competing claims, and while they are willing to act justly, they are not prepared to abandon their interests" (1999: 248). With these words Rawls rejects socially motivated contribution.

In chapter 12, I argued that when we accept markets, we embrace norms incompatible with egalitarian justice. If that argument is correct, Rawls's dismissal of socially motivated contribution is too perfunctory. Altruistic and social concerns are very different. The issue here is not altruism but finding terms of social cooperation acceptable to all. If cooperation requires that we have a sense of justice, why cannot this sense motivate contribution?

When we internalize norms of justice, those norms become part of our sense of self – I think of myself as one who fulfills my responsibility to my society. Hence a sense of justice can become part of my normative self-interest. I must contribute and cannot shirk these responsibilities without damaging my own sense of self.

These ideas are present in motives we already recognize. The psychic suffering which often accompanies prolonged unemployment is simultaneously moral and social. While we suffer diminished social dignity as a result of prolonged unemployment, the loss of dignity is grounded in a moral belief that each has a responsibility to contribute. Because the unemployed typically share that belief, the pain they experience is intensified. They feel they should be contributing (and be rewarded for it in the usual ways – one can also lose dignity if one's labor is regarded as having little or no social value, in market economies as measured by pay), but are unable to do so.

It is worth elaborating on how considerations of justice – it is part of our sense of justice that we should be contributing members of society – are simultaneously social, moral, and part of our self-interest. (These observations apply to other norms, but are less commonly recognized about norms of justice.) There is a tendency to contrast self-interest with morality. The Hobbesian tradition assumes that self-interest can be identified independently of the ways that norms contribute to our conception of ourselves and hence to the interests of the normatively constructed self (Freeman 1990; Gomberg 1997). The idea is very influential in economics and is assumed in rational choice approaches. Moreover, the separation of the normative from self-interest has become part of a certain common sense. But it is surely wrong. When we subtract our normative conception of who we are from our notion of self-interest, there is little left. There is something; survival, health, and physical comfort are strongly non-normative. Still, most of what we see as our self-interest, whether fulfilling responsibilities as spouses, parents, friends, teachers, or neighbors or, more broadly, sustaining dignity as contributors to society, is normative. Sometimes, the *internalization* of that normativity is obscured because it also has a social component: that is, while we lose dignity and status in the eyes of others when we are unemployed, this diminishment is the result of a shared norm, one that we too accept. There is internal, as well as external, shame.

Normativity – though not always conceptions of justice – is everywhere. Good neighbors keep their property clean and neat. Teachers encourage their students; they don't humiliate them. Sometimes the norms are not moral in that they don't concern responsibilities to people. We may seek a job with added prestige because we think it fitting that we be recognized. Consumer purchases may be motivated by their fulfillment of normative expectations: some cars or homes are *appropriate*, others not; minimally, some consumer goods are necessary to participate with dignity in community life. These are normative components of self-interest even when they do not concern justice or even moral responsibilities.

In these last few paragraphs I have rejected Rawls's assumption of "a definite limit on the strength of social and altruistic motivation." While altruistic motivation has limited strength, social motivation is powerful. People will sacrifice their lives and much else for normative reasons. I shall argue that norms of contribution are supportable; specifically, all can recognize that they form a reasonable basis for cooperative equality. If that argument is correct, then a society based on norms of contributive justice is possible. In that society, each would expect each of us (including herself) to contribute as she can. Our reasons to contribute would be more than adequate to motivate us.

Contributive justice and coercion

There are two ways that contributive justice is different from the familiar distributive justice of liberal egalitarianism. In chapter 4 and earlier in this chapter, I said that activity and contribution are the most important goods, not pleasures passively received. In chapter 11, I showed how the capabilities approach could be developed in a way consonant with contributive justice: extend capabilities to include the opportunity to contribute complex abilities. Nevertheless, that approach is still liberal in a way that contributive justice is not. At the center of contributive justice are *duties* of justice. This idea is anti-liberal. For liberals, justice is about freedoms and what we get. And the subject of justice is *institutions*, particularly what Rawls calls the basic structure, which should insure a just distribution. Contributive justice is about each of us and our reasons for contributing. Because, as chapter 12 argued, markets will not allow equal opportunity, we need norms of contributive duty.

Considered as something we desire, contribution is an opportunity. Considered as labor that we sometimes prefer to avoid, contribution is a duty. Even the contribution of routine labor is both. While we may think of it as a duty, the unemployed lack the opportunity to contribute labor in return for a wage and the dignity that wages give. Similarly, contribution of complex labor is a duty, even when it allows us to exercise complex mastery. This is particularly clear when we must choose how to develop complex abilities, whether to study astronomy or public health. In some circumstances there may be a special need and therefore a duty to study public health. A theory of contributive justice must defend both opportunities and duties to contribute by articulating supportable norms.

A conception of justice is put forward as a subject of possible *agreement* within a group. This is common terminology. But the agreement we need is not passive. To be effective without centralized coercion, contributive norms require *active support in the course of daily life*. Contributive justice is not a liberal theory – it is incompatible with freedom of market exchange. This may lead to the thought that contributive justice depends on centralized coercion. Rawls writes, "the use of the market system does not imply a lack of a reasonable human autonomy," suggesting that non-market alternatives are incompatible with autonomy (1999: 248). When Sen imagines a non-market economy, he imagines "a fully centralized system with all the decisions . . . regarding production and allocation being made by a dictator" (1999: 27). If duties of contributive justice could be enforced only by centralized coercion, this would show that we would not freely agree with them. So we must argue that contributive norms are supportable.

Sometimes philosophers write as if they were addressing God. What I mean is, they write as if their audience were someone all-powerful who could impose a solution to problems. They construct ideals often without addressing the question why ordinary people in the course of their daily lives would support those ideals.

There are two ways that proposals can be utopian; one is unobjectionable, the other not. My proposal to share routine and complex labor and to base contribution on the sense of justice rather than material reward is utopian in the sense that the proposed norms are distant from current ones. It is hard to imagine the details of their implementation and to see how to make the transition to a society with these norms. "Utopianism" of this sort is unobjectionable. The problems are inevitable when a proposal is a radical departure from current practice. Proposals that are utopian in this sense serve a useful function of stimulating criticism and reply; if the dialog leads to proposals that inspire increasing agreement, this process could affect social change, though we may not know what political processes would bring it about.

It may seem that my norms of contributive justice are too sketchy, but sketchiness is inevitable. A blueprint is inappropriate when we do not yet have enough experience to know how best to share labor. The problem is that not all children are encouraged to develop and contribute their talents. To solve that problem we need to start a discussion. If others respond, criticize, and think of better ways of creating a society where all children's abilities are fully developed, then I will have achieved what I wish.[5]

There is a more objectionable utopianism. One can imagine a market economy hedged in with safeguards for the disadvantaged and with redistributive norms that give every possible opportunity to those who fare poorly in market exchanges and especially to their children. Yet the proposals may be utopian in the sense that the egalitarian norms run counter to the ordinary workings of the market. If so, then the sense of justice that inevitably arises with market norms will be in conflict with the egalitarian imperative that the disadvantaged

---

[5]   *Non*-utopianism can be objectionable too. If we only think about proposals that we can implement now under current conditions, we are accepting too much pervasive injustice. We are not considering very different ways of living.

have every opportunity to improve their situation – as I argued in chapter 12. Moreover, markets entrench the power of elites with anti-egalitarian interests. Egalitarian norms will not make sense in everyday life, particularly if those with the greatest wealth (by the ordinary workings of the market) benefit from poverty and have disproportionate power. Or to imagine a "property-owning democracy" that is not capitalism is to imagine something that cannot exist.[6] This utopianism is objectionable not because it is far removed from current norms ("property-owning democracy" is much closer to them than contributive justice) but because it harbors contradictions that make its implementation impossible. That is what I meant when I wrote that philosophers write as if addressing God. Their proposals harbor internal conflicts that could be overcome by an all-powerful being, but they will not make sense to people in ordinary life given *other* norms that are left in place.

In chapters 4 and 9, I argued that stratified societies in general and "free markets" in particular require centralized coercion to establish property that is secure in the face of others' urgent needs. Here, and implicitly in chapter 12, I have argued, in essence, that egalitarian liberalism would require even more coercion to overcome the illogic of retaining markets and then enforcing equality.

What does it mean to say that norms of contributive justice are supportable? We must agree with the norms to the extent that we will *teach* them to the next generation and spontaneously *enforce* them because we agree that they form a reasonable basis for our shared life. Spontaneous enforcement consists primarily in according esteem based on conformity with norms. If we genuinely agree that it is wrong not to share opportunities for complex labor with others who are well qualified to do the same labor, then we will reinforce this norm through teaching, stories, gossip, and private and public criticism. If we agree with it, we will spontaneously disesteem any architect who refuses to train young architects and who tries to deprive others of the opportunity to design buildings or public spaces; we will make it known that we disapprove of this refusal to share complex labor. If we agree with the norm of labor-sharing, we will internalize that norm so that our own conformity with it becomes a ground of self-esteem; so any temptation to hoard opportunities can be more easily resisted because it would undermine our sense of our own moral decency. Our support for the norm should be robust in the face of reflection. That is, while we may learn the norm of labor-sharing as children, it should be the case that, on reflection, we can see the norm as a reasonable basis for cooperation.

When Sen and Rawls imagine a planned non-market economy, neither imagines it grounded in a shared conception of justice. Both seem skeptical that there

---

[6] "Property-owning democracy" is Rawls's term for a market society where concentrations of wealth and power are prevented through limits on bequest and inheritance; property is widely dispersed among society's members and great inequalities of wealth are prevented. See Rawls 1999: Preface and section 43; Krouse and McPherson 1988; and Rawls 2001: 135–40.

could be the reasonable agreement on norms of contribution and distribution that a conception of contributive justice would require. I admit that, given the distance between my proposal and current norms, I cannot offer a definitive defense of contributive justice. What I can do is sketch norms and argue that these norms would be widely supportable in daily life.

Contributive norms are supportable

Norms to provide the capability to meet the basic needs common to all of us – food, shelter, clothing, transportation, security, and health care among others – are supportable. We could justify these capabilities as Sen would: if we are to function in normal ways, we must have these goods. If there is to be equal freedom, it is reasonable that these basic needs be provided to all because they are needed.

I have given another justification. Distribution should advance contributive opportunities and duties. The norm of unconditionally distributing necessities gives each the opportunity to contribute and makes it possible for each to fulfill contributive duties.

Moreover, a norm of *entitlement* to basic needs strengthens a norm of contributing to society *from a sense of justice*. We each benefit from the production of needed things because we each receive from the common stock. Providing these goods for the common stock is a cooperative endeavor. So it makes sense that each of us, within the limits of what we can do, has a responsibility to contribute to their provision. Since we understand that the basic needs of each of us will be provided for unconditionally over our entire lives – whether we are ill, too young or too old, or otherwise incapable of contributing – and that providing these needs requires contribution of labor, it is natural for us to support a norm that we each contribute as we are able to the provision of needs. Even if we may not feel like working that day, we can see that, from a general point of view, the norm makes sense; we see reason to teach it and enforce it. We can incorporate it into our identities as a ground of esteem. Just as we would enforce it on others through informal sanctions of esteem, we would internalize it and "enforce" it on ourselves. Moreover, others would enforce it on us if we took without giving back. So contribution is justified as doing our part in return for being provided with what we need. In this way the provision of our needs justifies a norm of contribution. That norm is fully supportable; it would make sense in daily life.

There is a web of justice: a norm of entitlement to our needs presupposes contribution; a duty of contribution presupposes that needs have been met. Contribution is *primary* only in the sense that the ethical ideal of humanity as active, creative, and contributive distinguishes human beings. All organisms must have their needs met. Humans do this by providing for one another.

If we agree on a norm requiring us to contribute labor, then we will be esteemed for our contribution. Normative esteem attaches to people who conform to shared norms. First, we esteem ourselves for doing what is right. Second, others esteem us for the same reason. Routine labor is required by a conception of justice that creates equal and unlimited opportunity. Anyone who tried to avoid this labor would be criticized as someone who wished to shift this responsibility to others. Sharing routine labor, we also can be esteemed for contribution of complex mastery. Moreover, esteem for our contributions should be roughly in proportion to our contributions – assuming that we are aware of them. Contribution is rewarded by esteem, another reason it is in our interest to conform to these norms of contributive justice.

When I was explaining this to a class, my student Terrell Jackson remarked, "But on your view esteem will function just like money does in capitalist society." Terrell is very perceptive, but I reminded him of the differences as well as similarities. Yes, esteem should be roughly proportionate to contribution (though it is unclear that money is). But there are important differences from the ways money or material goods may reward individual contribution. Normative esteem, unlike money or material goods, is indefinitely expandable because as many can be esteemed for their contributions as contribute. So we need not compete for normative esteem, and my opportunities for esteem are unaffected by the esteem you earn for your contributions.

More important, because money and other material goods are in limited supply and often important for positional status, my material rewards diminish the opportunities of others to earn the same rewards. This effect tends to set individual material reward against considerations of justice, particularly equal opportunity. In contrast, the reward of normative esteem for contribution is grounded in a norm of justice. So the *individual reward binds us to norms of justice*. In a society bound by these shared norms of justice, normative self-interest strengthens justice and is strengthened by it. These norms of contributive justice make it possible for us to flourish together and to contribute to one another's flourishing.

A norm that all should contribute routine labor makes it possible for each to develop more complex abilities. Suppose routine and complex labor are shared. When one person takes advantage of her opportunities to develop and contribute a complex ability (to become an astronomer), her success does not diminish the opportunities available to another. Instead, by strengthening the community of astronomers, it helps to make others better astronomers. Sharing routine labor gives each of us a reason to wish to see others develop complex abilities. We will have buildings – including housing for everyone – that lift our spirits, a high level of nutrition and public health measures, beautiful urban landscapes and parks, captivating music, moving literature and plays, inventive and engaging crafts, searching philosophy, great science, and all the other imaginable things humans can create that make our lives good only to the extent that we develop everyone's abilities. So each has natural reasons to support a norm creating unlimited opportunity to develop and contribute complex abilities.

Some problems

I have argued that the norms sketched earlier in this chapter are supportable, that they would make sense as a shared basis for social cooperation. Still there are problems, particularly in applying the norm that each should have the opportunity to develop and contribute complex abilities. The development and exercise of complex abilities often require social resources. While mathematicians may need only a pencil, a piece of paper, and a wastebasket, astronomers and cosmologists need expensive equipment. Sculptors may need metal and metalworking equipment; gardeners, plants and trees; quilters, fabric and sewing machines. In addition to the resources needed to exercise abilities, there are resources needed to develop abilities. These resources are not likely to be of unlimited supply. So we must make choices. What norms should govern the provision of resources for the development and exercise of complex abilities?

The general answer I suggest is that resources should be provided to develop abilities that will be contributed to society. This implies a "condition" that resources should be provided *only* for abilities that are contributed. I accept that – at least for this historical epoch, when we live in the realm of necessity, that is, when the main task of humanity is to provide to all the conditions under which we can flourish. In fact the condition is crucial. It gives each of us a natural reason to support opportunities for others: those opportunities will be used to add to the good of the social group. Moreover, when the opportunity to acquire abilities is followed by "giving back" those abilities by teaching others, this tends to make opportunity expand; the use of resources to expand opportunity can lead to further expansion of opportunity. Suppose the devotion of resources to someone's opportunity will not be of some general benefit beyond the good of the person who has the opportunity. For example, suppose resources are devoted to developing computer games of ever-increasing difficulty, games that interest no one but their inventor. We do not have any very strong reason to support this use of resources. It is the "condition," that opportunities benefit others, that makes the norm supportable. But there are at least two problems: in what sense is it a condition? What counts as a contribution?

In what sense is it a condition? If Fred neither uses his quilts to keep warm nor shows his quilts to others, will we seize his fabric and sewing machine? If there was a shortage and someone lacked them who would use Fred's resources to make quilts for others, that situation would certainly create pressure to require Fred to share. That is, if we imagine these decisions being made on some basis besides "who has the money to pay for them," we have to imagine some norm for deciding who has access to resources. Certainly, willingness to "give back" to the social group is relevant. Here, as with the contribution of routine abilities, there would be a general expectation that people do their part. That does not have to imply nasty measures, but the expectations constitutive of norms have to be enforced.

The same issue arises with regard to the basic needs common to all of us (food, shelter, and the others); are these provided on the "condition" that we contribute routine labor to the social group? In the case of the contribution of routine labor, I would not imagine withholding food or essential goods. Just as giving individual material reward for contribution sets up an incentive structure contrary to considerations of equal opportunity and justice, so depriving people of material needs would have the same effect. In fact it is the same norm, stated negatively. If someone responded to the threat of being deprived of needs by contributing labor, she would be contributing for the wrong reason, for herself and her family, not because such contribution is owed as a matter of justice. A norm of withholding material needs from non-contributors would change the basis of social cooperation from considerations of justice to narrow self-interest independent of justice. Such a norm would weaken a social order based on shared norms of justice. Moreover, it would have negative impacts on any children of people who are not motivated to contribute, undermining the children's opportunity.

I would advocate withholding only esteem from those who would take from the collective without giving back in ways that they can. Withholding esteem from freeloaders is a natural response when we are engaged in projects for the common good and when "many hands make light work." Egalitarian peoples have enforced similar norms by withholding esteem, and such enforcement works in the sense that "freeloaders" are rare enough that they are not a problem. Besides, freeloaders do contribute: they serve as a social example of what *not* to be; they display to children and the rest of us the consequences (public disesteem, ridicule, gossip) of taking without at least trying to give back. This practice of withholding esteem from freeloaders strengthens the norm of creating a duty to contribute.

Withholding esteem, gossiping, and ridicule can be punishment just as cruel as withholding material rewards. So, one might wonder, "Why isn't the incentive structure of acting to secure esteem and to avoid social shame just as contrary to considerations of justice as acting to secure material reward?" I agree that if social sanctions for taking without giving back are experienced as purely *external*, then there is no great difference. But rewards and punishments that raise the question, "What is the right way for us to act?" – and all rewards and punishments grounded in social esteem are raising just this question – create the possibility for agreement on norms of esteem. Moreover, such decentralized social sanctions allow that one can argue that the criticism is not justified; this is what egalitarian peoples do. In many situations now social esteem is limited, and we compete for it. In a society of contributive justice, where labor is shared, opportunities for esteem are unlimited. So norms of contributive justice – even where enforcement by social esteem can turn nasty – honor each and allow each to flourish and win esteem simultaneously. Since all can agree on these norms, they can be internalized by all. Then they would not be experienced as external punishments but as the enforcement of norms that we can agree are fair terms of cooperation.

In the case of the resources required for exercising complex abilities, the situation is more complicated than it is for the basic material needs. By denying someone these resources, we would deprive him of those particular resources to exercise a complex ability. He could still make quilts by hand from scraps (the quilters of Gee's Bend showed that high art can be created even absent great resources). Or he could develop some other ability that might not require a lot of personal resources. Or he could conform to the norm that receipt of resources for complex abilities requires giving back: he could give his quilts to others or put them in a quilt show.

The main point, it seems to me, is this: when the social group as a whole devotes resources to each of us, there is an expectation that we participate in the common projects of society in a cooperative way. The expectation is reasonable and can be seen to be reasonable by all.

A further question raised by scarcity of resources is devotion of resources to projects in science or art (for example, opera) as opposed to activities that meet basic needs or appeal to many more people. Norms of meeting the basic needs of all are reasonable and can be seen to be reasonable by all. Because these norms allow us to flourish together and allow all to contribute, all can accept them as reasonable. Meeting basic needs has priority. As to the question of high culture versus mass culture, I would guess that with the sharing of routine labor, this contrast would be brought to a minimum. Not only would more people participate in the more complex, sophisticated intellectual and cultural activities, but as an inevitable consequence of wider participation, there would arise an even wider group that appreciate Mozart or Oscar Peterson or would be curious about what anisotropy in the cosmic microwave background radiation can tell us about the history of the universe. As a result, contributions in basic science become contributions to an ever wider group of people who can appreciate their significance.

The second problem with the proposal (that resources be provided for exercise of complex abilities on the condition that those abilities are contributed to the social group) was to clarify what counts as a contribution. We can contribute to smaller or broader groups; the greatest prestige is usually connected to positions which involve contributions to larger groups. I believe the reason for this is natural, as with the attachment of prestige to positions involving the exercise of complex abilities. We naturally esteem those who contribute to ourselves and to those to whom we are more attached. So there is a wider esteem for contributions to more people. More prestige will tend to be attached to positions that make these wider contributions.

If this argument is correct, this may explain the low prestige attached to parenting. Internally, no undertaking can seem more important, at least to some of us. Also, looked at objectively, we can see that parenting well is extremely important to the well-being of members of the next generation – it makes a difference how children are treated, whether they develop confidence in their talents and fearlessness in their thinking. Yet because we focus our efforts on this narrow task – just the raising of *our own* children – this responsibility does not carry much prestige, even if we are good parents.

She sings beautifully, movingly, a clear, sumptuous tone, with a wonderful sense of phrase and rhythm. But she sings only to her own children. Or she might sing for her (extended) family. Now broaden the group to which she contributes her ability: a church, a neighborhood cultural center, a regional opera, or a larger audience. Certainly we are imagining greater prestige attached to singing to these wider groups. Is this necessarily so? I think so, for the reason I gave. But the opportunity to sing to the widest audiences is necessarily of limited supply. How can that be shared by all who sing beautifully? I confess that my proposal to make positions of prestige of unlimited supply may here come up against a limit: in mass entertainment, these positions may be of limited supply.

We are investigating what counts as a contribution. This investigation raised the issue of breadth or narrowness of one's contribution. Narrow contributions are important, but they do not carry much prestige. So we found a residual inequality of prestige.

Focusing our efforts on narrow contributions can hinder opportunities to contribute to a larger group and gain greater prestige. Still, there is a compensation. Consider the case of being a good parent; the time and energy devoted to raising one's children has a big reward, at least in the ideal case: love and appreciation from one's children. This may be generally true of narrow contributions. They do not carry prestige, but they bring a more intense personal esteem that can be very important.

A theory of contributive justice must articulate norms of sharing labor which are naturally supportable because they lead to a better life for all of us. There are difficulties and unresolved issues, but norms of labor-sharing create the resources to provide both simple and complex capabilities to all equally. The norms make sense.

A fuller theory

The method of political philosophy, as I view it, is not to articulate and construct a conception of justice that expresses in rational form the ideals that are implicit in liberal democratic culture (the conception of method Rawls endorses in *Political Liberalism*). Rather, political philosophy engages in speculation – continuous with and informed by what we can know of human societies and their possibilities – about conditions under which human beings can flourish together. This conception of method marries consequentialist and contractualist ideas: our speculation is about the consequences of adopting various possible norms and institutional arrangements, but our norms and institutions should be ones on which all might agree. All can agree if they believe these social institutions advance the good of everyone in non-competitive ways; the good of one person advances the good of others rather than limiting the possibilities for others. This conception of political philosophy does not call for moral heroism in daily life: we do not ask people to put the good of others ahead of their own. Rather, we seek norms and institutions that allow all to flourish together.

Like Marx, I seek a form of social organization where "the free development of each is the condition for the free development of all" (Marx and Engels 1848: 87). The goal is to find a way to live together so that in seeking my good and the good of those I love I can at the same time promote the good of all. That is what I have tried to describe in the norms of labor-sharing and their consequences for human relationships. These norms would remove status rivalry – or rather bring it to a minimum – and give each a reason to promote opportunity for all. They would bring to a minimum the conflict between the point of view we take as individuals with particular desires, commitments, and attachments, and our impartial concern for the good of all. Seeking a shared conception of justice, we seek moral agreement on norms of contributing to the common good and of creating and sharing opportunities to contribute and other capabilities; these norms should be supportable by all.

Marxism, race, and opportunity

This book is about racism. It is about how to address the human costs of a society that must train some of its members for lives of disadvantage, lives of mind-numbing labor, social inferiority, and diminished social esteem. That much is necessary in societies that separate routine from complex labor and create mass unemployment. The diminished life expectancy, inferior housing and health care, ghettoization, low wages, and physical insecurity demonstrate how racism has worked itself out in the United States in the early twenty-first century – other periods in the 300-year history of racism in the United States would display different forms of racial inequality. Throughout this history, anti-black racism has displayed in an extreme form diminished life prospects that were experienced by many others who were not black. How can we address and eliminate this racism and unequal opportunity? How can we make opportunity equal for all?

As is well known, Marx believed that the organization of production is the key to explaining other aspects of social organization. Moreover, as a practical revolutionary he believed that workers must seize control of production and reorganize it for the common good of the working class; the seizure of production was the key to unlock other social changes in distribution and culture. The argument here is Marxist in spirit, if only in a general way. I have emphasized a particular aspect of the relations of production – the division between routine and more complex labor – as central to how education and much else is organized. The key to changing education and other elements which determine the opportunities open to each individual is to change the organization of production so that opportunity to perform complex labor is unlimited. Clearly, then, this way of looking at the relationship between education and production is Marxist in spirit.

In chapter 1, I pointed out how Rawls's view of the two moral powers and of the need for a theory of justice grew out of Rawls's conception of the historical context: problems of justice arise from European wars of religion, including the English Civil War of the seventeenth century. For my own egalitarianism of opportunity, the key historical context is different: in late seventeenth-century Virginia, who was to do the routine necessary labor of growing tobacco? Who toils? The answer I propose is that we all do it. By sharing labor, we create equal and unlimited opportunity.

Acknowledgments

The ideas for this book were sparked by two email conversations, one with the philosopher Elizabeth Anderson at the University of Michigan in 2000 and at about the same time with my sister Lynn McCarl, who has taught reading to young children. The conversation with Elizabeth Anderson was occasioned by her article "What Is the Point of Equality?" which I admired. Over a period of months we explored our disagreements, and much of chapter 7 attempts to answer objections she raised to my ideas. My sister Lynn experienced the joys and frustrations of teaching children who responded very differently to her instruction. Many arguments here are addressed to things she wrote.

In 2001 I wrote a draft of a paper on equal opportunity. John Deigh and David Miller kindly read it. Their criticisms led to many changes. A later draft was the topic of a small-group discussion of Chicago Political Theory, where Charles Mills and Stephen Engelmann gave criticism and encouragement; Isaac Balbus wrote a detailed critique that influenced much of the book. I rewrote the paper again, but that effort too was a failure. In the fall of 2002 I attended a conference at Bowling Green State University, "The Moral Legacy of Slavery," organized by Marina Oshana and David Copp. Presentations at that conference by Charles Mills, Lucious Outlaw, Bernard Boxill, Howard McGary, David Lyons, Tommy Lott, and others persuaded me that I should make anti-racism central to my work on opportunity. In the summer of 2003 I decided to "let the argument breathe" and rewrote my ideas as a short book. Jonathan Wolff kindly read ten chapters of that manuscript and offered detailed comments. His criticisms improved many pages of the book. Parts of the manuscript were read and criticized by Joan Roelofs, Richard David, Charles Mills, Carol Caref, G. A. Cohen, Fred Neuhouser, Hartry Field, Peter Stone, Joseph Carens, and Miriam Golomb. I owe all of you my thanks.

Chapters were presented at sessions of Association for Political Theory Conferences in 2004 and 2006; Steven Gerenscer, Johnny Goldfinger, and Eric MacGilvray offered helpful criticism. Anyone interested in political theory and political philosophy should get to know this delightful organization. Alex Makedon of the College of Education at Chicago State organized a colloquium where a chapter was presented and discussed. Phil Cronce made a chapter part of a Turnings Conference he organized at Chicago

State. Ron Munson and Eric Wiland made possible a visit to the University of Missouri-St Louis and were gracious hosts. Ben Berger and Jeffrey Murer were delightful hosts for a presentation at Swarthmore College, Michael Zuckert at the University of Notre Dame, Bob Schwartz, Margaret Atherton, John Koethe, and Fabrizio Mondadori at the University of Wisconsin-Milwaukee, and Loren Lomasky at the University of Virginia. I thank my hosts and audiences – especially comments from Robert Audi and Jim Sterba and the wonderful graduate students at Wisconsin-Milwaukee. Chicago State also offered course reductions for two semesters; these freed some time to write.

Marijke Rijsberman advised me that even well-written texts usually benefit by being shortened – her standard was to cut by one-third, which I nearly achieved. Many others have contributed to my ideas or offered encouragement: Mark Johnson, Kevin Triplett, Terry Rudd, John Rudd, Chris Rudd, Carol Caref, Marsha Vihon, Greko Tolbert, Valerie Brown, Tony Laden, Dan Brudney, Roland Wulbert, Emmett Bradbury, Cary Nederman, Dick Arneson, Mahesh Ananth, Phil Cronce, Floyd Banks, Terrell Jackson, Jerrell Johnson, Dave Gomberg, Dave Conklin, Sam Fleischacker, Saidou Mohamed N'Daou, Robert Bionaz, Lionel Kemble, the late Venson Currington Sr., and Judy Lawson.

For the past 20 years David Copp and Charles Chastain have encouraged my work. Chastain, who has read much of what I have written, raised his eyebrows when I suggested that my argument defended "contributive justice." That led me to rewrite everything to highlight that idea, which had been a throwaway phrase.

Also for 20 years it has been my privilege to teach at Chicago State University. I have learned much from my students, and what I have learned can be found on page after page here. My students in Social and Political Philosophy in particular have read and criticized the manuscript for the past three years.

Nick Bellorini at Blackwell shepherded the manuscript through the process of review and acceptance and was a strong advocate. I hope his confidence will be vindicated. Gillian Kane and Kelvin Matthews at Blackwell took me through the final stages. Two anonymous reviewers offered several useful criticisms and much encouragement. Bernard Boxill reviewed the manuscript and made extremely helpful comments. Harry Brighouse, originally anonymous but eventually revealed, read the entire manuscript twice, offering detailed criticism which strengthened the argument. Sarah Dancy was an excellent editor of the text.

My daughter Ruth Gomberg has allowed me to mentor her as she develops as a professional anthropologist. I am greatly indebted to her encouragement. My wife Mary Gomberg read the entire manuscript offering many criticisms that made it stronger. Even more, she has always encouraged me. Even more than that, for more than 40 years she has shared her life with me, and no words can express how much better my life has been for her companionship.

References

Sources that can be accessed on the World Wide Web are marked with an asterisk (*).

Allen, Theodore W. 1997. *The Invention of the White Race: The Origins of Racial Oppression in Anglo-America*, vol. 2. London: Verso.

*Allensworth, Elaine. 2005. *Graduation and Dropout Trends in Chicago: A Look at Cohorts of Students from 1991 through 2004*. Chicago: Consortium on Chicago School Research.

Aly, Bower. 1934. *Equalizing Educational Opportunity by Means of Federal Aid to Education*. Columbia, MO: National University Extension Association.

Anderson, Elizabeth. 1999. "What Is the Point of Equality?" *Ethics* 109: 287–337.

Anonymous. 1979. "Marxism and Material Incentives." *Progressive Labor Magazine* 13/1: 54–63.

Arneson, Richard. 1987. "Meaningful Work and Market Socialism." *Ethics* 97: 517–45.

Arneson, Richard. 1989. "Equality and Equality of Opportunity for Welfare." *Philosophical Studies* 56: 77–93.

Arneson, Richard. 1999. "Equality of Opportunity for Welfare Defended and Recanted." *Journal of Political Philosophy* 7: 488–97.

Baldwin, James. 1949. *Notes of a Native Son*. Boston: Bantam.

Balikci, Asen. 1970. *The Netsilik Eskimo*. Prospect Heights, IL: Waveland Press.

Barrett, James. 1987. *Work and Community in the Jungle: Chicago's Packinghouse Workers, 1894–1922*. Urbana: University of Illinois Press.

Barry, Brian. 2005. *Why Social Justice Matters*. Cambridge: Polity.

Block, Ned. 1995. "How Heritability Misleads about Race." *Cognition* 56: 99–128. Repr. in Bernard Boxill, ed., *Race and Racism*. Oxford: Oxford University Press, 2001.

Blum, Jerome. 1982. *Our Forgotten Past: Seven Centuries of Life on the Land*. London: Thames and Hudson.

Blum, Lawrence A. 1988. "Opportunity and Equality of Opportunity." *Public Affairs Quarterly* 2/4: 1–18.

Bowles, Samuel and Herbert Gintis. 1976. *Schooling in Capitalist America: Educational Reform and the Contradictions of Economic Life*. New York: Basic Books.

Bowles, Samuel, Herbert Gintis, and Melissa Osborne Groves, eds. 2005. *Unequal Chances: Family Background and Economic Success*. New York: Russell Sage Foundation.

Boxill, Bernard. 1984. *Blacks and Social Justice*. Totowa, NJ: Rowman and Allenheld; revised edition 1992, Lanham, MD: Rowman and Littlefield.

Braverman, Harry. 1974. *Labor and Monopoly Capital: The Degradation of Work in the Twentieth Century*. New York: Monthly Review Press.

Briggs, Jean L. 1970. *Never in Anger: Portrait of an Eskimo Family*. Cambridge, MA: Harvard University Press.

Briggs, Jean L. 1982. "Living Dangerously: The Contradictory Foundations of Value in Canadian Inuit Society." In Eleanor Leacock and Richard Lee, eds., *Politics and History in Band Societies*. Cambridge: Cambridge University Press.

Buller, David J. 2005. *Adapting Minds: Evolutionary Psychology and the Persistent Quest for Human Nature*. Cambridge, MA: MIT Press.

Burley, Justin. 2004. *Dworkin and his Critics with Replies by Dworkin*. Malden, MA: Blackwell Publishing.

Calavita, Kitty. 2005. *Immigrants at the Margins: Law, Race, and Exclusion in Southern Europe*. Cambridge: Cambridge University Press.

Carens, Joseph H. 1981. *Equality, Moral Incentives, and the Market*. Chicago: University of Chicago Press.

Carnoy, Martin. 1994. *Faded Dreams: The Politics and Economics of Race in America*. Cambridge: Cambridge University Press.

Cashin, Sheryll. 2004. *The Failures of Integration: How Race and Class are Undermining the American Dream*. New York: Public Affairs.

Castles, Stephen and Godula Kosack. 1973. *Immigrant Workers and Class Structure in Western Europe*. Oxford: Oxford University Press.

*Century Foundation. 2004. "Left Behind: Unequal Opportunity in Higher Education." Available at <http://www.tcf.org/Publications/Education/leftbehindrc.pdf>.

*Chen, Anthony S. 2001. "The Passage of State Fair Employment Legislation, 1945–1964: An Event-History Analysis with Time-Varying and Time-Constant Covariates." *Institute of Industrial Relations Working Paper Series*. University of California at Berkeley.

*Civil Rights Project. 2000. *Opportunities Suspended: the Devastating Consequences of Zero Tolerance and School Discipline*. Cambridge, MA: The Civil Rights Project, Harvard University.

Clark, Kenneth B. 1965. *Dark Ghetto: Dilemmas of Social Power*. New York: Harper.

Cohen, G. A. 1989. "On the Currency of Egalitarian Justice." *Ethics* 99: 906–44.

Cohen, G. A. 2000. *If You're an Egalitarian, How Come You're So Rich?* Cambridge, MA: Harvard University Press.

Cohen, G. A. 2004. "Expensive Taste Rides Again." In Justin Burley, *Dworkin and his Critics with Replies by Dworkin*. Malden, MA: Blackwell Publishing.

Cohen, Joshua. 1997. "The Natural Goodness of Humanity." In Andrews Reath, Barbara Herman, and Christine Korsgaard, eds., *Reclaiming the History of Ethics: Essays for John Rawls*. Cambridge: Cambridge University Press.

Conley, Dalton. 1999. *Being Black, Living in the Red: Race, Wealth, and Social Policy in America*. Berkeley: University of California Press.

Davis, Kingsley and Wilbert Moore. 1945. "Some Principles of Stratification." *American Sociological Review* 10: 242–9. Repr. in Lewis A. Coser and Bernard Rosenberg, eds., *Sociological Theory: A Book of Readings*, 3rd edn. London: Macmillan, 1969.

Davis, Kingsley. 1948. *Human Society*. New York: Macmillan.

Doppelt, Gerald. 1989. "Is Rawls's Kantian Liberalism Coherent and Defensible?" *Ethics* 99: 815–51.

Duffy, Kevin. 1985. *Children of the Forest: Africa's Mbuti Pygmies.* New York: Dodd, Mead.

Dworkin, Ronald. 1981. "What is Equality? Part 2: Equality of Resources." *Philosophy and Public Affairs* 10: 283–345. Repr. as chapter 2 in Dworkin, *Sovereign Virtue: The Theory and Practice of Equality.* Cambridge, MA: Harvard University Press, 2000.

Dworkin, Ronald. 1990. "Foundations of Liberal Equality." In Grethe B. Peterson, ed., *The Tanner Lectures on Human Values XI.* Salt Lake City: University of Utah Press.

Dworkin, Ronald. 2000. *Sovereign Virtue: The Theory and Practice of Equality.* Cambridge, MA: Harvard University Press.

Dworkin, Ronald. 2004. "Ronald Dworkin Replies." In Justin Burley, *Dworkin and his Critics with Replies by Dworkin.* Malden, MA: Blackwell Publishing.

Earle, Timothy, ed. 1991. *Chiefdoms: Power, Economy, and Ideology.* Cambridge: Cambridge University Press.

*Easterly, William. 2005. "Empirics of Strategic Interdependence: The Case of the Racial Tipping Point." Development Research Institute Working Paper No. 5, October, New York University.

*Engels, Frederick. 1850. *The Peasant War in Germany.* New York: International Publishers, 1966.

Farley, Reynolds and Maria Krysan. 2002. "The Residential Preferences of Blacks: Do They Explain Persistent Segregation?" *Social Forces* 80: 937–80.

Farley, Reynolds, Howard Schuman, Suzanne Bianchi, Diane Colasanto, and Shirley Hatchett. 1978. "Chocolate City, Vanilla Suburbs: Will the Trend toward Racially Separate Communities Continue?" *Social Science Research* 7: 319–44.

Farley, Reynolds, Charlotte Steeh, Tara Jackson, Maria Krysan, and Keith Reeves. 1993. "Continued Racial Residential Segregation in Detroit: 'Chocolate City, Vanilla Suburbs' Revisited." *Journal of Housing Research* 4: 1–38.

Fields, Barbara Jeanne. 1990. "Slavery, Race, and Ideology in the United States of America." *New Left Review* 181: 95–118.

Frederickson, George M. 1981. *White Supremacy: A Comparative Study in American and South African History.* Oxford: Oxford University Press.

Freeman, Samuel. 1990. "Reason and Agreement in Social Contract Views." *Philosophy and Public Affairs* 19: 122–57.

Freuchen, Peter. 1961. *Book of the Eskimos.* Cleveland: World Publishing.

Fried, Morton H. 1967. *The Evolution of Political Society: An Essay in Political Anthropology.* New York: McGraw-Hill.

Geddes, Andrew. 2003. *The Politics of Migration and Immigration in Europe.* London: Sage Publications.

Gilman, Antonio. 1995. "Prehistoric European Chiefdoms: Rethinking 'Germanic' Society." In T. Douglas Price and Gary M. Feinman, eds., *Foundations of Social Inequality.* New York: Plenum Press.

Gomberg, Paul. 1974. "Race and IQ: A Discussion of Some Confusions." *Ethics* 84: 258–66.

Gomberg, Paul. 1978. "Free Will as Ultimate Responsibility." *American Philosophical Quarterly* 15: 205–11.

Gomberg, Paul. 1989. "Marxism and Rationality." *American Philosophical Quarterly* 26: 53–62.

Gomberg, Paul. 1997. "How Morality Works and Why it Fails: On Political Philosophy and Moral Consensus." *The Journal of Social Philosophy* 28: 43–70.

Gomberg, Paul. 2002. "The Fallacy of Philanthropy." *The Canadian Journal of Philosophy* 32: 29–66.

Gomberg, Paul. n.d. "Can We Overcome Racial Division? On Group Identity and Self-Interest." Unpublished Manuscript.

*Gordon, Rebecca, Libero Delia Piana, and Terry Keleher. n.d. "Facing the Consequences: An Examination of Racial Discrimination in US Public Schools." Oakland, CA: ERASE Initiative.

Gould, Stephen J. 1981. *The Mismeasure of Man.* New York: W. W. Norton.

Grossman, Elizabeth. 2006. *High Tech Trash: Digital Devised, Hidden Toxics, and Human Health.* Washington: Island Press.

Gutman, Herbert. 1977. *Work, Culture and Society in Industrializing America: Essays in America's Working Class and Social History.* New York: Random House.

Haas, Jonathan. 1982. *The Evolution of the Prehistoric State.* New York: Columbia University Press.

Halpern, Rick. 1997. *Down on the Killing Floor: Black and White Workers in Chicago's Packinghouses, 1904–1954.* Urbana: University of Illinois Press.

Harris, Marvin. 1991. *Cultural Anthropology,* 3rd edn. New York: HarperCollins.

*Haveman, Robert and Kathryn Wilson. 2005. "Economic Inequality in College Access, Matriculation, and Graduation." La Follette School Working Paper No. 2005-032, La Follette School of Public Affairs, University of Wisconsin-Madison.

*Haycock, Kati. 2000. "No More Settling for Less." *Thinking K-16* 4: 3–12.

Herrnstein, Richard J. and Charles Murray. 1994. *The Bell Curve: Intelligence and Class Structure in American Life.* New York: The Free Press.

Hilgard, Ernest R., Richard C. Atkinson, and Rita L. Atkinson. 1971. *Introduction to Psychology,* 5th edn. New York: Harcourt Brace Jovanovich.

*Hill, Christopher. 1940. *The English Revolution 1640.* London: Lawrence and Wishart.

Hill, Christopher. 1961. *The Century of Revolution 1603–1714.* New York: W. W. Norton.

Hill, Christopher. 1972. *The World Turned Upside Down.* London: Penguin.

Hirsch, Arnold R. 1983. *Making the Second Ghetto: Race and Housing in Chicago, 1940–1960.* Cambridge: Cambridge University Press.

Hirsch, Fred. 1976. *Social Limits to Growth.* Cambridge, MA: Harvard University Press.

*Jefferson, Thomas. 1787. *Notes on the State of Virginia.* Chapel Hill: University of North Carolina Press, 1954.

Jones, Jacqueline. 1992. *The Dispossessed: America's Underclasses from the Civil War to the Present.* New York: Basic Books.

Jordan, Winthrop. 1968. *White over Black: American Attitudes Toward the Negro.* Chapel Hill: University of North Carolina Press.

*Kafka, Franz. 1913. "The Judgment." In *The Penal Colony: Stories and Short Pieces.* New York: Schocken Books, 1949.

Kamin, Leon J. 1974. *The Science and Politics of IQ.* Potomac, MD: Lawrence Erlbaum Associates.

Kant, Immanuel. 1798. *The Metaphysical Elements of Justice.* New York: Macmillan, 1965.

Kasser, Tim. 2002. *The High Price of Materialism.* Cambridge, MA: The MIT Press.

Katznelson, Ira. 2005. *When Affirmative Action Was White.* New York: W. W. Norton.

Kinder, Donald R. and Lynn M. Sanders. 1996. *Divided by Color: Racial Politics and Democratic Ideals.* Chicago: University of Chicago Press.

Kitcher, Philip. 1985. *Vaulting Ambition: Sociobiology and the Quest for Human Nature.* Cambridge, MA: MIT Press.

Kluegel, James R. and Elliott R. Smith. 1986. *Beliefs about Inequality*. New York: Aldine de Gruyter.

Kohn, Melvin L. and Carmi Schooler. 1983. *Work and Personality: An Inquiry into the Impact of Social Stratification*. Norwood, NJ: Ablex Publishing.

Kopina, Helen. 2005. *East to West Migration: Russian Migrants in Western Europe*. Aldershot: Ashgate.

Kornhauser, Arthur. 1965. *Mental Health of the Industrial Worker: A Detroit Study*. New York: John Wiley and Sons.

Kozol, Jonathan. 1967. *Death at an Early Age: The Destruction of the Hearts and Minds of Negro Children in the Boston Public Schools*. Boston: Houghton Mifflin.

Kozol, Jonathan. 1991. *Savage Inequalities: Children in America's Schools*. New York: Crown.

Kozol, Jonathan. 2005. *The Shame of the Nation: The Restoration of Apartheid Schooling in America*. New York: Crown.

Krouse, Richard and Michael McPherson. 1988. "Capitalism, 'Property-Owning Democracy,' and the Welfare State." In Amy Gutmann, ed., *Democracy and the Welfare State*. Princeton: Princeton University Press.

Lahav, Gallya. 2004. *Immigration and Politics in New Europe: Reinventing Borders*. Cambridge: Cambridge University Press.

Lamont, Michèle. 2000. *The Dignity of Working Men: Morality and the Boundaries of Race, Class, and Immigration*. New York: Russell Sage Foundation.

Lane, Robert E. 1991. *The Market Experience*. Cambridge: Cambridge University Press.

Lareau, Annette. 2003. *Unequal Childhoods: Class, Race, and Family Life*. Berkeley: University of California Press.

Layard, Richard. 2005. *Happiness: Lessons from a New Science*. New York: The Penguin Press.

Leacock, Eleanor and Richard Lee, eds. 1982. *Politics and History in Band Societies*. Cambridge: Cambridge University Press.

Lee, Richard. 1979. *The !Kung San: Men, Women, and Work in a Foraging Society*. Cambridge: Cambridge University Press.

Lee, Richard. 1982. "Politics, Sexual and Non-sexual, in an Egalitarian Society." In Eleanor Leacock and Richard Lee, eds., *Politics and History in Band Societies*. Cambridge: Cambridge University Press.

Lee, Richard. 1993. *The Dobe Ju/'hoansi*, 2nd edn. New York: Harcourt Brace.

Lee, Richard and Richard Daly, eds. 1999. *The Cambridge Encyclopedia of Hunters and Gatherers*. Cambridge: Cambridge University Press.

Lipset, Seymour Martin and Richard Bendix. 1959. *Social Mobility in Industrial Society*. Berkeley: University of California Press.

Loewen, James W. 2005. *Sundown Towns: A Hidden Dimension of American Racism*. New York: The New Press.

Lucassen, Leo. 2005. *The Immigrant Threat: The Integration of Old and New Migrants in Western Europe Since 1850*. Urbana: University of Illinois Press.

MacCallum, Gerald C. Jr. 1967. "Negative and Positive Freedom." *The Philosophical Review*: 312–34.

Macek, Josef. 1958. *The Hussite Movement in Bohemia*. Prague: Orbis.

McGary, Howard. 1999. *Race and Social Justice*. Oxford: Blackwell Publishers.

MacLeod, Jay. 1995. *Ain't No Makin' It: Aspirations and Attainment in a Low-Income Neighborhood*, 2nd edn. Boulder, CO: Westview Press.

McMichael, Philip. 1996. *Development and Social Change.* Thousand Oaks, CA: Pine Forge Press.

*Marks, Jonathan. 2005. "Anthropology and *The Bell Curve.*" In Catherine Besteman and Hugh Gusterson, eds., *Why America's Top Pundits Are Wrong: Anthropologists Talk Back.* Berkeley: University of California Press.

Marmot, Michael. 2004. *The Status Syndrome: How Social Standing Affects Our Health and Longevity.* New York: Times Books.

Marshall, Lorna. 1976. *The !Kung of Nyae Nyae.* Cambridge, MA: Harvard University Press.

*Marx, Karl. 1843. "On the Jewish Question." In Karl Marx, *Early Writings.* Harmondsworth: Penguin, 1975.

*Marx, Karl. 1858. *Grundrisse.* In David McClellan, ed., *Selected Writings.* Oxford: Oxford University Press, 1977.

*Marx, Karl. 1867. *Capital*, vol. 1. Harmondsworth: Penguin, 1976.

*Marx, Karl. 1891. "Critique of the Gotha Programme." In Marx, *The First International and After*, ed. David Fernbach. Harmondsworth: Penguin, 1974.

*Marx, Karl. 1894. *Capital*, vol. 3. Harmondsworth: Penguin, 1981.

*Marx, Karl and Frederick Engels. 1848. "The Communist Manifesto." In Marx, *The Revolutions of 1848*, ed. David Fernbach. Harmondsworth: Penguin, 1974.

Massey, Douglas S. and Nancy A. Denton. 1993. *American Apartheid: Segregation and the Making of the Underclass.* Cambridge, MA: Harvard University Press.

Mercer, J. R. 1988. "Ethnic Differences in IQ Scores: What Do They Mean?" *Hispanic Journal of Behavioral Sciences* 10: 199–218.

*Mill, John Stuart. 1869. *The Subjection of Women.* Indianapolis: Hackett, 1988.

Mills, Charles W. 1997. *The Racial Contract.* Ithaca: Cornell University Press.

Mills, Charles W. 2004. "Racial Exploitation and the Wages of Whiteness," In George Yancy, ed., *What White Looks Like: African-American Philosophers on the Whiteness Question.* New York: Routledge.

Mingione, Enzo and Enrico Pugliese. 1994. "Rural Subsistence, Migration, Urbanization, and the New Global Food Regime." In Alessandro Bonanno, Lawrence Busch, William H. Friedland, Lourdes Gjouveia, and Enzo Mingione, eds., *From Columbus to Con-Agra.* Lawrence: University of Kansas Press.

Moore, David S. 2002. *The Dependent Gene: The Fallacy of "Nature vs. Nurture."* New York: Times Books.

Morgan, Edmund S. 1975. *American Slavery–American Freedom: The Ordeal of Colonial Virginia.* New York: W. W. Norton.

Murphy, James Bernard. 1993. *The Moral Economy of Labor: Aristotelian Themes in Economic Theory.* New Haven: Yale University Press.

National Research Council. 1989. *A Common Destiny: Blacks and American Society.* Washington: National Academy Press.

Neeson, J. M. 1993. *Commoners: Common Right, Enclosure and Social Change in England, 1700–1820.* Cambridge: Cambridge University Press.

Neuhouser, Fred. 2002. "Rousseau and the Problem with Self-Love (*Amour propre*)." Presented at University of Illinois-Chicago on November 4.

Noble, David F. 1986. *Forces of Production: A Social History of Industrial Automation.* New York: Oxford University Press.

Nozick, Robert. 1974. *Anarchy, State, and Utopia.* New York: Basic Books.

Nussbaum, Martha C. 2000. *Women and Human Development: The Capabilities Approach.* Cambridge: Cambridge University Press.

Oakes, James. 1983. *The Ruling Race: A History of American Slaveholders*. New York: Vintage Books.

Oliver, Melvin L. and Thomas M. Shapiro. 1995. *Black Wealth/White Wealth: A New Perspective on Racial Inequality*. New York: Routledge.

*Orfield, Gary. 2001. *Schools More Separate: Consequences of a Decade of Resegregation*. Cambridge, MA: The Civil Rights Project, Harvard University.

Painter, Nell Irvin. 1979. *The Narrative of Hosea Hudson: His Life as a Negro Communist in the South*. Cambridge, MA: Harvard University Press.

*Presley, Jennifer B., Bradford R. White, and Yuqin Gong. 2006. *Examining the Distribution and Impact of Teacher Quality in Illinois*. Edwardsville, IL: Illinois Education Research Council.

*Progressive Labor Party. 1982. "Road to Revolution 4." New York: Progressive Labor Party.

Rawls, John. 1993. *Political Liberalism*. New York: Columbia University Press.

Rawls, John. 1999. *A Theory of Justice*, rev. edn (1st edn 1971). Cambridge, MA: Harvard University Press.

Rawls, John. 2001. *Justice as Fairness: A Restatement*, ed. Erin Kelly. Cambridge, MA: Harvard University Press.

Ray, Joseph M. 1941. *Equalization of Educational Opportunity*. Austin, TX: The University of Texas.

Reed, Adolph Jr. 2002a. "Unraveling the Relation of Race and Class in American Politics." *Political Power and Social Theory* 15: 265–74.

Reed, Adolph Jr. 2002b. "Rejoinder." *Political Power and Social Theory* 15: 303–17.

Roemer, John E. 1998. *Equality of Opportunity*. Cambridge, MA: Harvard University Press.

Rogers, Heather. 2005 *Gone Tomorrow: The Hidden Life of Garbage*. New York: The New Press.

Rothstein, Richard. 2004. *Class and Schools: Using Social, Economic, and Educational Reform to Close the Black-White Achievement Gap*. Washington: Economic Policy Institute.

*Rousseau, Jean-Jacques. 1755. *Discourse on the Origin of Inequality*. In Steven M. Cahn, ed., *Classics of Modern Political Theory: Machiavelli to Mill*. New York: Oxford University Press, 1997.

Ruse, Michael. 1990. "Evolutionary Ethics and the Search of Predecessors: Kant, Hume, and All the Way Back to Aristotle?" *Social Philosophy and Policy* 8: 59–85.

Sahlins, Marshall. 1972. *Stone Age Economics*. New York: Aldine de Gruyter.

Sassen, Saskia. 1988. *The Mobility of Labor and Capital: A Study in International Investment and Labor Flow*. Cambridge: Cambridge University Press.

Saxton, Alexander. 1990. *The Rise and Fall of the White Republic: Class Politics and Mass Culture in Nineteenth-Century America*. London: Verso.

Schelling, Thomas C. 1971. "Dynamic Models of Segregation." *Journal of Mathematical Sociology* 1: 148–86.

Schelling, Thomas C. 1972. "A Process of Residential Segregation: Neighborhood Tipping." In A. H. Pascal, ed., *Racial Discrimination in Economic Life*. Boston: Heath.

Schmidtz, David. 2005. "History and Pattern." *Social Philosophy and Policy* 22: 148–77.

Schor, Juliet B. 1998. *The Overspent American: Upscaling, Downshifting, and the New Consumer*. New York: HarperCollins

Sen, Amartya. 1992. *Inequality Reexamined*. New York: Russell Sage Foundation.

Sen, Amartya. 1999. *Development as Freedom*. New York: Anchor Books.

Shapiro, Thomas M. 2004. *The Hidden Cost of Being African American: How Wealth Perpetuates Inequality*. Oxford: Oxford University Press.

Shipler, David K. 2004. *The Working Poor: Invisible in America*. New York: Alfred A. Knopf.

Shostak, Marjorie. 1983. *Nisa: The Life and Words of a !Kung Woman*. New York: Vintage Books.

Siegelbaum, Lewis H. 1988. *Stakhanovism and the Politics of Productivity in the USSR, 1935–1941*. Cambridge: Cambridge University Press.

Sigelman, Lee and Susan Welch. 1991. *Black Americans' Views of Racial Inequality: The Dream Deferred*. Cambridge: Cambridge University Press.

Slade, Giles. 2006. *Made to Break: Technology and Obsolescence in America*. Cambridge, MA: Harvard University Press.

Smedley, Audrey. 1993. *Race in North America: Origin and Evolution of a Worldview*. Boulder: Westview.

*Smith, Adam. 1776. *An Inquiry into the Nature and Causes of the Wealth of Nations* ed. Edwin Cannan. Chicago: University of Chicago Press, 1976.

Solomos, John. 2003. *Race and Racism in Britain*, 3rd edn. New York: Palgrave Macmillan.

Tajfel, Henri and John Turner. 1979. "An Integrative Theory of Intergroup Conflict." Repr. in Michael A. Hogg and Dominic Abrams, eds., *Intergroup Relations: Essential Readings*. Philadelphia: Psychology Press, 1991.

Takaki, Ronald. 1979. *Iron Cages: Race and Culture in 19th-Century America*. New York: Oxford University Press.

Taylor, Paul C. 2004. *Race: A Philosophical Introduction*. Cambridge: Polity.

Terman, Lewis M. 1916. *The Measurement of Intelligence*. Boston: Houghton Mifflin.

*Thomas, Laurence. 1990. "In My Next Life I'll Be White." *Ebony*, December.

Thompson, E. P. 1975. *Whigs and Hunters: The Origin of the Black Act*. New York: Pantheon.

Tilly, Charles. 1986. *The Contentious French: Four Centuries of Popular Struggle*. Cambridge, MA: Harvard University Press.

*Tocqueville, Alexis de. 1850. *Democracy in America*, 13th edn. New York: Harper Perennial, 1988.

Trigger, Bruce. 1990. "Maintaining Economic Equality in Opposition to Complexity: An Iroquoian Case Study." In Steadman Upham, ed., *The Evolution of Political Systems: Sociopolitics in Small Scale Sedentary Societies*. Cambridge: Cambridge University Press.

Turnbull, Colin M. 1961. *The Forest People: A Study of the Pygmies of the Congo*. New York: Touchstone.

Turnbull, Colin M. 1982. "The Ritualization of Potential Conflict between the Sexes among the Mbuti." In Eleanor Leacock and Richard Lee, eds., *Politics and History in Band Societies*. Cambridge: Cambridge University Press.

Walter, John. 1980. "Grain Riots and Popular Attitudes to the Law." In John Brewer and John Styles, eds., *An Ungovernable People: the English and their Law in the Seventeenth and Eighteenth Centuries*. New Brunswick, NJ: Rutgers University Press.

Walzer, Michael. 1983. *Spheres of Justice: A Defense of Pluralism and Equality*. New York: Basic Books.

Werth, Alexander. 1964. *Russia at War 1941–1945*. New York: Dutton.

Westen, Peter. 1985. "The Concept of Equal Opportunity." *Ethics* 95: 837–50.

Wiessner, Polly. 1982. "Risk, Reciprocity and Social Influences on !Kung San Economics." In Eleanor Leacock and Richard Lee, eds., *Politics and History in Band Societies*. Cambridge: Cambridge University Press.

Wilson, William Julius. 1987. *The Truly Disadvantaged: The Inner City, the Underclass, and Public Policy*. Chicago: University of Chicago Press.

Index